HEI

AND

THE CHRISTIAN LIFE

HEROISM
AND
THE CHRISTIAN LIFE

Reclaiming Excellence

Brian S. Hook and R. R. Reno

Westminster John Knox Press
Louisville, Kentucky

Scripture quotations, unless otherwise indicated, are from the New Revised Standard Version of the Bible, copyright © 1989 by the Division of Christian Education of the National Council of the Churches of Christ in the U.S.A., and are used by permission. Scripture quotations marked RSV are from the Revised Standard Version of the Bible, copyright © 1946, 1952, 1971, and 1973 by the Division of Christian Education of the National Council of the Churches of Christ in the U.S.A., and are used by permission.

Book design by Sharon Adams
Cover design by Pam Poll

First edition
Published by Westminster John Knox Press
Louisville, Kentucky

This book is printed on acid-free paper that meets the American National Standards Institute Z39.48 standard. ∞

PRINTED IN THE UNITED STATES OF AMERICA

00 01 02 03 04 05 06 07 08 09 — 10 9 8 7 6 5 4 3 2 1

LIBRARY OF CONGRESS CATALOGING-IN-PUBLICATION DATA
Hook, Brian S. (Brian Stewart), 1964–
    Heroism and the Christian life : reclaiming excellence / Brian S. Hook and
R. R. Reno. — 1st ed.
        p. cm.
    Includes bibliographical references and index.
    ISBN 0-664-25812-3 (alk. paper)
    1. Courage—Religious aspects—Christianity. 2. Courage in literature.
3. Christian life.
I. Reno, Russell R., 1959– II. Title.

BV4647.C75 R46 2000
241'.4—dc21

                                                                99-086534

Worthy is the Lamb that was slaughtered
to receive power and wealth and wisdom and might
and honor and glory and blessing!
Revelation 5:12

≫ — ≪

Contents

Acknowledgments

This book had its genesis in a simple question: Can the Christian life be heroic? That question first shaped the basis of a course, which we taught together, and the course provided the impetus for the book. It is often true, especially in the classroom, that the question is more important than the answer, but as we came to see, for the Christian writers whom we study, the answer to this question is affirmative and vital. By and large they are concerned that we see women and men as enlarged and perfected by God's grace. We hope that readers are not only challenged and enlightened by our exploration of their poetic and rhetorical arguments but also prompted to return to these authors themselves, who represent the convergence of grace and ambition with such eloquence.

Many are due thanks for their contributions to this study. First, thanks are owed to the students who took part in the first seminar that we taught together and engaged so enthusiastically in the question, and to students who attended subsequent classes on the figure of the hero in antiquity and read and responded to preliminary chapters of this book. Several scholars read individual chapters and offered their insights. Fidel Fajardo-Acosta, Robert Lamberton, and Sheila Murnaghan lent their wisdom and encouragement to the direction of chapter 2; Geoff Bakewell and Gregory Carlson, S.J., helped sharpen the arguments of chapter 4. Patrick Murray gave his usual close and sage reading to the introduction and helped us refine our overall vision of the book. Ross Wagner's critical observations aided in the revisions of chapter 5. Robert and Blanche Jenson read selected chapters and offered their encouragement. Of course, any errors or weaknesses that remain are our own.

We express our appreciation to Nick Street, our editor at Westminster John Knox Press, who encouraged this project from the start and guided it to conclusion, and to the other editors at WJK who have made the process a relatively painless one.

Finally, we offer our thanks and love to our wives, Elizabeth and Juliana, for helping us, in active and passive ways, realize our ambitions for this book and for ourselves. We dedicate this book to them.

Chapter One

The Challenge of Christian Heroism

Can the Christian life be heroic? Does Christianity promote human greatness? How much, if at all, can a life of discipleship embrace human excellence? Is faith the engine of achievement? At first glance, these seem silly questions. Of course the Christian life can be heroic. Martyrs go to their deaths with courage. Saints attend to the sick and poor with fortitude. Popes resist the spirit of the age with implacable conviction. Monks scale the heights of ascetic self-denial. Modern men and women wrest a meaningful faith out of the grip of a cold and impersonal scientific worldview. At every turn, Christian faith seems a powerful thing, motivating believers to change their lives and to witness in the world with force and vigor. Surely, one might think, this spiritual potency and worldly influence is the very essence of heroism.

Our goal is not to question this initial response to the question of whether the Christian life can be heroic. Certainly, there are Christians who have lived, and died, heroically. Rather, we hope to investigate the odd and difficult relationship between what is Christian and what is heroic. To call someone a "hero" draws attention to his or her distinctive character and achievement. The hero is worthy of praise and emulation. Christianity, in contrast, points beyond the disciple and toward Jesus

1

Christ. John the Baptist expresses just this dynamic when he says of Jesus, "He must increase, but I must decrease" (John 3:30). No matter how remarkable the sacrifices of a saint or the ascetic achievements of a monk, Christianity teaches that praise goes to Christ alone. The ancients knew nothing of this heroic humility and spiritual poverty. These virtues, so important in the vision of Christian heroism, signal a strange conjunction: the great virtue of faith involves renouncing the honor and glory normally accorded the great. This odd vision—that the highest human achievement is conjugated in the language of self-denial—is at the center of Christian thinking. So, even if we immediately agree that the Christian life can be heroic, we must acknowledge that a conjunction of heroism with faith challenges our assumptions about each.

Nietzsche was one of the greatest and most perceptive critics of Christianity. Unlike so many modern doubters, he did not think Christian faith incredible because captive to superstition and belief in miracles. Instead, Nietzsche thought Christianity was incredible because it was inhumane, a nihilistic form of life that ate away at the inner springs of life. The very project of Christian discipleship, he observed, is rooted in self-denial. This, he argues, leads to a "transvaluation of values." Instead of viewing human life as an expressive expansion of innate human energy and creativity, Christianity treats sensuality, ambition, and the desire to rule over others as so many vices to be suppressed. This ascetical turn against oneself, the Christian assumes, opens the door to salvation and spiritual growth. Indeed, this project of self-denial is so fundamental that even spiritual achievements must be renounced as one's own. By grace alone do the faithful subsist, even in their faith. By the power of Christ does the church endure. For the heroic Christian, the Olympian feat of self-denial, the very power to deny oneself is not one's own. Achievements of discipline and self-denial are deflected outward. As the razor's edge of renunciation cuts into passion and pride, the saint says, "Not I, but Christ in me."

For Nietzsche, this is an impossible self-evacuation, and it leads to nihilism, a hatred of life itself. Eager to make God our hero, we subject our natural egoism to perpetual attack. "Not my will," says the disciple of Jesus, "but thine." In this miasma of self-denial, the mere thought of personal power and achievement strikes the believer with horror. "How can I imagine myself worthy of glory when everything I do is stained with pride and diminished by sloth? How can I claim prerogative and merit when God has done so much for me?" With just these patterns of self-judgment and spiritual submission, Nietzsche argues, the harsh acids of the ascetical "No!" corrode our will to live. The upshot is a world-weariness, a discouragement and exhaustion born of perpetual efforts to repress the human claim upon life in order to make room for the divine claim. We must disappear so that God can be all in all.

However bitterly Nietzsche opposed Christianity, he could not rest with the conclusion that Christianity diminished and destroyed human power and potency. The way of discipleship is no illusion, no spectral and pious morning mist that evaporates with the first warm rays of reality. Christian heroism seems an actual possibility rather than a contradictory assault upon humanity; the ascetical "No!" seems to rebound to a "Yes!" As a simple matter of fact, Nietzsche admits, Christianity and its vision of spiritual poverty has effected tremendous personal and cultural changes. As Nietzsche puts the matter, "Rome has been defeated beyond all doubt," and that defeat was effected by the comically weak force of "three Jews" (Jesus, Peter, and Paul) and "one Jewess" (Jesus' mother, Mary).[1] An apparent strategy of impotence—renouncing one's own power—generates remarkable potency. Indeed, the very *inhumanity* of self-denial testifies to a remarkable ambition, an ambition that cannot help but win Nietzsche's grudging admiration. To want to be more than human—and to have the willpower to undertake radical renunciations, even the paradoxical renunciation of will—strikes Nietzsche as incredible, and for that very reason, remarkable. Something striking emerges out of the other-worldly ambition of the Christian form of discipleship, and although it is deeply at odds with classical ideas of heroism, the life of faith has its own glory, its own achievements. And this glory and achievement eclipsed pagan antiquity, as Nietzsche knows (and regrets), winning the contest for the soul of the Western world.

We need not enter into the labyrinth of Nietzsche's complex joust with Christianity. The basic insight is clear: Christianity charts an enigmatic path toward human excellence. Consider a contrast between the archetypal hero of classical literature, Achilles, and the father of Christian faith, Abraham. These two figures, the one central to the literature of Greek culture and the other to the scriptural narrative of Christianity, are strikingly different. Achilles is a warrior, swift-footed, efficient, and triumphant on the plains of Troy. Abraham is a nomad, called out from his people to be the father of God's chosen people. Achilles is the paragon of fighting prowess. Abraham is the paradigm of faithful obedience. Achilles is a hero of action. As he is presented in Homer's great epic, the *Iliad*, Achilles faces a fateful choice: either a long life in anonymity or a brief life of glory. He chooses glory, and this choice requires him to be present on the battlefield as the dominant figure. The dramatic action of the *Iliad* is devoted to crafting the proper setting for this presence. Achilles must come into the glory of his heroism in just the right way. In contrast, Abraham's heroism is found in his obedience. The Genesis narrative turns on God's choices and commandments, not Abraham's. His significance as father of a chosen people is a gift rather than an achievement. Unlike the *Iliad*, the book of Genesis depicts Abraham's conformity to that gift, a conformity that is revealed most dramatically through the trial of his faith on Mount Moriah. And in the test, the difference between Achilles and Abraham is extraordinarily vivid. Achilles asserts himself in the test of wills and the test of arms. Abraham gives his beloved son in obedience in the test of faith.

What are we to make of this difference between Achilles and Abraham? Does the notion of "hero" bridge this difference? Can we call Abraham a hero, and if so, then must we ascribe to Achilles a false or superficial heroism? These are not simply scholarly questions that might interest the historian of ideas, as if Achilles and Abraham were antique figures who have lost their relevance and allure. They illuminate Nietzsche's intuition. The Achillean ideal of human excellence has a universal appeal. He is a man of intense loyalties, physical beauty, excellence in the arts of war, and a charismatic presence. In him, Greek culture saw aristocratic virtues: an indomitable spirit, an unwillingness to enter into compromises of convenience, a commitment to emotive eloquence, and passionate action. However much we might reject the *ethos* of the Greek warrior and aristocrat, the sheer drama of Achilles' achievement retains an appeal. He is nothing if not a powerful presence, and considering our own attraction to charismatic politicians and our admiration for dominant athletes, even if our heroes are narrower and less grand, we continue to recognize an Achillean form of heroism. We make celebrities out of stunningly beautiful models. We adulate the raw masculinity of male movie stars. We seem perennially fascinated with leaders who exhibit decisiveness in times of trial. No matter how much sociologists and psychologists try to persuade us that social forces are the dominant factors in history, we are attracted to Great Men and the influence we imagine they exert on human affairs. Surely, then, Achilles lives as a heroic archetype.

But if Achilles lives on, then can Abraham be a hero? Abraham is important in the Christian reading of the Old Testament because he so completely embodies the first virtue of Christian discipleship: faith. Abraham does nothing. God does all. And Abraham is great because his faith allows him to participate in all that God has done for and in him. Abraham empties himself, "hoping," as Paul describes him, "against hope" (Rom. 4:18). He leaves the land of his ancestors and turns his back on whatever hope for status and honor might flow from tribe and community. He even forsakes the hope of an earthly legacy by willingly binding his only son for sacrifice. In all things, Abraham is obedient, and for this reason, Abraham's life seems a study in self-denial, the evacuation of all he might have or possess, an empty vessel that awaits God for fulfillment. For Christianity, this "hope against hope," this patient obedience, does not diminish; rather, it secures a higher, divinely ordained glory. As the letter to the Hebrews describes his role, "Thus Abraham, having patiently endured, obtained the promise" (6:15).

In our society of achievement, this path of self-denial seems alien. Nietzsche's rebellion against the ascetical imperative echoes endlessly. Surely, we think, our greatness lies in our accomplishment, in what we do for ourselves, and not in what others do in and for us! Submission cannot ennoble. Obedience cannot provide the basis for glory. And yet, this is not entirely so. We champion those who die in the line of duty or for a cause larger than themselves. We have a fascination with the odd emptiness of ascetic self-denial. No matter how "impossible" we might think the age-old Christian ideal of celibacy, priests and nuns exert a remarkable power over our imaginations. There can be a strange power in having less. We might be horrified by the story of Abraham's ascent of Mount Moriah to sacrifice his son, but beneath that horror we cannot help but feel a certain envy, or even a fear that comes whenever we encounter great power. To believe so strongly in something other than oneself that one can give up all—surely that is a remarkable kind of strength. Indeed, the fanatic possesses a wild imprudence that oversteps much of what we imagine insuperable. How can one risk financial disaster, social ostracism, personal harm? The Abrahams of the world seem insensible to such anxieties, and as a consequence, they possess a special power. Rome could only be defeated by those who were impervious to her blandishments of glory and riches and who did not fear her deadly punishments.

Achilles and Abraham. These two figures do not simply typify two intuitions that animate our sense of what is most admirable in human affairs, they also define a contrast that Nietzsche saw at the center of Christian discipleship. However much Christianity might wish to deny the triumph of Achilles as the hero of martial perfection, from the earliest martyrdoms to the classics of early modern Christian poetry, that denial has always been paired with an insistence that Christian discipleship has its own distinctive, even aggressive power. The accounts of martyrdom emphasize the agonistic context of persecution. The desert monk does not conquer Satan by force of arms, but he does triumph. The Christian knight is not to be admired for his swiftness of foot or his fury in battle, but for his purity of heart and soul, God's charisms, and these virtues lead to victory and are worthy of our admiration and emulation. As Nietzsche recognized and acknowledged, however much he may have hated the consequence, faithfulness is heroic. Renunciation has a real potency, so much so that Nietzsche treats "the Crucified" as his most powerful adversary. Far from the superannuated, pietistic residue of past credulity and irrational faith, Christianity is the only power that Nietzsche thinks can rival his own vision of heroic existence.

We do not intend to declare a victor in Nietzsche's contest with the Crucified. Instead, we wish to understand more clearly what Nietzsche found so incredible and counterintuitive: the power of saying, "Not my will, but thine." It is our conviction that Christianity affirms the human impulse toward excellence. Indeed, it promises fulfillment of that impulse. Faith in Christ is not, finally, a diminishment, a renunciation of oneself to a vanishing point. To use Nietzsche's terminology, Christianity is not nihilistic; it does not evacuate us of the will to life. However, it is equally our conviction that the form of Abraham, the pattern of faithful obedience, is constituted by self-denial. Faith is not a happy-clappy embrace of oneself; it is not a therapeutic project of self-acceptance. Nor is faith a careful balancing act between spiritual discipline and worldly endeavor, as if the disciplines of faith must be pruned in order to place "realistic" demands on our lives. Discipleship is not a way of half measures; it involves a renunciation of any number of independent projects so that the will of God might predominate. This evacuation of the self, according to Christian teaching, is the royal road to excellence and the fulfillment of our greatest powers and aspirations.

In order to grasp this ideal of heroic self-denial, we will undertake close literary analysis of classical and Christian texts. Our goal is to receive instruction from these literary performances, both about the nature of heroism and the Christian insistence that an obedient faith is active and potent. As we read, our attention flows to these texts as cultural artifacts. As such, we largely suppress text-critical questions of composition and concerns of historicism. Our reading is informed by a scholarly acquaintance with secondary literature, but our conviction is that these texts have sufficient internal force as literary documents to motivate effective reading without excessive recourse to extratextual data. Precisely because questions of human excellence and its full enactment so dominate the material we have chosen, our efforts to understand the odd and difficult conjunction of heroism and the Christian life will run through channels already carved by the currents in these texts. Interpreting these texts, then, shall be the way in which we pursue the question of how the Christian life can be heroic. Reading well both requires and stimulates thinking clearly.

These depictions of heroic personalities in poetry and narrative, in hagiography, and even in theological tracts raise three important literary challenges: the recognition of the hero, imitation of heroic exemplars, and the hero's participation in surpassing achievement. These literary challenges of poetic depiction and didactic purpose reflect difficulties of thought and of life. For the problems of poetic and narrative presentation are challenges of the imagination. And as Nietzsche makes clear in his own struggle with heroic discipleship, the incredible is as much a function of imaginative boundaries as common sense. We must *see* the hero as a human being whose excellence surpasses others; otherwise, the very term "hero" becomes an empty, honorific title we apply, either out of convention or simply to designate that someone is out of the ordinary.

First, the excellence of human life is made public and visible through patterns of *recognition*. Heroism is not an abstract quality; it is not an innate property that shimmers, like gold, simply by virtue of its mere essense, without exercise or enactment. Nor is heroism a solipsistic conceit, a forceful way of expressing our likes and dislikes. Quite the contrary, heroism is deeply communal. It demands and evokes acknowledgment. We can be heroes in our own minds, or we can imagine that a parent or friend is heroic, but only as others laud and magnify deeds and character, only as the hero is recognized, does a heroic gestalt emerge. The secret and private hero is, finally, no hero at all. The patterns of recognition are many. In our study of the *Iliad*, we consider the standard patterns of recognition that Homer presupposes, the rewards of victory that reflect communal esteem and are displayed by heroes for all to see. Yet in these standard patterns, we detect a problem. Supreme in battle, Achilles reaches toward a greatness that exceeds the normal means of communal recognition, and this produces poetic difficulties that reflect real limitations of the human imagination. Although acknowledged by all to be the greatest warrior, the heroism of Achilles seems to extend beyond recognition. The man whom all Greeks acknowledge as the greatest warrior slides toward a private and unrecognized excellence. He moves beyond the frame of heroic recognition.

The second theme is *imitation*. The excellences manifested in a heroic life evoke the greatest possible compliment: the desire to imitate, to acquire and manifest a similar greatness. To be sure, this imitation may be pale and shallow, but the allure of heroic achievement is consistent. Our analysis of Plato's depiction of Socrates and his trial illuminates the literary challenges of imitation. The very greatness of Socrates is manifest in his teasing irony. He is part of a heroic tradition of public excellence and achievement, and yet, he is exactly opposite, a man of no particular standing in the community and without obvious appeal. The effect, we shall argue, is paradoxical. Drawing upon, but transgressing the standard heroic tropes of the Homeric epics, Plato presents Socrates in such a way that he both stimulates and deflects imitation. The hero attracts and repulses. Not surprisingly, Nietzsche found Socrates almost as troublesome as Jesus. Socrates is incredible. He fits no trajectory of human aspiration. Yet Plato is able to present Socrates in such a way that, instead of provoking readers' exasperation and dismissal, their imitative desire is redoubled. The more difficult the task of imitation, the more effort must be brought to bear. The remarkable grip that Socrates exerts over the history of Western philosophy testifies to the effectiveness of Plato's manipulation of the patterns of heroic imitation.

Finally, aspiration can stretch the imagination beyond what seems possible. If we so enlarge the horizon of excellence, we must struggle to see how mere finite creatures can fully *participate* in such surpassing achievement. By our reading, this is Vergil's singular preoccupation in the *Aeneid*. Vergil's Rome is bathed in transcendent and eternal glory, and in his epic, he wishes to show how the destiny of one man, Aeneas, is fundamentally connected to this transcendent and eternal glory. His hero is not accidental; he has an essential role to play, and for just that reason, Aeneas participates in his heroic achievement. The literary effect is crucial and twofold. First, Vergil prevents the overwhelming glory of eternal Rome from eclipsing the significance of human endeavors. The greatness of Rome is not so transcendent that men can only serve; one man, at least, has a founding role for which he is not only destined but is also fit, both in virtue and passion. Thus, the greatness of Rome admits of human participation. But the electric charge runs both ways. For, to the extent that a man can participate in the greatness of Rome, he too is transcendent and eternal. The hero is connected to the highest and most surpassing excellence, even an excellence that begins to encroach on Olympus. The hero's character, then, is enlarged with divine purpose and potency.

Our strategy is to isolate the literary challenges of recognition, imitation, and participation, artificially perhaps, in three classical texts—the

Iliad, Apology of Socrates, and *Aeneid*—in order to prepare ourselves to engage the Christian literary project. Through these close readings of classical texts we hope to refine our literary imaginations in order to consider, more closely, Nietzsche's intuition that, in spite of its self-denying form, Christianity makes a claim upon our heroic aspiration. Achilles does not simply oppose Abraham. Rather, as our reading of Christian literature makes clear, the claims of faith involve an assumption about the relationship between the human person and surpassing excellence and power. The writer of the Gospel of Matthew, no less than Vergil in the *Aeneid,* bends his art to the task of showing how Jesus participates in divine glory. The writer of the Gospel of Mark, no less than Homer, wishes to underline the striking claim of recognition evoked by Jesus. Paul and other early Christian writers, no less than Plato, intend to incite our desire to imitate Jesus. Our claim is not that they agree about the nature and shape of the hero. Quite the contrary, as Nietzsche recognized, the classical world's vision of human excellence is very much at odds with the Christian ideal of discipleship. Our claim is that the works we consider are preoccupied with the question of surpassing excellence, how it is recognized and imitated, and the means by which a human being might participate in it. Our task as readers is to see and outline the dynamics of recognition, imitation, and participation, so that we might better understand the heroic ideal commended, whether Homeric, Platonic, Vergilian, or Christian.

But this is not an objective study, at least not in intent. We do not simply wish to see and outline diverse forms of the heroic ideal. Our purpose is apologetic. We want our readers to grasp the distinctive form of Christian heroism, the form that so agitated Nietzsche because he saw it so clearly. We wish to study heroism, in these various texts, so that both we and our readers can see self-denial as a form of human excellence. This is by no means easy. The vast modern consensus is that we should be in charge of our own destinies. We ought to believe only that for which we can discern sufficient evidence. We ought to take credit only for that which is wrought by our own hand. We ought to demand of ourselves and others only that for which we can find good reason. We ought to make room in our lives and the lives of others for our own unique self-expression. In each instance, characteristic modern "oughts" seek to encourage quite specific forms of human excellence—critical reflection, responsible creativity, and moral restraint appropriately pruned to make room for legitimate self-expression. A humanistic heroism—the Achilles of critical freedom and rational judgment—seems to collide with the Christian ideal of discipleship, and this makes the heroic obedience of Abraham incredible to the modern believer.

We are not so sure. Again, Nietzsche is our guide. He thought that his age was blind to heroic ideals, Christian or otherwise. A domesticated form of self-denial that he labeled "pity" so predominates that none are permitted to entertain ambition. Normalcy and a herd mentality demand conformity. People do not reject traditional Christianity, then, because it involves a childish conformity. They do not disbelieve out of the strength of a critical confidence. They do not turn away from obedience because they possess new powers of freedom. Instead, Christianity is rejected out of fear. The degree and intensity of self-denial seem altogether beyond the pale. Christianity is too much, not too little, too ambitious, not too childish. Christianity is incredible, but not in the way that belief in the tooth fairy is incredible. It is incredible much as Vergil's claims on behalf of Aeneas are incredible. We do not want to think that the pathways to excellence are so narrow and fraught with labor and sacrifice. We want human excellence to be a workaday project from which we can take holidays and enjoy our weekends. We want achievement to come in bite-sized pieces that are easily digested. We want heroes, but heroes we can pigeonhole and who do not draw us into all-consuming projects of imitation. We want role models whom we can balance off against each other so that they cancel out each other. In the end, then, the problem is not that Christian discipleship makes an implausible claim upon heroism—although, as we shall see, Spenser and Milton thought such a claim required great poetic labors—but rather that the modern humanist is allergic to the larger and more demanding claims of heroism.

Our primary goal, then, is to recover the role of excellence, both in the literature we study and in our own lives. We wish to combat the devaluation of heroism. This devaluation takes place in three ways. First, heroism is so widely democratized that it fails to signal a human excellence worthy of recognition and admiration. Second, heroism is often sentimentalized when we use the term to affirm anyone who might command our respect. Third, we seem to have developed a notion of the incidental hero, whose latent excellence goes unrecognized until an odd and extraordinary event reveals it. All three tendencies undermine the notion of heroic life, and as such, diminish our capacity to imagine lives devoted to excellence.

The tendency toward democratization or leveling is powerful. One of the most pervasive contemporary ideas of heroism is that anyone who is true to himself or herself is a hero. This is expressed in several ways. Any deed or career or personality can be perfected and therefore be heroic. One can be a heroic office clerk. One can be a heroic schoolteacher. One can be a heroic mom or dad. This may entail an element of self-knowledge and choice: the heroic mom must know herself to be destined as a mother and choose to assume that role with full commitment. But she could just as well be destined to be a heroic stockbroker, with a parallel self-knowledge and commitment. The point is that heroism is, in principle, available to all. Special qualities that mark classical heroism are absent. One need not be beautiful or strong or intelligent or simply lucky. Similarly, the attributes of Christian heroism do not hold sway. Heroism is found in the act of self-affirmation, not self-denial. One needs only to choose oneself. One need not be chosen by God. Democratic heroes, then, are well-adjusted middle-class folks who are committed to their social roles. Is it any wonder that this democratization of heroism fails to inspire excellence?

The sentimentalization of heroism runs on different tracks. A hero is anyone that we might admire. To children, no matter how old, parents or grandparents may be heroes. To avid students, their teacher is a hero. The older boy down the street may be a hero. The local Boy Scout leader is a hero. At each point, "hero" serves as an exclamation mark that people use to express admiration. To a certain degree, this participates in the classical meaning of heroism. A hero must be recognized and admired. However, the sheer fact of admiration is insufficient. A classical and Christian hero is presented as one who deserves the admiration of all. The sentimentalized hero is essentially private. I admire my dad. Maybe you ought to as well, but my description of him as a hero marks the psychic power he holds over me as his son, not the qualities that command universal admiration. Like so much else in contemporary culture, the public realm of excellence thins as we turn toward spheres of private relationships for satisfaction and fulfillment.

Incidental heroism is a remarkable phenomenon. From time immemorial, both good and bad luck have been woven into accounts of human excellence. Whether the fundamental luck of having a divine mother or of being predestined by God, or the more episodic luck of being in the right place at the right time, the heroic is colored by fate. Nonetheless, the airline pilot who lands the crippled plane, the fireman who rescues the child, the soldier who holds his ground: these episodes capture our imaginations simply by their seemingly heroic form. We do not wonder about the circumstances. We do not inquire into motivations. Is anyone who saves a child from a burning building a hero? Clearly the child's mother, the fireman, and the casual bystander have very different relations to that act. Yet we are uninterested in a pattern of past action or character, or in seeing the character and the action as inseparable and mutually defining. Is the fireman an ordinary guy who just happened to find a child in one of the bedrooms? Does the fireman possess an excellence, or was he merely in the right place at the right time? Perhaps because heroism is so democratized and sentimentalized, we hunger for some unique form of human behavior which is genuinely distinctive and worthy of emulation. Starved for "real heroes," we latch onto the extraordinary act and elevate the agent to the status of hero. The problem is that heroes are people who possess remarkable virtues and abilities, and are not unique acts. Since true heroism entails recognition and emulation, the incidental hero fails. If we want to be that kind of hero, then we should play the lottery so that we can be generous once we win.

These devaluations of heroism diminish our ability to identify human excellence. If everybody can be a hero, if "hero" is just another name for someone you love and respect, if heroic action begins to fade into sheer luck, then the full operation of heroic description atrophies. The distinctive patterns of character, action, and destiny which are intimate to classical heroic narratives no longer cohere. The mysterious embodiment of holiness and the otherworldly power of spiritual achievement that runs through the lives of the saints like an electrical charge are similarly eclipsed. There are many explanations for this loss of a fuller language of heroism. Some might say that a cultural pluralism has undercut our confidence in determinate patterns of human excellence. Others might say that natural science has so despiritualized the cosmos that we tend to see the extraordinary merely as a genetic or chemical oddity. We see no reason to dispute either claim. Nonetheless, we are inclined to think the present fragmentation of our sense of the heroic may have more to do with the inherent difficulties of presenting and representing the heroic in language and narrative. Both the classical and Christian texts that we will consider struggle to bring the distinctive character and achievement of their heroes into full form. Not every text (or drama or film or news broadcast or sporting event) shares that struggle. That our age has such a thin view of the hero, and a concomitant inarticulateness about the proper shape and embodiment of human excellence, can be attributed to a simplification of our heroic tradition, which fails to train us to see with any real precision the difficulty of manifesting and recognizing excellence.

We want to bring the reader, then, into the inner aspirations of these heroic narratives, not only to read well but also to recover the ability to think about, and strive toward, the heroic. Heroism is elusive, and the texts we consider in this book are important because they develop strategies for effectively narrating the power of heroic life. Fluency in that language might also train us to see and acknowledge the excellences and achievements of our own day. But more importantly, such fluency may help us see what Nietzsche saw—the potent aspirations of faith. Perhaps, then, the Christian claim to *save* will come out from behind the spiritual platitudes and into view as a stunningly ambitious and controversial claim about the power and fullness of human life. Our readers may still reject that Christian claim upon their souls. But if they understand the nature of Christian heroism, at least they will, with Nietzsche, reject it as incredible because it is fearlessly ambitious, not because it is childish and easy.

Our project has three parts. First, we attend to heroic figures from the classical period, beginning with the figure of Achilles in the *Iliad.* Our goal is not to develop a theory of the development of the hero in antiquity, nor as we shift from Achilles to Socrates to Aeneas, do we wish to discern a unifying definition of "the hero." Both are admirable goals, but ours is more modest. We wish to treat the Homeric epic and its Vergilian counterpart, as well as the Platonic dialogue, as fully formed literary performances from which we might learn the range and depth of heroic enactment. As parts of a unified cultural tradition that constitutes the background for Western Christianity, the texts give us the basic fluency necessary to talk about the role of recognition, imitation, and participation in Christian literary depictions of heroic discipleship.

The second part of our study directly engages foundational Christian texts. No account of Christian heroism can bypass the canonical narratives of Jesus of Nazareth. His achievement is presented as triumphant: cosmic in scope and divine in power. And yet, Jesus' life is remarkably thin. Although Jesus often silences his critics, heals the sick, and casts out demons, the canonical stories move beyond the standard heroic *topoi* of effective speech and triumphant action. The narrative flows toward his suffering and death on the cross. Our job as readers is to see how the Gospel writers depict this form of heroic achievement. The Gospel of Matthew works to bind Jesus' destiny to messianic fulfillment, and thus show how Jesus participates in divine glory. The Gospel of Mark presumes this participation, and turns attention toward evoking patterns of repentance and faith which constitute the proper recognition of Jesus' greatness. The followers of Jesus who came to be called Christians accepted the literary arguments of the Gospel stories, and thus faced the question of imitation. How does one follow the messiah? How can one emulate the man, who unlike any other man, is worshiped as one with the God who hates idols? Paul grapples with the difficulty of imitating the God-man, and in so doing, makes the bold claim that discipleship entails a transparency to Jesus. Faith does not imitate on the basis of independent, personal effort; rather, faith opens the believer for the mimetic power of grace that shapes us into the form of Christ. After Paul, the martyr and the monk both accept the scriptural claim that Jesus saves, and both are presented as paradigmatic imitators to be imitated. Their lives testify to the power of God to fill that which has been emptied in discipline and self-denial.

The third and final part of our study focuses on early and late modern accounts of heroism. Spenser and Milton are early modern poets whose literary ambitions are to join the most vivid forms of heroic life to Christian discipleship. Spenser's great cycle of allegories, *The Faerie Queene*, is a sustained effort to show that the heroic warrior fits the pattern of faithful dependence on Christ. The allegories of quest link ambition to obedience in order to formulate a picture of active and conquering discipleship. Milton's *Areopagitica* argues that Christian virtue untested is diminished rather than perfected. His epic account of the highest human heroism in *Paradise Regained* turns on the enduring and obedient virtue of Jesus perfected through the testing temptations of Satan. In both cases we see vigorous attempts to redeem the Christian claim that the Christian life is heroic. Two late modern figures forsake the ambitions of Spenser and Milton. Heroism, for Bonhoeffer, is an insufficiently ambitious language for describing the full power and achievement of discipleship. Thus, he removes distinctively human predicates from the life of discipleship. Christ is too powerful to be possessed; his achievement on the cross overflows into our lives and can never be recognized as ours. Discipleship is, finally, Jesus acting in and through our obedience to his commands. In a very different way, Camus also rejects heroism. Heroic ambition is an impulse to reach beyond our common humanity, and for Camus, the aspiration toward heroic enactment numbs us to the quite ordinary bonds of friendship and fellow feeling. Where Bonhoeffer would have us live in Christ alone, Camus wishes to bathe us in the particularity of human existence. For both, the ways in which heroic language highlights and exalts human excellence distract from that power which gives life. For both, the hero is set apart, and for just that reason, is severed from the true source of human fulfillment.

Perhaps Camus and Bonhoeffer are right, and the idea of heroism does distract from what *is* most important. It may be egocentric and draw us away from either God or our collective fate as beings in solidarity against death. In the end, we as authors have no strict investment in the language of heroism. In fact, our readings of some of the most important texts in classical and Christian literature highlight how difficult it is to employ this language, to make the hero real, to connect heroism to what *is* most important. The *Iliad* struggles to frame Achilles as a recognizable human figure. The writer of the Gospel of John works to fix Jesus in our minds as fully human. In both cases the special qualities of these heroes threaten to keep them at arm's length. Nonetheless, as we undertake this study, we have an investment in the heroic reach toward excellence. Whether or not our readers share the epic ambitions and attraction to heroic language that so clearly animate authors such as Spenser and Milton, to the extent that any of us wish to expand our imaginations, and perhaps our souls, we must come to terms with the heroic theme that runs like a red thread through all the texts we consider. We may resolve that we are fated to be normal, mediocre, comfortable, and sane, but we should not regard such a fate as heroic. Whether at the end of the day our powers and destinies permit heroic action, we should allow ourselves to be bitten by an ambition to reclaim excellence.

Chapter Two

The Presence of the Hero: Achilles

Character gives us qualities, but it is in our actions that we are happy or the reverse.

Aristotle, *Poetics*

Despite the great battle scenes, the *Iliad* is not about war. However poignant its observations about the futility of strife, it is not about the anonymous struggles of men or the meaninglessness of killing and dying. The *Iliad* is neither a poetic political manifesto in which Oriental despotism struggles against nascent democracy nor a structural mediation between the polarities of war and peace. These are components of the epic. Warriors from different lands meet in battle. Men exchange blows, and the sound of armor clattering to the ground echoes through the entire work. The ongoing war on the plains of Troy serves as the backdrop for the *Iliad*, but the action itself concerns the presence and absence of one man—Achilles—a man of inimitable excellence. The *Iliad* is far more than a catalogue of military engagements precisely because it takes with complete seriousness Achilles' furious desire for honor and recognition. His desire is matched by his excellence, but his desire will not be satisfied. Through Achilles' desire and his dissatisfaction, the poet presents the difficulty of awarding appropriate honor.

Heroic recognition is the overwhelming concern of all the characters in the *Iliad*, for the dynamics of honor and glory are intrinsic to the so-called heroic code. The desire for honor and recognition competes with and, in many cases, conquers the concerns of family, city, love, life, and death. But this desire and the forms of its satisfaction operate on several different planes and involve several different words in Greek. When Achilles is wronged by Agamemnon, his concern is primarily for *tîmê,* or what the Greeks owe him, both material and immaterial, in return for his person and his services. The kind of recognition designated *tîmê* is usually translated as "honor." But Achilles is also concerned with a different and less tangible kind of recognition, his *kleos,* which is often translated as "fame" or "glory" and is virtually synonymous with epic poetry itself. This is the recognition by future audiences who will hear of their achievements, and it is understood and hoped for (or dreaded) by most of the characters within the epic. For Achilles, it will come only with his death at Troy. *Kleos* is the key to the fundamental definition of the Homeric hero: he is one whose acts and achievements attract the attention and command the memory of all who come after. The hero embodies *kleos* actively, and *kleos* in turn creates him.

The preeminent hero at Troy is Achilles. The person and actions of Achilles in his unsurpassed excellence overwhelm ordinary settings. The Greeks agree that he is invaluable, a man of stellar skill, and yet he remains strangely elusive and difficult to honor appropriately. The structure and art of the *Iliad* are bent by the poet to the task of exposing the fullest possible scope of Achilles' power and substance as a man.[1] The epic only succeeds if that power and substance come to full presence in the dramatic action. The key to our reading of the *Iliad* is an awareness that the poet does not simply deploy common heroic tropes to manifest and frame the distinctive features of Achilles. Those tropes are certainly present in the text. Achilles is handsome. He is passionate in action and victorious in battle. He possesses an endurance beyond his peers and is favored by the gods. Yet the greatness of Achilles is not fully revealed in these standard heroic features. He is the most excellent human being, and as such, he exceeds the standard tropes. The *Iliad* testifies constantly to this excess, both in the voice of the narrator and in the voice of Achilles himself. No matter what the ethical system, no matter what heroic definition, Achilles seems too large for it.

Our interpretive claim is that the narrative action, both in structure and substance, presents Achilles within and yet surpassing the standard forms of heroic enactment, aware of his own excellence and dissatisfied with the inadequacy of recognition. The *Iliad* is never a shrine to Achilles; the magnitude of his dissatisfaction does not inspire awe. Nor does the *Iliad* founder on the problem of heroic magnitude and its proper poetic expression. It presents the difficulty of recognizing true glory. The epic brings heroic excellence and achievement into the fullest possible view, but acknowledges, even reinforces, our intuitive sense that the superhuman approaches the inhuman.

This difficulty of recognition testifies to the distance of the extraordinary hero from ordinary humanity. It dominates the literary efforts of the great poets and philosophers whom we consider in the following chapters, as well as the Gospel writers and those whose works are animated by the convictions of Christian faith. Within the Christian frame of reference, God is entirely different from man. Yet, in Jesus, the divinely superhuman is linked with the ordinary—and, in poverty, suffering, and death, even with the "sub-ordinary"—human form. In the language of the Christian creeds, Jesus must be recognized as both God and man. In this way, Christianity will appear to renounce the heroic, reaching far higher and far lower. The suffering Messiah is both above and below the range of honor and glory that defines the great men of antiquity.

We must engage the limits of the epic medium, both in Homer and Vergil, as well as the Platonic alternative, in order to fully appreciate this decisive shift in heroic presentation. For the classical texts we consider are not insensitive to the ways in which excellence drives beyond common assumptions about heroism; they thrust against the boundaries of honor and glory. In so doing, they anticipate difficulties that Christianity intensifies. Thus, to the extent that we can see Achilles as a hero too large for the epic frame of reference, as beyond recognition, we will train our literary imaginations to see Jesus and his disciples as early Christian writers intended: as "above heroic" and "below heroic." Further, we can prepare ourselves to understand the ambitious efforts of the Christian poets, Spenser and Milton, to reshape the classical epic form in order to serve Christian purposes.

At the most basic structural level, the *Iliad* is framed by two scenes of supplication which call for appropriate recognition, and both testify to the fact that seeing and recognizing are extraordinarily difficult. In the first book, Chryses pleads for the return of his daughter Chryseis, and he offers an appropriate ransom. Agamemnon rejects this ransom and withholds the girl. Faced with this refusal, Chryses prays to Apollo for vengeance, and the god obliges and sends a plague upon the Greek camp. Agamemnon is forced to yield up Chryseis to stay the hand of Apollo, but in so doing, he demands a proper replacement. He turns to Achilles and demands his war prize, the "fair-cheeked" Briseis. Achilles, second to none in battle, is enraged. He refuses to fight, predicting that the day will come when Agamemnon and his followers will long for the presence of Achilles. Everything that follows in the *Iliad* is a ramification of Achilles' refusal. A remarkably similar scene concludes the *Iliad*. Achilles has returned to battle to avenge the death of his beloved friend Patroclus. He has killed Hector, Patroclus's killer and the greatest Trojan warrior, and in rage, he withholds the body of the slain hero, refusing to permit his burial. Just as Chryses the father approaches Agamemnon, who possesses his child, at the opening of the epic, so Priam, the father of Hector, supplicates Achilles. Achilles recognizes Priam's claim upon the body of his son, and returns the dead Hector for proper burial.

These two scenes are important for our reading of the *Iliad* because the first introduces and the last recapitulates the basic pattern of withholding, supplication, and return which dominates the larger narrative structure of the epic. Both scenes involve children withheld. Both feature fathers as supplicants who plead for the return of their children. Both conclude with return and restoration. The centerpiece of the pattern is Achilles, who withholds himself from battle. He will not fight against the Trojans, even as they threaten to destroy the Greek forces. An embassy of Greek heroes, who supplicate him with various arguments, entreats Achilles to return. Like Agamemnon at the outset of the *Iliad,* Achilles rejects the terms of the supplication, both material and rhetorical. Yet, also like Agamemnon, subsequent events force him to relent. He returns to the battlefield, and the Trojans feel the full force of his heroic presence. The pattern is complete, but the narrative is not closed. Given the extremity of his character, his destiny, and his passion, Achilles' choice to return to battle carries exceptional narrative momentum and consequence, just as Agamemnon's failure to return Chryseis implicates Achilles and his rage, and carries the whole of the epic in its train. His heroic presence overflows the scene of his return and is revealed and enlarged in the exchange with Priam.

Guided by the framing scenes of withholding, supplication, and return, we want to take a close look at the way in which the *Iliad* crafts the full sweep of Achilles' heroic enactment. Heroic *kleos* is won by actions; heroism requires performance. Our conviction is that Achilles' performance is revealed through the conventions of heroic manifestation and recognition, but it stretches the boundaries of heroic storytelling. The *Iliad* constantly suggests the overabundant excess of Achilles' heroism. Paradoxically, this excess is dramatized in his absence from the scenes of battle which are rightfully the most appropriate context for his distinctive excellence, and emphasized in the inadequacy of standard forms of heroic recognition. By withholding himself, Achilles draws attention to his inestimable glory. Without him, the Greeks are doomed; with him, they are victorious. And yet, in the scenes of supplication and in his return to battle, the *Iliad* testifies to the difficulty of actually seeing and affirming the excellence of Achilles. Restitution is not enough. Killing Hector is not enough. Dragging his body around for days is not enough. The excess of Achilles is contained, but only temporarily, during the final supplication of Priam. With this in mind, then, we must turn to the three-fold pattern of withholding, supplication, and return so that we can understand more fully the need for and difficulty of heroic recognition, both for the hero and the poet.

The Absences of Achilles

Achilles first suffers from the loss and absence of Briseis, which, more broadly, is the absence of due recognition for his heroic excellence. He then inflicts his own absence upon the Greeks by his withdrawal from battle. His absence stands like a shadow over the subsequent conflict. By Zeus's decree, Achilles is the determinative focus of the battle. The Greeks will lose as long as he is absent. Both absences, of Achilles' honor and his presence in battle, are intertwined as cause and effect, and together they drive forward the action of the epic.

Let us look, then, at the first withdrawal. Agamemnon is angered by the role of protector that Achilles plays in the return of his prize, Chryseis, to her father. Feeling, perhaps, the implicit challenge that Achilles poses by guaranteeing the safety of Calchas as he prophesied against him, Agamemnon wishes to put Achilles in his place, "I don't care about you. I have no regard for you or your anger," Agamemnon says, and he declares that he shall take Briseis from Achilles as replacement for Chryseis. This he shall do, says Agamemnon, "so that you may know well how much greater I am than you" (1.180–87).[2]

Briseis is taken from him, and Achilles feels the pain of her departure. But even more, Achilles feels a competitive, bitter anger. Agamemnon takes Briseis in order to demonstrate his self-proclaimed superiority over Achilles. The *Iliad* is Achilles' epic, as the poet proclaims from the first line—is it only Agamemnon who does not know that Achilles is the "greatest of the Achaeans"?[3] Achilles' greatness is even mandated by his father Peleus, who tells him, as Nestor reminds Patroclus, "always to be the best and to be superior to others" (11.784), a maxim that lies at the heart of Iliadic ambition. But superiority is ambivalent enough to allow

Nestor to say in consecutive lines to Achilles that he is superior "since a goddess gave you birth" and that Agamemnon is superior "since he rules more men" (1.280–81). Agamemnon asserts his superiority as ruler by taking away Briseis. For Agamemnon not only withdraws the comfort and succor of a beautiful woman. In doing so, more significantly, he withdraws the prize that Achilles has won in battle, demonstrating that he, and not Achilles, distributes the spoils of war. Achilles' loss is, then, more public than private. Achilles speaks with great passion about her, but Briseis is not primarily important to Achilles as a romantic interest—he chillingly speaks of his love for her in the past tense[4]—or even as a person. Instead, she personifies Achilles' honor. Though she is not equivalent to his honor, she represents it when she is with him, and unfortunately, represents his dishonor when she is not. To Achilles, her representational significance is greater than her personal significance—but again, he never distinguishes the two, nor does the poet. By removing from him the "fair-cheeked" prize of battle, Agamemnon strips Achilles of honor before the entire army, asserting his own, higher, status.

As Briseis departs, so does the objective *tîmê* of Achilles. By withdrawing this spoil of victory, honor, Agamemnon fails to recognize the greatness of Achilles, and this infuriates and afflicts him. It is this absence he wishes to redress, this honor he wishes to restore. At the very least, decides Achilles, Agamemnon will know the foolishness of his mad action. His first impulse is to make that foolishness obvious by killing Agamemnon: Is the victim greater than the victor? But Athena stays his arm; Achilles cannot take the direct path to vindication. Instead, he pledges to make manifest Agamemnon's mistake by withdrawing from battle. To dishonor the greatest has a price. In his absence, predicts Achilles, "you will be able to do nothing," for the "man-slaughtering Hector" will have his way and many men will drop and die (1.241–42). If Agamemnon wishes to lord his greatness over Achilles, then so be it. Soon Agamemnon will see who is, indeed, the greater. And when he does, he will beg for Achilles' presence.

That Achilles refuses the battlefield is remarkable. By remaining in his tent, Achilles forsakes the forum for his own heroic enactment. War, however much it might depend on the strong arms of a few champions, is a communal effort. Honor and glory go to individuals, but the recognition of achievement, the bestowal of honor, and the memory of glory require the fellowship of comrades. *Tîmê* and *kleos* cannot be gained in private, and Achilles' absence from the battlefield runs the real risk of the greatest humiliation: subsequent absence from the memory of generations to come. Old Nestor, who more than other heroes sees with the clarity of age, brings just this possibility to Patroclus's attention. Nestor perceives that Achilles' absence is fatal, and he bends all of his persuasive energies toward ensuring his return. When Achilles sends Patroclus to investigate the fate of the Greeks, Nestor speaks to him. Reminding him of his own glory, Nestor warns Patroclus that Achilles has taken a dangerous path. Achilles may be blessed by the gods with excellence greater than all others, "but," Nestor continues, "Achilles will enjoy his own excellence (*aretê*) alone; and I think he will shed many tears, too late, when the people have perished" (11.761–63). Such tears will not fall from sympathy for the dead. Achilles will weep, suggests Nestor, because none will sing his praise, nor will there be anything to sing of.

The narrative action of the *Iliad* is governed by these initial withholdings or absences. They throw the heroism of Achilles into question. Objectively, the dishonor entailed in the loss of Briseis compromises Achilles' greatness. Although we readers know that Achilles will surpass Agamemnon, and although the various characters in the epic never seem to doubt that Achilles is the greatest of warriors, the fact of dishonor remains. Achilles is acutely aware that he must respond to it appropriately in order to regain his honor. In large part, Achilles' own withholding or absence is part of this response, a response validated by Zeus. However, for a hero whose passion for glory is not limited by worries about failure, this is a risky strategy. By withdrawing, Achilles renounces the communal conditions for heroic enactment and recognition. He cannot possess his glory in loneliness. And precisely because Achilles is so indispensable to his allies, his absence puts the entire communal project at risk of ultimate failure. And with that failure would come the loss of all possibility of conventional, human honor. So both the initial loss of Briseis, which afflicts Achilles, and the subsequent absence he inflicts on his comrades strike us as an eclipse rather than a manifestation of heroic excellence. The dishonor lowers his status, and his response involves a retreat into inaction. Neither are auspicious narrative conditions for rendering visible the fullness of a heroic character.[5]

THE SUPPLICATION OF ACHILLES

The theme of withdrawal was apparently one familiar from earlier epic poetry, and its outlines are in place in Athena's promise to Achilles of "three times as many gifts" (1.212–15). We can reconstruct the pattern: the dishonored hero refuses to participate, his absence reveals his worth, and he receives his due recognition at his return.[6] In the ninth book of the *Iliad*, the Greek leaders send an embassy to supplicate Achilles, hoping to entice Achilles into this familiar epic pattern. The Greeks have suffered setback after setback and realize that they cannot defeat the Trojans without Achilles. So drastically have the tides of battle shifted that they fear that they may themselves be defeated. So the Greek leaders send Odysseus, Phoenix, and Ajax, armed with the offer of glorious compensation, to ask Achilles to return to the fight. The three ambassadors each make different appeals to Achilles in speeches. Achilles shifts his position slightly in response to each one, but still refuses. Like Agamemnon before him, who refused the entreaties of Chryses that involved common appeals to the standards of heroic practice, Achilles will not accept the standard coin of honor and recognition.

The supplication of Achilles by the Greeks in the ninth book is the pivotal moment of the *Iliad*'s plot, not only because it intensifies the drama of Achilles' absence by recapitulating the decisions of book 1, but also because this attempt to repair the breach between Achilles and Agamemnon reveals both the depth and ambiguity of Achilles' own purposes in withdrawing from the conflict. The Greeks intend to offer him the deprived honor, *tîmê,* in the form of enormous wealth. Such compensation is very much in keeping with the heroic atmosphere of the *Iliad.* It has been promised to Achilles by Athena in the first book of the *Iliad,* when she descends from heaven to check Achilles' rage and to prevent him from killing Agamemnon in front of the entire army after Achilles was wronged. "I will say this to you, and it will be a thing accomplished: three times as many glorious gifts will be placed before you for the sake of this outrage. Hold back, obey me" (1.212–15). Before approaching Achilles, Nestor advises such a reconciliation. In the assembly of leaders following a series of military defeats, he says to Agamemnon, "You disgraced an excellent man whom even the gods have honored . . . but even now, let us consider how to make amends and win him back with glorious gifts and conciliatory words" (9.110–13). Agamemnon understands the need for reconciliation, and, accepting Nestor's advice, he offers the requisite gifts, which include gold, horses, cities, even his own daughter. Thus, with the imprimatur of the gods and by the wise advice of Nestor, an embassy of heroes enters Achilles' tent with exactly the kind of recognition that they assume he wants. His honor has been taken away. Now an offer has been made to return that honor, and more.

During the embassy, each of the heroes reiterates the offer of restored honor, though each in a different way, according to his distinctive character. Odysseus makes the first entreaty. He appeals to Achilles' sense of communal solidarity, pointing out the seriousness of the danger facing the Greeks (9.247–51). He evokes Achilles' father, who, he says, warned against "the bad complication of quarrel" that stands in the way of honor (9.257). He commends the magnitude of the gifts offered by Agamemnon, which he itemizes in detail (9.260–99). Though the litany of gifts is great, and though in the standard epic pattern the withdrawal of a hero is properly reversed with just such a supplication, Odysseus is aware that Achilles may so hate Agamemnon that he rejects his offer. He ends his speech with a final appeal, one that is far more serious. The Greeks are in retreat for one very important reason: Hector is at the front of the Trojan forces. By returning, he observes, "you might kill Hector," and "all the Greeks would honor you like a god; and you would win great glory (*kudos*)" (9.302–4). As a warrior profoundly sensitive to the desire for glory, Odysseus is reminding Achilles that return to battle provides the chance to meet the greatest enemy warrior, one who has been avoiding a direct fight for nine years, and whose defeat would yield the highest possible return of honor and glory. What could give a true hero greater incentive to return to battle?

Achilles' response makes quick work of the offer of gifts that Odysseus so carefully describes. The standard economy of heroic recognition holds no allure. Men fight, says Achilles, and whether they die, run, or fight valiantly to victory, it matters not. By taking away his prize of honor, Agamemnon has made a mockery of the entire system of heroic recognition through gift giving. Achilles will no longer fight under those terms. And yet, in that speech of redoubled determination to stay out of the battle, he does acknowledge the last of Odysseus's appeals. He reports that his mother has told him that he has two destinies. One entails returning home to a long life in which the fullness of his glory is lost. The other rests very much with the fury of Hector, for it entails remaining to fight by the city of Troy and to enjoy a glory everlasting (9.411–16). Odysseus was right in his final appeal. Achilles does know that the only way to remedy the dishonor brought on by Agamemnon is through a return to battle. However much Agamemnon may have perverted the economy of honor and recognition, Hector is abroad and the possibility of heroic enactment remains. But Achilles refuses that possibility. He is utterly determined to withhold himself from battle, and, as if to place an exclamation point on his absence, he announces his plan to depart in his ships at dawn.

This speech is Homer's rhetorical masterpiece because it marks, in Achilles' own words, his character, his passion, and his difference. As such, it has invited intense interpretive scrutiny.[7] Achilles places a competitive value (his personal honor) over cooperative values (community and victory) with a passionate finality.[8] None of the Greeks disagrees with the fact that he has been inappropriately treated, and that Agamemnon is in the wrong,[9] but all seem to feel that the gesture of compensation is adequate and that Achilles should be satisfied. Yet he is not. Achilles is willing to court the risks of withdrawal from conflict, a move that, as Odysseus suggests, might lead to the ultimate disaster: the destruction of the community that is necessary for heroic recognition itself. There are two obvious ways to interpret Achilles' determined refusal of Agamemnon's gifts. Both are guided by plausible interpretive intuitions. One sees Achilles as superseding the standard economy of heroic recognition altogether. The other insists that the standard economy of heroic recognition is a necessary part of the Iliadic worldview, and as such, Achilles cannot function outside its constraints. Our view is that Achilles must enact his heroic glory within the standard economy—it is the only functional system of honor in the epic—but that his presence as a hero exceeds its boundaries of recognition.

Modern readers are tempted to see Achilles' response to Odysseus as a rejection of the heroic way of life, as if Achilles is claiming an independence from a system that he has seen through. The language itself is particular to Achilles and has encouraged some scholars to interpret Achilles' speech as the expression of a new, tragic worldview by the man who has eclipsed the old, epic one.[10] By this reading, Achilles is a hero not only of the battlefield but also for his moral clarity. In the extremity of his experience, he grasps the essential falsity of the Greek social system of honor and shame. Whether a man flees or fights matters little, since the trappings of heroism are awarded arbitrarily. Accordingly, Achilles refuses the supplication of Agamemnon's emissaries because, for the first time, he realizes that, finally, all that matters is the fulfillment of his desires, aspirations, and destiny. One need not be recognized as a hero by the "official culture." Conviction and authenticity are enough.

There are several problems with such a reading, but it retains an attractive power. Achilles does differentiate himself from patterns of common expectation. Ajax's exasperated speech testifies to Achilles' determination to flout the official culture. And further, when he responds to Odysseus, Achilles gives vivid expression to the fact that the significance of his life overflows the bounds set by the standard patterns of heroic recognition. As Achilles observes, even the greatest "possessions are not equal compensation for my life. . . . For cattle and fat sheep are things that can be taken, and tripods possessed, and golden maned horses; but a man's life does not come again, not by stealing nor taking, whenever it passes the fence of his teeth" (9.401, 406–9). Achilles is able to see himself outside the conventional accoutrements of honor. At the very least, he conceives of a want greater than the system can provide. His life exceeds all these things.

As attractive as this reading might be, a disdain for tripods and golden-maned horses is at odds with the dominant ethos of the *Iliad.* The heroes are motivated by the acquisition of glory and honor, which for some amounts to a zero-sum game. The glory that one gains in killing is the glory won from the one being killed, and this glory is bound up with the armor of the defeated. Victories are followed by stripping the armor of the vanquished, or commandeering his horses. To the victor goes the glory made manifest in the esteem and prerogatives that come to the victorious.[11] Another important character in the *Iliad,* Sarpedon, like Achilles the son of a divinity, articulates the close identification of glory and honor that Achilles calls into question. He speaks to his companion Glaucus:

> Glaucus, why are we two honored most with first place, with
>   choice meats and with full cups, in Lycia where
> all look on us as gods? We hold our allotted land on the banks of
>   the Xanthus, good for vines and fields of wheat.
> Now we two must go among the front ranks of Lycians,
> to stand and throw ourselves into the battle's raging heat,
> so that any of the heavily armored Lycians would say,
> "Not without glory do our kings hold sway in Lycia,
> they who eat the rich meat and drink the honeysweet wine; for, to
>   be sure, their fighting strength is noble, when they fight among the
>   front ranks of the Lycians." O friend, if
> we two could flee this war and live forever, ageless and deathless, I
>   would never fight in the front ranks again,
> nor send you into the battle where men win glory. But now
> the fates of death hover around us, thousands of ways to die, which
>   no man can escape or ward off—so let us go in to fight.
> Let us give a triumph to someone, or let him give one to us!
>
> (12.310–28)

This principle of noblesse oblige is the obverse of Achilles' complaint. We have been honored, the two Lycian kings say, so we must prove ourselves worthy of it. And their stances on death are also opposite. Since we will all die, it is better to die with glory than without it.[12] The honor (*tîmê*) that the heroes receive takes the material form of privileged lands, foods, and seats, but in a larger sense it is essentially immaterial. Honor designates status earned as well as conferred; it marks that which is due to a person by virtue of character and achievement. But there is a great deal of ambiguity in the definition of what is due. The particular standards for honor, for its bestowal and receipt, vary within a range, and this allows for debate and disagreement about the right course of action within the ethical framework that governs the Greek community.[13] However, the basic structure of expectation is clear. As Glaucus and Sarpedon have been given honor in concrete and abstract ways, their glory has been recognized. But just as clearly, they earn their honor and achieve their glory by fighting.

Exactly how this economy of manifestation and recognition functions in the epic is the object of much scholarship. In general, it seems clear that the reciprocity is not a tightly regulated exchange, that is, a fixed number of gifts in return for a fixed number of deeds. The reciprocal actions are done as favors and as expressions of gratitude; and the gifts themselves are merely symbolic of the honor that the hero has won, which has true and lasting value. Achilles, however, is not quarreling about the subtleties of reciprocal action. He is rejecting the very currency of heroic recognition by refusing to entertain Agamemnon's gifts. An important difference between Achilles' and Sarpedon's speeches signals the reason for this stark refusal. Sarpedon's words express an interpersonal reciprocity between leaders and their people (the Lycians, in Sarpedon's case). In contrast, Achilles' concern is the lack of reciprocity between leaders of equal status.[14] Thus, Sarpedon finds compelling reasons for fighting, while the lack of true reciprocity undermines the motive for Achilles to fight.

In view of this difference between Sarpedon's clear affirmation of the standard economy and Achilles' equally clear refusal of a supplication based on such reciprocity, we might ask whether Achilles speaks and acts from within that heroic framework, or as an outsider, having seen through it? The weight of scholarship is currently leaning toward Achilles as a participant of the system and not as an outsider, and we agree with this interpretation of the context for Achilles' refusal. Achilles takes pains to explain his refusal to the Greeks who have come to him in terms of the ethical structure of reciprocity that they all understand. Achilles' refusal is not then a general statement about the inherent meaninglessness of honor, given the fact of death; it is a specific rebuttal to Agamemnon, who has perverted the meaning of the system. Achilles realizes that no apology from Agamemnon is communicated, and thereby there is no true recognition of his wrongful treatment of Achilles. Agamemnon's gifts are no longer symbolic of Achilles' honor, but are equated with it, and that is unacceptable.

Achilles demands recognition, and all the interpersonal and communal elements such recognition entails, not mere compensation and enticement.[15]

However much his withdrawal from battle separates him from the standard economy of heroic life, Achilles is not offering an alternative vision. He is complaining that a misuse of the standard economy of achievement and recognition by Agamemnon destroys the only source of meaning that gifts and rewards have. The gratitude that has never been there, as Achilles recognizes, is not a fault of the system but of Agamemnon, who is unable to give it. For this reason, not only is Agamemnon not persuasive, but Achilles seems to say that he will never be. Achilles goes on to cite his adherence to the ethic in the lines that follow (9.328–37): he sacked eleven cities by land, twelve more by sea (the siege of Troy allowed such secondary conquests of neighboring cities), and brought the spoils back to Agamemnon for redistribution.[16] But Agamemnon did not parcel out honor as the ethic would suggest; he kept a disproportionate amount for himself. He compounds the transgression by taking back the gift that Achilles had already been given, the woman Briseis, whom Achilles claims to have loved. In this light, Achilles is not criticizing the system of the heroic ethic. He is faulting Agamemnon for not observing it. According to this interpretation of the refusal, Achilles is not presenting an alternate view of life and heroic values. He is a participant in the system, and defined by the system, and its greatest adherent. He does withdraw, but not in order to find a new, nonheroic way to define achievement and worthiness, but to hold out for a fuller and more fundamental recognition within the heroic framework.

We have considered two options for reading Achilles' refusal, one that individualizes and exempts him from the system, one that involves and integrates him fully into it. Let us propose a third.[17] Although Achilles' great speech in the ninth book seems to be a summation of the general value of human life and of the honor due to the individual, such an interpretation does not make sense contextually. Achilles is not explaining the limitations of the system in itself. He is explaining (and this is crucial for our reading of heroic enactment in the *Iliad*) the limitations of its application *in his own case*. For Achilles, the problem with the standard economy is that the specific conditions of his particular life, both the conditions of his dishonor and the unique destiny, which he must choose, exceed the patterns of achievement and recognition. Agamemnon cannot come up with enough gold to restore Achilles' honor. The prospect of future rewards is entirely inadequate for the recognition that Achilles desires and for the destiny he foresees.

In view of the particular conditions of Achilles' refusal, it is not surprising that the Greeks listening to him are not persuaded. None of them seems to understand quite the extremity of Achilles' position. Ajax, the last to speak, pointedly expresses his incomprehension. The man he sees before him is otherworldly. Achilles is savage and pitiless, impervious to the needs of his friends. He is forgetful of the honor that has already been bestowed upon him above all others. But most poignantly, Ajax suggests that Achilles is inhuman. He points out, accurately, that even relatives will sometimes accept compensation for a kinsman or child slain, and he cannot comprehend why Achilles so values one woman, to the extent that he refuses the offer of seven from Agamemnon. Ajax makes a claim for friendship and affection (*philotês*), which the others make before him but not as strongly, striking again the other theme that runs powerfully alongside honor throughout the *Iliad*.[18] And to him, Achilles answers approvingly: "You seem to have spoken everything pretty much in agreement with my spirit" (9.645). Achilles then explains that even so, he cannot forget his rage, and at the memory of Agamemnon's slight his heart "swells with fury." Ajax is the most basic outline of the Greek martial hero, a reduction to the lowest common denominator of strength and love of glory, and Achilles agrees with him without being persuaded at all.[19] At this point in the narrative we are invited to wonder exactly what Achilles' relationship to the system is. He complains that it must be based entirely on proper interpersonal reciprocity and recognition, and yet he cannot articulate a heroic form of life in a way fully intelligible to those who are supposed to share it.[20]

The extremity of Achilles' speech echoes that of his situation and of his character. The system is inadequate, in the final analysis, even if practiced perfectly, for his need for heroic enactment. Achilles has reached a point, perhaps even precipitated it himself, where there is no clear correlation between honor, excellence, and the heroic ethic. The system gives no honor to those who hang back, who are absent from the fight, who cannot persuade, who are outside the community. Achilles approaches such an absence. However, this isolation cannot be viewed as an exemption or dismissal from heroic achievement and recognition. Even in refusal and isolation his excellence is recognized. His potential worth as a great warrior seems objectively agreed upon by all. We suggest that Achilles is neither simply within or outside the standard heroic assumptions that animate Ajax. In other words, Achilles possesses something that overwhelms the standard economy of achievement and recognition. He is not outside, but rather too large for the conventional frame.

He is not isolated, but he exceeds. He is therefore beyond the full recognition that a warrior like Ajax assumes to be the proper function of the standard economy.

Achilles defines appropriateness and excess differently. Warriors who shirk battle are liable to the severest reproach and censure—to do so is to commit a moral wrong. The terms of shame, reproach, and transgression are more varied than the terms of honor and appropriateness and have received more study.[21] The two concepts that receive the most attention are *aidos* and *nemesis*. Roughly, *aidos* corresponds to the emotion provoked by the thought of failing to act in ways appropriate to one's social and moral role and being seen by others to do so, while *nemesis* is the disapproval provoked in those who witness such a failure.[22] Significantly, the position of Achilles receives very little censure. During the embassy, Phoenix says to him that "up to now your anger is not *nemessê-ton*," that is, it does not seem inappropriate or unjustified to anyone (9.523). Only in the final book, when Achilles continues to drag Hector's body around Patroclus's tomb on the twelfth day after Hector's death, does Apollo protest to the gods and suggest that Achilles is in danger of incurring the *nemesis* of the gods (24.52–54).[23] Achilles feels no *aidos* and provokes no *nemesis*, nor is his action *nemessêton*. This is an element of his character, something that he understands of himself and that the others understand of him. What is inappropriate to one's role depends on individual circumstances,[24] and Achilles' status seems to preclude the indignation of others. Of course, Achilles himself feels *nemesis*, perhaps more quickly than any other person. Patroclus, the most gentle character, urges him *not* to feel it if he pities the Greeks, who are Achilles' enemies (16.22), and Patroclus initially refuses Nestor's invitation to stay because Achilles is prone to *nemesis* (11.649).[25] Again, Achilles is not outside the ethical system of shame and resentment, but his experience of it is presented uniquely, from the vantage point of near-perfection.

This interpretation of Achilles' relationship to the ethos that informs his supplicants is reinforced by his response to Phoenix. In that response, Achilles reveals the insufficiency of the honor contained entirely within the standard economy of recognition. As the voice of memory, Phoenix recounts past models of withdrawal, supplication, and return: "we've heard the songs of heroes past, when choking anger possessed them. Yet they were won with gifts and words" (9.524–26). He proceeds to tell the story of Meleager, who similarly withdrew from battle and was offered great gifts to return. But Meleager refused until the final moment, and then returned without the gifts, to a lesser glory.[26] Phoenix knows

Achilles as well as anyone, and perhaps he sees through the threat to leave at dawn. The story of Meleager is a cautionary tale: beware testing the limits of the standard pattern of withdrawal, supplication, and return, for beyond certain limits, returns diminish.

Achilles' response to Phoenix is stunning: "Old father, I have no need for this honor: for I know that I am honored by the decree of Zeus" (9.607–8). Phoenix knows his warlike nature, yet he does not seem to know exactly what Achilles seeks. Whatever it is, it rests, says Achilles, "in Zeus' decree" (9.608), but it remains unexplained. Just as Achilles sees and can express a life that moves beyond the standard economy, he also sees a glory and honor outside the system, one residing in the hands of the gods. Achilles seems to envision a form of honor that transcends stripping armor from the vanquished and rounding up the horses of riderless chariots, an honor "by decree" rather than an honor that flows from heroic performance and the songs of poets.

What kind of honor can exceed the very bounds of epic? The figure of Paris offers a window on this question. The cause of the war, Paris is often viewed as simply a nuisance, a nonheroic precipitator of events greater than he is, a subtragic trigger for a real heroic venue. But he has the patronage of a goddess, Aphrodite, whom he chose, and whose favor keeps him virtually inviolable. And of course, he has Helen. In a narrative in which women (and the "possession" of them) bear a strong correlation to one's *tîmê*, Paris must be viewed with some esteem: he won and keeps the most beautiful woman in the world in the face of popular disapproval and personal censure.[27] Paris's limitations on the battlefield prevent him from winning the honor available there. But he shares with Achilles the fact of possessing a form of excellence, in his case, extreme physical beauty. Like Achilles, Paris incarnates the gap between some forms of human excellence and an ethic that is bound up in balances and measures. The inability of the *Iliad* to find a fitting role for Paris testifies to the way in which his particular excellence exceeds the frame of heroic enactment.

Achilles is as close to human perfection as the *Iliad* can conceive. He has a beautiful form as does Paris, but unlike Paris, Achilles is very much at home on the battlefield. The problem facing the poet is that however fitting the plains of Troy are for a portrayal of Achilles the hero, the full force of his presence overwhelms the normal bounds of heroic engagement, victory, and reward. The entire scene of supplication in the tents of Achilles drives home just how difficult this problem is. Achilles wants what the epic seeks to portray. He wants to perform great deeds on the field of battle, and to have those deeds, and potency of his character that made such deeds possible, recognized in the fullness of his heroic glory. This desire marks a heightened ambition, one the defines Achilles' character, but without active engagement, without returning to the battlefield where Hector rages, it is an impossible ambition.

THE RETURN OF ACHILLES

As with many other supplications in the *Iliad*,[28] the supplication of Achilles ends successfully: he does return. But he is not won, as the others imagine, by glorious gifts and conciliatory words. He reenters the field of battle only when his beloved friend Patroclus is killed by Hector, and his own armor, which Patroclus wears into the field, is stripped and worn by Hector. Upon his return Achilles receives all the gifts promised in the previous books, but the death of Patroclus and the grief of Achilles put them in their proper light, which is the very light that Achilles articulates in his great refusal of book 9. Gifts do not measure honor, nor does honor come only with gifts. Enactment is necessary. Patroclus echoes the initial prayer of Achilles as he exhorts the Myrmidons to fight "to honor Achilles, by far the greatest of the Greeks . . . and that Agamemnon might know his madness, who gave no honor to the greatest of the Greeks" (16.271–74).[29] The death of Patroclus does not change the issue of Achilles' return from one of generic honor to a personal vengeance. The return of Achilles is still a matter of his peculiar honor. The death of Patroclus intensifies the issue by weaving in the motive of vengeance. In a sense, the death of Patroclus also purifies the issue of honor, for in his death the death of Achilles is clearly foreshadowed,[30] and in avenging him, Achilles demonstrates his heroic excellence at a level beyond the capacity of the standard economy of honorific recognition.

The sending of Patroclus seems at odds with Achilles' refusal, but it represents Achilles' softening in the face of a fourth, beloved suppliant. Patroclus returns from his errand for information and repeats Nestor's wish that he wear Achilles' armor into battle and lead their men, and he animates his supplication with his own grief at the Greek suffering. Achilles yields. He cannot forget his treatment at Agamemnon's hands, and nothing has happened to change that, but he relents to Patroclus and allows him to beat back the immediate threat of defeat. But he puts a strict limitation on Patroclus. He is only to ward off the disaster from the ships, and not to attack Troy itself. Achilles expresses the reason clearly: "so that you win for me great honor and glory from all the Greeks, and that they might send back my beautiful girl and provide many glorious gifts in addition" (16.84–86). Patroclus is not to usurp Achilles' role. And he does not.

Patroclus dies, and Achilles' hope for his return is brutally crushed. We maintain that this blow to Achilles does not replace his larger goal of achieving the honor that is his due. A personal and private purpose does not replace Achilles' communal and public ambition to achieve a surpassing glory. As Zeus himself planned, the death of Patroclus serves as the impetus of Achilles' return. Achilles, whose particular condition is so resistant to the communal standards and expectation of heroic motivation and action, but whose singular desire is to triumph within those standards and expectations, is swayed by his particular affections. Patroclus's death secures the success of his supplication; Achilles returns to battle and ensures the victory for which Patroclus knew he would be essential.

The bond of Patroclus and Achilles precedes the start of the Trojan War by years.[31] Nestor reminds Patroclus that his father, Menoetius, charged him as the elder to watch over Achilles, give him advice, and guide him, even though Achilles is superior in nobility and is stronger (11.785–89). Achilles exempts Patroclus from his wish that all Greeks and Trojans die, and he is willing to share the ultimate honor and glory with him. As much as he loved or loves Briseis, Achilles would prefer her death to Patroclus's (19.59–60). Achilles even says that news of his father's or son's deaths would not cause him more grief than the death of Patroclus does (19.321–27). His love for Patroclus is profound, and his desire to avenge his death is intense. But after Patroclus's death, Achilles' rage is in no way at odds with the standard motivations for returning to the conflict. Achilles' campaign against Hector is motivated by honor along with love and grief. Not just a private impulse born of personal feelings, it is a public endeavor undertaken for glory. Vengence is added to desire for glory.

Though communal, Achilles' return to the conflict and his pursuit of honor take on a further affective and personal quality. Achilles knows that he must kill Hector, and he knows that his death will follow Hector's. The choice of his life is made: a short, glorious one without a homecoming (16.88–93). Achilles' short life is a theme throughout the *Iliad*, especially in the scenes with Thetis and during the embassy, and no mention of his fate fails to evoke what must come with it. After he accepts his death, he claims its corollary: "But now let me win noble glory" (16.121), and he longs to make the Trojan women wail and tear their cheeks and know how long he has been absent. What glory Patroclus enjoyed has been taken by Hector. The armor of Achilles, which Patroclus wears into battle, represents his brief, borrowed honor, and when Patroclus dies, it is stripped from his dead body by Hector, and put on. That redoubles Achilles' fury. He wants to reclaim the armor, and his glory and that of Patroclus which it represents, and to humiliate Hector, just as he wanted to reclaim Briseis and humiliate Agamemnon.

And he does so. The streams of passion converge and intensify his commitment to action. Leaving a wide wake of bodies, Achilles finally confronts Hector, kills him, and recovers his armor. Yet, the armor represents the essential problem of enactment for Achilles at this point in the narrative. What kind of honor comes with winning armor that is one's own to begin with? Just as Agamemnon's gifts merely restore Achilles to his earlier status within the standard heroic economy, so also the recovery of his armor simply restores. In neither case does Achilles move forward into a fuller status or honor. All along Achilles has desired more. His passion continues to push him forward.

A HEROISM OF EXCESS

Why doesn't the *Iliad* end with the death of Hector? Several of its driving themes are completed: Achilles' own death is assured, as is the fall of Troy, though neither will happen within the narrative of the *Iliad*. The cycle of withdrawal and supplication is completed with Achilles' return. Achilles' wrath reaches its highest level of enactment in the death of Hector, one that can only be repeated, not surpassed. As we shall see, Vergil ends the *Aeneid* with its parallel scene of the death of Turnus, with Aeneas incensed and enraged. But Vergil has a larger frame of destiny and empire into which Aeneas must meaningfully fit. Homer does not; he goes on. He does not allow his hero to attain his glory by killing his greatest enemy and dragging his body while Hecuba and Andromache lament. The armor of Achilles that Patroclus wears and Hector strips, the symbol of his own honor and his death and which is significant between books 16 and 22, receives little attention after Hector's death. It is stripped from Hector's body and thrown in Achilles' chariot (22.368–69, 399). Achilles' wrath remains insatiable. In the final two books, the poet recasts the theme of excess and of "enough" and resets the stage of recognition.

Book 23 begins with the end of the day of Achilles' rampage, which began in book 19. The book opens with mourning and relentlessness, but after fifty-six lines, night comes, and sleep. While Achilles sleeps on the beach, the ghost of Patroclus visits him and reproaches him for not burying his body, for without burial the shade of Patroclus cannot enter the

Underworld. Still asleep, Achilles promises to obey the ghost and asks for a final embrace: "But stand near me, and let us embrace a little while and take pleasure once more in destructive sorrow" (23.97–98). It is the same request that he makes of his men earlier that evening (23.10). But the shade slips through his arms three times "like smoke" and sinks beneath the earth—there is no satisfaction, no joy to be found in "destructive grief." The social and religious rites have to be fulfilled. Awakened, Achilles utters what he has learned: "Indeed, even in the house of Hades, there is a shade and image left, but there is no life in it at all" (23.103–4). The epic itself calls little attention to this scene, but scholars have noticed its importance. It begins a process that reestablishes the communal bonds of heroic and human recognition and reciprocity.[32] The scene signals an otherworldly limit on Achilles' possessiveness and isolation and draws him back within the normal frame.[33] This prepares for the final resolution with Priam, for just as Achilles cannot keep the body of Patroclus, he will not be able to keep the body of Hector.

Achilles' dream is followed by the funeral of Patroclus, and the pendulum swings back violently toward the theme of unbounded desire and excess. Achilles pours more blood on the pyre—of sheep, cattle, four horses, two dogs, and twelve Trojan captives—than can be burned, and he has to pray to the winds to aid in the conflagration. The day of the funeral is followed by funeral games that Achilles hosts, but in which he does not compete. He gives a reason for not competing in the chariot race: his immortal horses "are surpassing in their excellence" and he would win first place (23.274–79). The mention of his immortal horses recalls his own immortal heritage, for the horses were gifts to his father from the gods on Peleus's wedding day, and his own surpassing excellence.[34] But the surpassing excellence of Achilles, an excess embedded in his divine heritage, does not hold sway. Instead, Achilles officiates with an unusual calm and beneficence, demonstrating excellence of a different sort.[35] He awards prizes to every competitor. He even gives a prize to Nestor, who doesn't compete, out of respect. More importantly, a conflict of honor, recognition, and excellence arises in the chariot race, recalling the conflict between Achilles and Agamemnon at the start of the epic. Achilles wants to award second prize to Eumelus, whose chariot wrecks. Another competitor, Antilochus, complains, and Achilles graciously provides an additional gift. A third competitor, Menelaos, is angered and contests the prize to Antilochus, the younger man. Here, however, Antilochus defers and gives the prize to Menelaos. Menelaos is then free to demonstrate his generosity and lack of offense by giving it back, and so he does. The tone in this complex exchange of honor wounded and then healed is set by the magnanimity of Achilles and followed by the others.

The funeral games do not yield perfect conciliation. The poet adds an artful twist. The final contest is spear throwing, and Agamemnon enters. Achilles recognizes him as the superior spear thrower on the field and awards him a prize without a contest. While this is usually read as restoration of heroic reciprocity between Achilles and Agamemnon, and it is in part, Achilles denies Agamemnon one crucial feature of heroism: a stage for enacting his superiority. Achilles recognizes Agamemnon, for he awards him the standard gifts due the champion. However, this recognition is imputed rather than earned. This recalls Agamemnon's status as "ruler of men," conferred by unspecified loyalties that brought the Greeks to Troy, rather than loyalty clearly earned or achieved. Like the spear contest, then, the overall place of Agamemnon is recognized, but unenacted. Agamemnon has honor, but not achievement.

Achilles' recognition by the Greeks is complete at the end of book 23. He has earned glory, for his killing of Hector manifests his *tîmê* as the greatest warrior. During the funeral games he reintegrates himself into the community, awarding prizes to the victors though he does not participate himself, for he is above challenge. But his insatiable fury continues. Whatever he has achieved through victory seems insufficient. Book 24 opens with Achilles lying awake, restless, remembering Patroclus and weeping. He binds Hector's body to his chariot and drags it three times around Patroclus's tomb, and he does this for eleven days.[36] His excess offends Apollo, who protests, and after a council, Zeus forms a plan. Hector's body will not be stolen away, but Achilles must surrender it. And in this surrender, Zeus promises to attach great glory, *kudos*, to Achilles (24.110).[37] He will receive proper compensation in the form of gifts "which will gladden his heart" (24.119). In language reminiscent of his refusal to accept gifts from Agamemnon, Achilles expressly denies that he will accept any ransom when Hector asks for this concession as he dies (22.337–53).[38] However much the funeral games may have reintegrated Achilles back into the economy of heroic recognition, he still refuses to accept its currency.

But Priam is not Agamemnon, nor is Achilles the same man after the death of Patroclus. Priam invokes Achilles' own father, Peleus, just as the members of the embassy in book 9 do. This time, however, Priam reminds Achilles of his father. Priam's resemblance to Peleus lies in his wretchedness, in a paternal loss that no honor can restore, and not in his paternal exhortations to strive for glory. Neither Peleus nor Priam will have a son return alive from battle. In his encounter with Priam's grief, the magnitude of Achilles' passion for honor and grief is finally matched by another's equally powerful passion. Achilles does not respond with pity, as if Priam were a pathetic old man. He receives the gifts of Priam as signs of the honor that one hero gives to another, calling yet another hero to the scene as he asks the shade of Patroclus not to take offense. He then uses some of the cloth Priam brings to wrap Hector's corpse, thus beginning the funeral rites and nullifying Andromache's lament.[39] Achilles and Priam weep together, eat together, marvel at each other's stature and appearance, and recognize that to live is to suffer and endure. This reciprocity of heroes seems to mark the greater glory that Zeus has promised.

This new *kudos* is one that only Priam and the audience recognize. This is crucial for our reading of the *Iliad*. Only they see and know the greatness of Achilles' magnanimity, manifested in his willing return of Hector's body as part of the economy of gift, ransom, and exchange that Priam offers. The transaction takes place at night, unrecognized by the Greek army. Achilles remains the greatest warrior, and his inclination to wrath is still in place; he warns Priam not to "stir up my spirit more in pain, or I may not spare even you, though a suppliant, in my tents, and so transgress the commands of Zeus" (24.568–70). But he restrains his wrath and feels sympathy.

Given his extremity of rage, which he demonstrates throughout the epic, Achilles' final restraint expresses his greatest achievement. Achilles allows his relocation into the human order and accepts its limitation. The limitation works in two ways. His fury ends; his martial achievement, reenacted again and again in the treatment of Hector's corpse, is finished. However, the excess that marked his wrath does not diminish. He does not diminish his passion; instead, it becomes an appropriate part of his character as it extends to his sympathy. In this way, the final book of the *Iliad* extends the nature of heroic enactment. In Achilles' actions toward Priam, it redefines excellence as Achilles' magnanimity,[40] and his achievement in terms of restraint.

Achilles' restraint is far from restful and consummating. The "more" he yearns for, which the epic subsumes into *tîmê*, is extended in the final scene, but it is no more reachable. Unlike the signs of honor that are so visible throughout the poem—the armor stripped and horses corralled— this achievement and the excellence it manifests remain unrecogniz- able. The Greeks are back in their own tents, sleeping, and they do not recognize the heroism of the greatest man because they are "less" than Achilles. The gods may look on with interest or disinterest, but they cannot recognize Achilles with tears and words of admiration, as does Priam, because they do not suffer. Well does Achilles describe himself to Priam as *panaôrios*, "completely out of all season" (24.540). He is referring, specifically, to his imminent death, but equally well to his character and its *tîmê*. The stage is enlarged in the final book—the many scenes of battle are not replaced but expanded toward filial and fraternal love—and yet that stage remains too small. The system that recognizes excellence requires reciprocity, a community of heroes who witness great achievement and acknowledge it with the signs of honor and praise. As the *Iliad* draws to a close, Priam departs, and Achilles is alone. He is neither part of the conventional world of heroic reciprocity, nor able to participate in an alternative, somehow perfected heroic world. In Achilles' final scene, excellence is realized, not in the heroic exchange of gifts and stories but in suffering and endurance.

Achilles' final loneliness makes the *Iliad* an essentially tragic poem. Heroism requires a stage and a performance. Human excellence should mean something within the affairs of men; it should become public so that it can be honored and held up for imitation. The excellence must be embodied and enacted, and the audience must recognize and understand the enactment. But for Achilles, a meaningful frame for his greatness is desperately hard, if not impossible, to find. Achilles finds himself surpassing the standard heroic forms of enactment; but the stage is not large enough, and the audience sleeps. Not even the gods can provide a meaningful frame of reference. They need nothing, lack nothing, and suffer nothing; and most importantly, they do not die.

True, Homer depicts a final, dramatic scene. With Patroclus, we are reader-shades, looking on as Achilles embraces Priam. Achilles is singular in his unbounded passion, so violent in battle and so profound in love, and the epic evokes the passion vividly. But the passion is not an achievement, and we are unsure just what we should see and acknowledge as great. It is not the military victories, not the magnanimity at the funeral games, not even the tears and embrace of Priam—Achilles is always something more. Thus, Achilles remains an unfinished figure of restlessness, absorbed into commonality of human life—suffering and endurance. He is, as he says, "completely out of all season." There is not room in epic poetry for a man whose defining feature is not a victory won or goal achieved, but an unquenchable potency of character, a relentless desire for more.

Has Homer failed to grasp the full potential of epic poetry? Can we rewrite the *Iliad* to render Achilles more fully visible as the greater warrior, the perfect man? No. Homer's ambition to render in verse the heroic excellence of Achilles, the greatest of the Greeks, is embroiled in the tensions between excellence and recognition. To make Achilles more easily recognizable means to make him more common, more a representative than singular. Epic poetry necessarily depends on patterns of heroic recognition and is based on the assumption that the achievement makes the man, and not the man the achievement. The tropes of heroic description—the taunts, the engagements, the clattering armor of fallen warriors, the celebrations of victory—depend on conventions that shape distribution of honor and the recognition of glory. Achilles is the greatest man, so great that he will not, he cannot, allow the presumptive measures of heroic achievement to constrain the scope of *his* achievement. As Homer recognizes, this edge of excess sets Achilles apart and drives him beyond his comrades, both in fury of battle and magnanimity of conciliation. Achilles, then, cannot be both the measure and measured; he cannot be both the exemplar of a heroism that exceeds all other heroes, and at the same time, be ranged among the heroes, even as the highest in rank. Thus he must be alone, beyond the reciprocity of heroic recognition, unmeasured because the measure.

These problems were by no means unfelt in classical culture, and they find expression in poetry and philosophy. The *Odyssey* and the works of the tragedians echo the essential problem of Achilles—a magnitude and intensity of character that exceeds the bounds of communal recognition—and offer different responses to it. Others reject the Homeric ethic entirely. Plato's vision of philosophical, moral excellence is a direct response to the apparent failure of Homeric excellence in ancient Athens. Plato offers Socrates, whom he and many others had seen and knew, as an alternative measure of achievement. Vergil's *Aeneid* proposes a remarkable revision of epic heroism. Instead of a singular hero who actively epitomizes excellence, Vergil offers a singular destiny (and city and people) that confers greatness upon an individual, Aeneas, who gradually inhabits his role. Vergil insists upon a recognized hero, even in an epic about surpassing achievement.

And what of Christianity? In our reading, Christianity intensifies the Homeric approach. As a hero, Jesus is singular and surpassing. He is not to be measured, for he serves as the measure. His identity and purpose exceed the scope of human life. And yet, he is fully human, and he must be recognizable and ultimately real in human terms. However shaped by the excess of divinity, Jesus is not driven outside the boundaries of communal reciprocity. By changing literary genres and employing an entirely new approach to heroic depiction, the Gospel stories offer a hero greater than Achilles—not a child of a god, but very God himself—who is ordinary to the point of vulnerability and humiliation. In this way, unlike Achilles, Jesus is not a finally incomplete man whose passion cannot rest in a singular and public achievement. As he dies on the cross, the literary claim of the New Testament is that Jesus enacts the full potency of his character as the Son of God. As the Gospel stories argue so vigorously, he does so in a way that fulfills rather than exceeds messianic expectations. This therefore allows the community of faith to recognize Jesus by giving him the honor that is his due: worship.

Chapter Three

Irony of Presence and Absence: Socrates

Oedipus: All your meanings are too vague—all riddles.
Tiresias: Aren't you the best born at discovering such things?
Oedipus: Yes, mock me there—you'll discover me great!
　　　　　　　　　　　　—Sophocles, *Oedipus the King*

Extreme excellence and its communal recognition, the tension of the *Iliad,* is unresolvable. A movement toward one or the other destroys the balance. A simpler recognition would compromise the godlike excellence of Achilles by quantifying it. His heroic greatness cannot be measured in tripods, golden-maned horses and fair-cheeked maidens. However, too great an achievement defies recognition. True *kleos,* both glory and its appropriate acknowledgment, requires an admiration that includes some kind of sameness and familiarity. The *Iliad* dramatizes the fact that Achilles' greatness cannot become more recognizable without becoming, at the same time, more common and less exceptional. It is the genius of Homer that he manages both to frame Achilles and to allow him to exceed the frame, that he enables his readers to recognize and understand the magnificent dissatisfaction of Achilles as he strains the confines of standard heroic forms. We are invited to share in Achilles' dissatisfaction and to feel, with him, that human ambition and desire for greatness exceed that which may be possessed and enjoyed with others. This, and not Achilles' fateful choice of glory over long life, is the enduring tragic element of the *Iliad.*

The power of Homer's epics shaped the Greek world, both its literature and its values. Like the Bible in America several generations ago,

Homer's epics were the texts that Greeks knew best and shared as a cultural currency; beyond the local differences of civic institution and religious practice, all Greeks were bound by particular visions of excellence embodied in the figures of Achilles and Hector, Odysseus and Penelope. The Athenians were no exception. Athens, unlike some other Greek cities, did not derive its history from Homer's story of the war on Troy, but it did derive literary forms and social values from the influence of Homer's heroes. Tragedy is the most significant literary legacy.[1] The tragedies, especially those of Sophocles, offer a sustained revision of the Homeric forms of heroic excellence. The tragedies present a heroic distinctiveness that is less martial, less conventionally enacted (defeating enemies, winning races, or casting spears great distances); it is seen more against a civic and domestic backdrop. Tragic excellence tends toward extremisms of character that seem emblematic. Oedipus is relentless intelligence; Antigone is obedience to the unwritten laws of familial bonds. The Sophoclean characters possess a distinctive power. But their heroic excellence is not Achillean, superhuman and surpassing in scope; rather, the Sophoclean hero is more a reduction of humanity to a singular and redoubled feature. These heroic figures lack the enlarged fullness of Achilles, and as a consequence, they fit more easily into the human frame of reference.

This shift in heroic portrayal from surpassing achievement to intensity of character and purpose refocuses the tension between excellence and recognition without relieving it. Sophoclean heroes often embody singular features, features we share with them, but to such an extreme degree that their characters border on the repulsive. As a result, these heroic figures seem unable to evoke a key element in the full recognition of greatness: our desire to follow them in imitation. Without the desire to imitate, heroic recognition migrates away from human aspiration and striving. In the *Iliad*, Achilles is surpassing, but the true extent of his achievement is invisible in the too small mirror of the "heroic code." Even though Achilles is invisible to the Greeks in the solitude of his tent at the end of the epic, his beauty and passion are enviable to us, and his heroic form remains an ideal for subsequent generations. Many readers of the *Iliad* offer Achilles their imitative desire, which the epic reckons as much a part of the devotional economy of recognition as the tripods and maidens his peers offered him on the plains of Troy. If we are unable or unwilling to imitate, then our relation to heroic achievement necessarily changes. We can marvel at Antigone's endurance, for example, her almost mad insistence upon familial duty. We can even fear this highly focused passion, knowing that human beings are nearly as powerful as gods when the many tethers of communal habit and diverse loves are cut away by singular commitment. This amazement (and horror) is a recognition entirely different from the imitative urges of devoted admiration. Without this admiration, even as we acknowledge the remarkable power of the Sophoclean characters, we can give them only a negative form of *kleos,* like that which Helen dreads for herself and Paris in the *Iliad:* "that we will be the theme of songs for generations" (6.358–59). Imitative aspiration is as important to heroic recognition as laurel wreaths and swift horses.

An ancient writer tells us that the young Plato wrote tragedies, but when he met Socrates, he consigned his poetic efforts to the flames.[2] True or not, this story dramatizes one of the most important features of the Platonic effort to perpetuate the Socratic form of life: it is essentially antitragic. For Plato, our pursuit of human excellence need not founder on the limitations of human recognition. Plato's hero is neither plagued with Achillean dissatisfaction nor burdened with Sophoclean curse and ostracism. Plato wishes to depict a life that does not exceed the communal frame of reference. Unlike Achilles, alone in his tent, Socrates is visible before the city of Athens and surrounded by his friends. Yet, at the same time, he wishes to avoid the fate of Sophoclean heroes. The unique power of Socrates is not an intensification of a common human feature. Socrates is a man of moderate passions, not driven by intense hatred or unrestrained curiosity or a fevered sense of duty. Plato's hero, Socrates, is a model of human perfection who is both visible and enviable, for when we see him as he truly is, Plato's dialogues suggest again and again, we cannot help but want to imitate him. Indeed, given the moderate ordinariness of the man, imitative desire emerges as the only appropriate form of recognition. We cannot give Socrates any glory other than our desire for wisdom and virtue; we honor Socrates with self-examination.

Plato's ambition is clear, but his success less so. A difficulty arises from the strange combination of ordinary communal life and the special excellence which characterizes Socrates. Since he is a man of simple origin, modest means, and without special physical attraction, we see ourselves in Socrates. But he is Homeric in his achievement—original in his philosophical way of life, fearless in the face of death, triumphant in argument—and we strive to be like Socrates. Yet, how can we both see ourselves in Socrates and want to change ourselves in imitative discipleship? How can he be part of our ordinary life and embody an extraordinary excellence that is as encompassing and surpassing as that of

Achilles? Plato's genius rests in his refusal to release his readers from the tension of these questions. Socrates is an ironic hero, and the key to his irony is the absolute seriousness and indispensable significance of both the ordinary and extraordinary features of his life.

We propose to investigate Plato's ironic hero through a close reading of the *Apology of Socrates*. There, Socrates and his excellence are the focal point of recognition. The *Apology* depicts the hero in a public forum of the law court, a civic instrument of accusation and defense designed to expose the character of the contestants. On the basis of what is said, the judges must discern guilt and innocence, to confer a properly public recognition in the form of verdict and punishment. The court is not, of course, infallible, but in the public realm, it is final. From this depiction of Socrates' rhetorical performance, we will be able to discern the outlines of Socratic excellence and begin to probe the difficulties of an antitragic, ironic heroism that places the hero at the center of civic affairs rather than on the battlefield, as in Homer, or, as in Sophocles, at the margins of ordinary human life.

THE HERO ON TRIAL

Because it is a public *agon*, a trial is an essentially heroic milieu.[3] This heroic setting of public speaking is otherwise alien to the Platonic presentation of Socrates.[4] In the course of his speech we learn that he has had public roles (32b–d). For example, Socrates served as president of his tribe. His term of office was not, he reports, inconsequential. While serving in that office, he refused to judge collectively the ten generals who had failed to recover the dead after a naval battle. The laws required judging each in turn, and Socrates resisted popular cries for immediate and collective punishment. Even as he reports his courage in the matter, however, Socrates does not suggest that he spoke against this unjust civic action. He simply refused to cooperate. The same holds true for another public moment Socrates reports. When called before the oligarchy to bring in Leon the Salaminian, Socrates simply went home rather than cooperate. In neither case, then, does Socrates meet public challenges as one who speaks forcefully and to the public. Indeed, extant classical texts which are so full of the words of Socrates record no public speech by him other than his *Apology*. In view of the uniqueness of the moment, we rightly expect the *Apology* to disclose an aspect of the Socratic character not otherwise available.

The immediate purpose of Socrates' speech is to defend himself against the charges brought against him by Meletus, Anytus, and Lycon: that he does not believe in the gods of Athens and that he corrupts the youth of Athens. These charges initiate the contest, and prior to Socrates' speech the accusers have offered their own speeches justifying the charges. What is so important about Plato's account is that Socrates does not limit himself to responding to those who have spoken before him. The trial will not be a contest between his wit and intellect and the perhaps malicious mean-spiritedness of his accusers. Instead, Socrates' rhetoric will expand both the scope and strength of his adversaries. At the maximum reach of his speech, Socrates will appear to contest with the very city of Athens and its Iliadic traditions.[5]

Socrates' opening words signal his intentions. At the outset, Socrates reports that upon hearing the speeches of the accusers, "I, for my part, almost forgot myself, so persuasively did they talk . . . " (17a).[6] Though he is emphatic that their words are false, Socrates is willing to allow, even eager to insist, that the accusations have power, even the power to make him forget his own identity. The first part of Socrates' defense speech is taken up with an explanation of the true source of the power. Socrates must bring into view the underlying persuasive force of the accusations brought against him in order to properly defend himself. But more importantly, his listeners must see Socrates' true adversary so that they can properly grasp the superiority of his speaking. A public combat with his enemies, exposed in their full power, will allow Socrates to manifest his own distinctive power and excellence.

Socrates exposes the real force opposing him by making a distinction between his first accusers and those who had just spoken of him before the court. The first accusers are many and venerable. As Socrates says to those who brought the charges, "Many accusers have come before you against me, speaking long ago, too, many years ago—but saying nothing true" (18b). And he recounts their words: "There is a certain Socrates, a wise man, a ponderer over heavenly matters and one who has investigated things under the earth and who makes the weaker argument the stronger" (18b–c). For Socrates, these older accusers give power to the speeches given by those who have brought the charges before the court. For years, these first accusers have sown the minds of most Athenians with the charges that Socrates is a man of scientific knowledge and sophistic speech.[7] This gives an air of familiarity to the accusations brought to the court. "Yes," responds the mind of the judge, "what Meletus is saying is true. Everybody knows that Socrates does those sorts of things." As a consequence, the first accusers, those who have spoken against Socrates from the beginning, "are more dangerous" (18b), even "enemies" (18c). They act upon the trial, even in their absence, with greater force than those who make the later accusations; and because they are absent, "they are the most difficult to get through" (18d4). The prejudices formed against Socrates by their constant speaking against him have made the later accusations seem commonsensically true.

The identity of these first accusers is unclear. Aside from a reference to Aristophanes' comedy *The Clouds* (19c),[8] which criticizes Socrates' way of life as impious and antisocial, Socrates is surprisingly vague. He says that "it is not even possible to know and speak their names" (18d). This demurral is odd. Can Socrates remember no names? Socrates seems to fear naming his opponent directly, but not for the normal reasons men fear to name the powerful. The body of opinion that animates the first accusers is so vast, so integral to Athenian public life, that he cannot say it stems from this man or that man. The prejudice against him is the common opinion of Athenians who have observed his way of life. Not surprisingly, then, when he describes the goal of his speech, he comes very close to saying that he intends to speak against the judges themselves, "to remove from you this prejudice" (19a). But Socrates does not seem to want to say plainly that Athens and its citizens are against him. He does not want to clearly identify the source of the underlying power of the accusations, knowing that this would make obvious the fact that he is speaking against nearly the whole of Athens, including the judges before him.

Why is Socrates unwilling to set himself against Athens, to say to his listeners, directly, that they are the accusers, not the judges? We could say, of course, that a too direct confrontation might be a poor defensive strategy, but Socrates gives ample evidence that his speech is not calculated to achieve legal victory. Moreover, in a number of places, his speech offends the judges, and he must plead for calm. Clearly, Socrates is not afraid to offend. A better explanation of Socrates' odd refusal to "name names" is the antitragic vision of Socratic heroism. If Socrates battles directly against the city, then he sets himself against Athens, and his victory risks either tragic isolation or Achillean excess. Socrates does not want to become an Achillean figure, alone in his tent, exceeding the heroic frame of reference, denouncing the heroic enterprise of the Trojan War. To avoid this fate, Socrates must both expand the scope of the contest, even to the point of allowing the *agon* to border on a combat against Athens, while at the same time, he must not exceed Athens in victory or reject Athens in contempt. He must be part of Athens, a citizen among citizens, while at the same time, he must fight against the almost intuitive assumptions of the city.[9]

THE SOCRATIC *ARETÊ*

This antitragic heroism not only requires Socrates to be ambiguous about the true identity of his adversary but also requires him to be clear about his distinctive excellence and achievement. His speech must manifest greatness, but that greatness cannot overleap his listeners. This leads to a twofold scheme that recurs throughout the *Apology:* self-deprecation and self-exaltation, or more specifically, "I possess nothing, and knowing that fact is the greatest possible excellence." This combination of apparent underselling and overselling generates the distinctive irony of Socrates' speech and obscures his character even as it adds clear details and develops forceful analogies. Socrates' response to his first accusers follows this twofold scheme and foreshadows the irony that builds throughout the *Apology* as a whole. And this irony, so central to Socrates' self-presentation, makes imitation of his heroic achievement both attractive and difficult.

Socrates begins his defense against the first accusers by denying that he has anything to do with speculations about "things beneath the earth and in the heavens" (19b). These sorts of speculations, which his judges may associate with disbelief in the gods of the city, do not occupy Socrates, or so he says.[10] To prove his claim, he appeals to the experiences of his judges, "Now tell, if anyone ever heard me talking much or little about such matters" (19d). None has, for, as Socrates says, he is not wise like the foreign teachers such as Gorgias of Leontini, Prodicus of Ceos, and Hippias of Elis, whose teaching is so powerful that they persuade young men "to associate with them and pay them money and be grateful besides" (20a1–2). According to Socrates, then, he lacks whatever extraordinary knowledge is necessary to create followers and generate revenue.

This denial of speculative, foreign knowledge does not meet the charge of atheism, at least not directly.[11] Socrates is silent about whether he believes in the gods of Athens. He only denies that he is involved in the sophistic speaking and teaching that is, perhaps, popular among the youth of Athens and threatening to traditional belief. Socrates takes this public phenomenon—the new teaching and the reaction among the young—to be the real issue that motivates his first accusers. The established figures of Athens worry that certain new teachings about things above and things below undermine the Athenian *nomos*. Socrates does not say that he opposes these new teachings, and this is surprising, for a convincing denunciation of sophistry would strengthen his defense by reassuring his judges that their prejudices are well founded. He only says that he has nothing to do with such teaching, and that he possesses none of its power to influence young men.

In repudiating inaccurate assumptions, we see Socrates as self-deprecating. He seems to be saying that he is but an ordinary man with no special teaching, no special powers, who has no influence, bad or good, on public affairs. Inauspicious in age and appearance, Socrates' daily life is antiheroic. Socrates tells the judges in the *Apology* that he is seventy years old, not an age of beauty and vigor. Indeed, as long as the primary vehicle for heroic enactment is the battlefield and other fora of physical competition, the aged have little claim on power and its resulting *kleos*.[12] A man of self-proclaimed poverty, Socrates describes his life as a series of private inquiries and discussions, some conducted in the marketplace, others in private homes. We can talk about Socrates' "enactment" in competitive terms, because his conversations do involve a form of contest, but they are not unlike everyday bargaining. Further, the forum for these engagements is the Athenian *agora*, the marketplace and the spiritual antithesis to the battlefield. More importantly, the ways in which Socrates "wins" his discussions is highly ambiguous. Socrates himself does not claim to have the knowledge that the others lack; he claims only to know that he lacks it. As a heroic enactment, then, the Socratic practice of examining others does not manifest anything clearly: whatever the excellence is that allows Socrates to "defeat" his opponents remains unknown. As such, this daily life must strike the judges as singularly unheroic. Socrates seems an entirely insubstantial man, a peculiar epiphenomenon, an odd figure who adds color to Athenian life, but not a threat to Athens and her ancient traditions.

But appearances often lie, and as Socrates proceeds in his defense, we see that he does not want the judges to stop at this point. Socrates does not want them to think him innocent by virtue of his insignificance. He takes on the persona of the judges and gives them the voice of accusation, "But Socrates, what then is this trouble about you? Where have these prejudices against you come from? For certainly this great report and talk has not come about while you were busying yourself no more than other men, unless you were doing something other than most people; so tell us what it is" (20c). This response to Socrates' self-deprecation, which Socrates himself provides, is then affirmed by Socrates in his own voice. "The man who says this," admits Socrates, "seems to me to be right" (20d). The common opinion against Socrates did not appear out of thin air. Socrates is not an otherwise insignificant man who has suffered the misfortune of being singled out and cursed by malicious rumor and false accusation. Socrates promises to explain this underlying prejudice, and although, as he reports, this explanation may seem delivered in jest, it is the "whole truth" (20d5).

This "whole truth" begins with the report that he has a reputation for "a sort of wisdom (*sophia*)." Although he teaches nothing like that taught by the foreign sages, Socrates allows that he possesses a wisdom, so this reputation, however confused or inaccurate, is not altogether mistaken. To explain this wisdom, Socrates tells how his old and now dead friend Chaerephon, "once went to Delphi and made so bold as to ask the oracle this question . . . , he asked if there were anyone wiser than I" (21a). The oracle replied that there is no one wiser than Socrates. The mere fact of this oracular pronouncement does not create the reputation that seems to be at the bottom of the accusations against Socrates.[13] Instead, this reputation grows from the way in which Socrates investigates the truth of the oracle. Socrates believes that the oracle was riddling (not false), even though its reply seems straightforward. This testing of the oracle's "riddle" quietly invokes Oedipus, who famously fails to test the oracle's meaning and fatefully takes it at face value. Socrates surpasses Oedipus's error easily. Socrates is "conscious within himself" that he is not the wisest (21b), but he assumes that the god could not lie, so he must discover what the god intended. How, he asked, could none be wiser, if he is wise in nothing? To answer this question, he went to various men who seemed to possess a certain kind of wisdom. He then examined these men to learn the nature of their wisdom, only to discover that, unable to explain what they did or sought to do, they did not have the wisdom they thought they possessed. Politicians could not explain the nature of justice. Poets could not explain why they wrote as they did. Craftsmen, though practiced in their art, arrogantly assumed competence in matters beyond their expertise. These examinations (*elenchoi*) finally provided Socrates with the answer to the riddle of the oracle: he is wiser than others only in "just this little thing . . . that what I do not know I do not think I know, either" (21d). None has wisdom, and therefore the highest wisdom is to know that one has no wisdom. Though this wisdom is "little," it cannot be surpassed.

The inquiries that led to the answer of the riddle of the oracle were not popular, ending as they did in demonstrations of ignorance. Of this

Socrates is aware. He tells the court that he came to see very quickly "that I was hated," and this put him at risk of malevolent public opinion, especially since, as he reports, "those held in greatest repute seemed to me to be almost the most deficient" (22a3–4). The mighty fell before his questions with an especial thud. "Now from this investigation, many hatreds have arisen against me, and such as are most harsh and heavy to bear, so that many prejudices have resulted from them, even this prejudice, that I am called by the name of 'wise' " (23a). The oracle and Socrates' efforts to prove its truth are, then, at the root of the grumblings against Socrates which now give such power to the charges brought against him. The voice of the god has directed Socrates toward his unsettling way of life.

The divine origin of mission and character is a standard heroic trope. However, both the way of life (questioning Athenians as they go about their everyday affairs) and the "achievement" of that way of life (showing that he is wiser than others in "just this little thing" of knowing that he does not know) seem the antithesis of heroism. In fact, Socrates seems almost pathetic, like a man who has spent his life compiling a grammar of Hittite, unique only in his awareness that such an achievement is "just a little thing." But far from pathetic, Socrates describes his life by direct appeals to heroic analogy, building toward the grandest of images, the opposite of the aged irrelevance that opens his defense speech.

Socrates refers to his own "wandering" and "labors" in language that evokes Heracles. The simple reference to Heracles' wandering and labors suggests several things. Heracles is driven to his tasks by Hera; Socrates, by comparison, is driven to his by Apollo. The divine motivation for both amount to necessity, not choice.[14] Heracles' labors cleanse the earth of several monsters, and as such can be seen as a civilizing, though destructive, effort. Likewise, Socrates sees his work as civilizing: he makes the Athenians better citizens and better humans through his painful and destructive work. Heracles' "labors" were also "miseries," and with the parallel Socrates emphasizes the hugeness of his task as well as its unpleasantness, which took the form, in his case, of the general loathing that his examinations caused.[15] However, more significant than the specific analogies of divine mission and great labor, is Heracles' parallel to Socrates in the elastic significance of his heroism.[16] Ultimately, the indeterminate quality of Heraclean heroism, unquestioned but plastic, fits Socrates as much as the specific analogies. With a life so ordinary, even diminished, and with a self-irony that makes his heroic discourse seem almost like joking (as he realizes—see 20d), Socrates offers this plastic and flexible hero as an analogy to his own life.

Socrates does not stop with Heracles; he pushes his heroic claims further. In order to guide his listeners to the real issue at stake, Socrates accuses himself once again. Someone might ask, he says, "Are you then not ashamed, Socrates, for having followed such a pursuit, which now results in your risk of being put to death?" (28b). The charge is sharp and Iliadic; it returns us to the heroic world of *aidos* and *nemesis.* If we take our communal context seriously, if we see the polis as a reliable mirror in which we might view ourselves, then the ignominious penalty of death, the strongest form of communal censure, must give pause. Here, Socrates' difficulty is crystallized. How can a hero be honored by death? His response occupies the rest of the *Apology,* and it requires him to extend himself rhetorically. For this question echoes the difficulty of speaking against Athens. A nontragic hero must receive adequate recognition. Therefore, just as Socrates must speak against Athenian opinion without turning the ethos of the city into his adversary, so also must he explain how the looming punishment of death does not dishonor his distinctive achievement.

To respond to this self-accusation Socrates compares himself to Achilles. Achilles, we remember, likewise feels no shame for his withdrawal from battle—but Achilles' "audience," the Greek army, feels no indignation. Socrates does not focus on the similarity of their shamelessness,[17] but on the similarity of their deaths. As Socrates recalls to his listeners, Achilles' mother, the goddess Thetis, warns him that if he kills Hector, then he will die soon thereafter. But Achilles, "when he heard this, made light of death and risk, and feared much more to live as a coward (*kakos*) and not to avenge his friends" (28c–d). This image of the great man Achilles, the child of a goddess, supreme in beauty and strength and speed, roused in passion to destroy the man who has killed his friend, hangs over the conclusion of Socrates' defense speech. Like Achilles, he disdains death in the service of his passion, which takes the form of serving the oracle. This passion, which necessarily entails questioning the wisdom of others, has given Socrates an intensity of character, a power that overwhelms all obstacles, even the threat of death. Socrates warns the judges that they should have no illusions about compromises in which punishment will be waived if he agrees to renounce his peculiar habits. Against this possibility Socrates says, "Men of Athens, I respect and love you, but I will obey the god rather than you, and as long as I breathe and am able to continue, I will not cease from philosophy or from exhorting you and pointing out the truth to any one of you whom I happen to meet, saying just what I usually say" (29d). Socrates steers the Athenians away from their concerns about money and reputation and honor (*tîmê*), and toward a concern for understanding and truth and "the soul, how it may be the best possible" (29d). As he enters into the final part of his defense speech, Socrates offers a judgment of himself: he sees the life of philosophy as the object of his deepest passion and divine mission, and like Achilles, he will gladly choose the deeds that serve that passion rather than escape death.

Amidst the glorious comparison with Achilles, Socrates returns to the minuscule and ordinary. Where Achilles is destined to kill Hector and thus ensure the fall of Troy, Socrates' divine mission directs him to spend his life "in philosophy and in examining myself and others" (29a). Because of Socrates' (or, perhaps more accurately, Plato's) success in providing the word "philosophy" with a high mission and heroic coloration, we are likely to miss the absurdity of the comparison. Achilles sweeps over a battlefield littered with bodies and overrun with risk, and triumphs. Socrates talks to unsuspecting, intellectually defenseless Athenians who are more concerned with their practical affairs than his questions about the nature of virtue. When he is not talking to these innocents, he is conversing with devoted young disciples who are disinclined to disagree. Socrates is aware of this absurdity. Of his life and the choice he makes to test the oracle, Socrates is confident: "I believe that no greater good ever came to pass in the city than my service to the god" (30a5–7). Yet, while speaking so confidently about his unique contribution to the city, a contribution of Heraclean labor which required a passion of Achillean proportions to complete, Socrates swings wildly to a ridiculous and diminishing image. "If you put me to death," he warns, "you will not easily find another, who literally, to use a rather absurd figure, is attached by the god to the city just as to a great thoroughbred horse, which on account of his size is rather sluggish and needs to be aroused by the stinging of a gadfly" (30e1–5). This image, following so closely the high rhetoric of Achillean passion and unique contributions to the city, captures the enigma of Socratic excellence: the close association of the highest rhetoric of achievement and an ordinary (if eccentric) way of life.

This close association provides the irony of Socrates' heroism. Socrates is Heraclean in scope, Achillean in passion; he is an insect, a man who differs from the everyday merchant and craftsman in only one little thing, the irritating wisdom that he knows he is nothing special. He has a divine mission and the power to set an entire city against him; he is a minor irritant, one who seeks no influence in politics and claims to attract young disciplines against his own will. He is a hero, better than any other man (see 29b); he is a performance artist who does nothing more than amuse bystanders as he unravels the foolish conceits of others (see 33c). In each juxtaposition, what is visible to the Athenian judges is an old, impoverished man who is very clever with words, but obscure in his purpose and irritating in his effect. In the *Apology,* Socrates never repudiates this visible figure, not even indirectly by consigning it to mere outward appearance. Instead, he seems to commend just this odd figure to his listeners as a divinely ordained and heroically enacted life. He presents himself, an old man with no knowledge other than the knowledge that he has none, as Achilles' successor, the greatest of heroes.

This dual self-presentation is the key to Socratic irony.[18] Throughout his defense speech, Socrates seems to be saying both more and less about himself, and both at the same time. With his eye on Achilles, he seems to be winking when saying that his excellence is "just a little thing" of knowing that he does not know, as if we do not all recognize how difficult it is to break the magic circle of reflective complacency and really question our beliefs. But elsewhere, with his eye on the sedentary and leisurely life of questioning and self-examination, he seems to be winking when he piously proclaims his life as the greatest gift to Athens, as if we did not recognize how "philosophy" is a prerogative of the idle and an easy temptation to self-indulgence. Yet, neither side, the little world of conversation nor the expansive world of heroic achievement, is dispensable. Without the "little thing" that typifies his ordinariness, the substance of his excellence would disappear into the rhetorical employment of heroic analogies. His life *has* been absorbed by private conversations. But without the heroic analogies, he cannot express the greatness of his way of life. Only in close association with the excellences of the heroic past can the surpassing virtue of his own life be visible. Faced with the need to be seen *both* ways—as ordinary and extraordinary—Socrates (or the man whom Plato has crafted out of the raw material of his memory; it does not matter which) smiles, and talks out of both sides of his mouth.

HONOR FOR THE HERO

The judges of the court seem unable to grasp Socrates in his rhetorical conjunction of insect existence and heroic life. They declare him guilty. According to the laws of Athens, Socrates has the right to propose an alternative penalty to the sentence of death demanded by his accusers. Socrates takes this as an opportunity to speak directly to his worth or honor, to propose to his listeners a suitable recognition of his great labors on behalf of Athens and in the service of the gods. Because his excellence is an ambiguous mixture of ordinary and extraordinary, his approach to punishment has the same irony as his defense speech. After acknowledging that he expected to be condemned, Socrates restates the nature of his heroic labors on behalf of Athens. His goal was to persuade "each of you to care for himself, how each may be most good and most wise, before he cares for any other of his interests, and to care for the state itself before he cares for its interests" (36c).[19] Socrates seeks what is best, both for each citizen and for Athens. But a representative group of Athenians, the very people he sought to instruct, have rendered a guilty verdict and thus rejected his efforts. Clearly, then, Socrates has failed to achieve his goal. Athens does not care enough for goodness and wisdom to recognize his labors. Rather than commending him, the court condemns. In view of this failure, we may justly ask what reward (or punishment) is proper to a great hero who seems unable to influence those around him, one who labors but does not make progress.

Socrates' first proposal is so purely heroic that it is preposterous in view of his situation. Instead of punishment, says Socrates, "I must propose something that is just and in accordance with what I deserve" (36e).[20] Since his divine mission so benefits Athens, Socrates proposes as his "punishment" free meals in the prytaneum, the equivalent in Athens of a town hall. This is an honor Athenians give to their greatest benefactors and to Olympic champions. Socrates offers this "punishment" just as seriously as he puts forward the heroic characterizations of the defense speech as indispensable analogies to his excellence. In view of his divine mission, he can hardly allow that he deserves anything bad (37b). Virtue must be honored and vice punished. As a just and beneficent man, he deserves no punishment, only the highest honor.

Socrates concludes this part of his speech by offering to pay a small sum, immediately increased through the intervention of his friends to a recognizably punitive amount. The jurors reject both of his proposals. That the judges reject Socrates' proposed punishment is hardly surprising. However innocuous he may seem, Socrates cannot justly be ignored or brushed aside. The seemingly appropriate fine that Socrates proposed, though not seriously, is just as impossible as the preposterous reward of free meals, which Socrates defended so ardently. A fine would have been appropriate for an insignificant troublemaker. The meals at state expense would have been appropriate for an Iliadic hero. Socrates is both—or neither—and the judges rightly see that this ambiguity prohibits either form of recognition. So they decide in favor of death, and in so doing, the insignificant troublemaker is brought even closer to the Iliadic hero. Achilles' choice to avenge Patroclus's death guarantees his own death. Socrates' decision to test the Delphic oracle leads to the same end. Thus, the judgment of the court seals the analogy with Achilles. Ironically, in this decision, a decision that Socrates prophesies they will come to regret, Athens recognizes her hero.

No one at the trial seems to have recognized Socrates properly. His enemies think him worthy of punishment rather than honor. His friends think his death a great evil and wish to help him avoid such a dire punishment. Neither group realizes that his perfect virtue prevents him from being harmed at all. His heroic excellence secures a happy fate. This misrecognition is very different from the failures of recognition that characterize Achilles' relationship to other Greek warriors in the *Iliad.* There, Achilles exceeds the standard economy of recognition. His excellence is too enlarged for normal honors of tripods, horses, and maidens. Socrates' excellence is elusive rather than enlarged; it is dispersed into the ordinariness of his life rather than concentrated into an overwhelming passion that overruns the banks of heroic enactment. Whatever passion Socrates has for justice, it does not fill up and then burst the standard forms of Athenian civic life. He is a public figure.[21] Most of Athens talks about his endless questioning and the young men who follow him around. Moreover, most Athenians seem to recognize a certain excess: his sharp verbal skills, his deflating attacks on the pretensions of the mighty, his remarkable influence over his followers. Yet this public life and its attendant excess do not overstep the standard frame of reference; this life exists entirely outside the world of political grandees, mighty military deeds, and moving public speeches. Socrates shares with Athens this standard pattern of life, but his life runs on different rails.[22]

In view of this disjunction, we should not be surprised that Socrates combines ordinary life and heroic ambition, modesty and arrogance. This humility and arrogance reach a crescendo in the final scene of the *Apology*. The standard view of what is best, embodied in the collective prejudice of the court, has failed to harm Socrates. Instead, as his concluding words make clear, contrary to what everyone around him thinks, the decision of the court has actually rewarded Socrates by doing what is best for him. As he says, "I see clearly that it was better for me to die now and be released from these affairs" (41d3–5). He has received an honor greater even than meals at the prytaneum, and this allows him to say, with equanimity, "I am not angry with those who condemned me or with my accusers" (41d6–7). Everything has worked out for the best. The most virtuous man has received the blessing of communal recognition. The court has rewarded him with what is better rather than what is worse. Socrates is given the kind of tripods, horses, and maidens he properly deserves: death, the most common of things, an "honor" that we will all enjoy. Thus, in the final scene as Socrates embraces his death, the irony of Socratic heroism is recapitulated. The best honor for the best man is that which eventually comes to us all.

THE IMITATION OF IRONY

The difficulty of seeing how death is a blessing testifies to the difficulty of seeing Socrates as he apparently saw himself (or as Plato saw Socrates; it does not matter for our reading). The combination of honor and shame, of Achillean imagery and analogies to insect life, of private life and great public service to the city, make Socratic heroism difficult to identify and, as a consequence, difficult to imitate. We can see the distinctive power of tragic heroes, their towering passions and consuming hatreds. In contrast, Socrates' character is alluring. He is committed to virtue, unwilling to curry favor and ingratiate himself to prevailing power, dedicated to his own distinctive mission, fearless of death, and magnanimous toward those who seek to harm him. The fact that subsequent ancient philosophy comes to treat Socrates as exemplary testifies to his attractiveness, even though his character and the excellence it manifests are enigmatic. We want to imitate Socrates, but we are not exactly sure who he is. We have difficulty conceiving of heroic conversation. Just as Socrates' central role in subsequent philosophy is telling, so also is the profound diversity and even conflict among the schools who claim Socrates as their inspiration. Surely we are dealing with a slippery figure when his life can be the exemplary model for Stoics and Cynics, as well as Academics and Skeptics.[23]

Plato was Socrates' greatest disciple and was acutely aware of the difficulties of imitating that life in action. Just because Socrates is uniquely accessible, so immediate and attractive, so enrolled in the familiar give-and-take of the everyday, does not mean that his way of life is easily reproduced. In the *Symposium,* a dialogue framed by multiple layers of recollection of Socrates and his distinctive excellence, Plato provides a scene of recognition that is freighted with failed imitation. The dialogue recounts an evening that Socrates shared with friends exchanging impromptu speeches in honor of love. After Socrates has revealed the teachings he claims to be those of his mentor, Diotima, on the power of love to give birth to philosophical discourse and contemplation, Alcibiades, a beautiful young man, perhaps the most Achillean figure of his own day, bursts into the room. With the arrival of Alcibiades, Socrates playfully exclaims, "I shudder at his madness and his passion for having lovers" (213d6). Alcibiades embodies the "power and courage of Eros," which Socrates had just finished commending as the indispensable impulse toward the truth (212b8). In the spirit of the evening, Alcibiades speaks of love, but he does not praise eros; rather, he praises Socrates as that man most able to arouse the ardor of others.

Alcibiades' speech on Socrates is a companion piece to the elusive attractiveness of Socrates' speech to the court in the *Apology*. He tells his friends of the irresistible attractiveness of Socrates. Comparing him to Achilles, Alcibiades states that Socrates commands wonder and the imitative desires of those who seek excellence (221c). In fact, this attractive power is so great that Alcibiades desires him to the point of madness, and by his desire is "enslaved by the man as no one ever was by any other" (219e3–5). The allure of Socrates is like that of the Sirens; like Odysseus, Alcibiades says that he must "run away holding my ears, in order not to grow old sitting here beside him" (216a6–8). However, this enslaving love seems inexplicable. Socrates' outward appearance repels. But more importantly, Socrates' love for handsome people, combined with his apparent "ignorance of everything," seems crude and untutored. Socrates is an old man with a strangely lascivious and naive character, a rustic who leers but does so without seeming to desire what normal people do, either from everyday life (money,[24] fame) or from the objects of his love (sexual satisfaction, emotional and financial support). In short, Socrates appears to Alcibiades just as he presents himself to the Athenian court in his defense speech: an ironic combination of grand and lowly. He is both an Achillean hero and an insect, an alluring ideal and a civic failure, triumphant over death itself and condemned by Athenian justice.

Alcibiades expresses this strange combination with the image of carved statues of silenus, which, though repulsive on the outside, when opened, reveal something "so divine and golden, so marvelously beautiful, that whatever Socrates should bid must straight-away be done" (216e7–217a2). Alcibiades uses the image of the sileni repeatedly to express the essential irony of Socrates' life.[25] Even his arguments are like sileni. They "appear quite ridiculous at first, they're wrapped round on the outside with words and phrases like the hide of an outrageous satyr" (221e1–4). Yet these seemingly ugly conversations about the lowly things of life such as "packasses and smiths and cobblers and tanners" are actually "utterly divine, and contain within themselves countless images of virtue" (222a). Throughout, Alcibiades' account of Socrates bears an essential similarity to Socrates' own self-presentation in the *Apology*. Everything about Socrates is strange in this way: he is both unattractive and attractive, mired in the everyday and in things crucial for the attainment of highest things, both ignorant and the source of true wisdom.

There does seem to be one difference between the *Symposium* and the *Apology*. Where the *Apology* suggests failed recognition, Alcibiades reports that the power of Socrates is so great that he shapes those who love him by sheer attractive allure. As Alcibiades reports, through his love for Socrates, he has "been bitten by something more painful, and in the most painful place one can be bitten—in the heart or soul or whatever one must name it, struck and bitten by arguments in philosophy that hold more fiercely than a serpent whenever they seize on a young soul with natural talent" (218a2–6).[26] Socrates has a near divine and irrevocable influence, an almost physical power over those who feel his attractiveness. To know the good is to do the good—to see the inner beauty of his soul, the strange truth of his odd way of speaking, the dignity of his undignified poverty is to imitate Socrates. However, as the voice of irresistible imitation, Alcibiades is a witness to the failure of Socrates, not his success. Soon after the dramatic date of the events in the *Symposium,* charged with the desecration of religious statues guarding the entrance to public and private buildings, and with the drunken mockery of the Eleusinian Mysteries, Alcibiades deserted to Sparta rather than face trial. In Sparta, he betrayed Athenian military secrets and campaigned against the city, accelerating its defeat in the Peloponnesian War. Alcibiades embodies the charges of the corruptive influences that, at his trial, Socrates argues are unjustly leveled against him. Alcibiades sees Socrates just as he presents himself to the people of Athens—as a silenus, as a combination of pesky insect who possesses "just the little thing" of knowing that he does not know and the Achillean hero who has the power to lead Athens to wisdom and virtue—yet Alcibiades fails to imitate the beauty he finds so attractive.[27]

While the young Alcibiades of the *Symposium* may speak naively about the powerful allure of Socratic beauty, in the *Apology*, Socrates is not unaware of the difficulty of imitating his ironic heroism. After hearing of the decision to execute him, he prophesies to those who have condemned him. They seek to rid themselves of his irritating questions, but Socrates predicts that after his death many others will rise up to imitate him. However, warns Socrates, these men "will be harsher, inasmuch as they are younger, and you will be more annoyed" (39d). His imitators will continue his way of life, questioning claims to wisdom and unmasking their ignorance, but they will lack his restraint. As such, they will attack ignorance directly, demanding that Athens recognize and conform to genuine wisdom. They will insist that philosophers should emerge out of the shadows of private life and assume the public roles appropriate to their superior virtue. In short, they will imitate Socrates in everything except his irony, forgetting that their wisdom is "just that little thing" of knowing that they do not know. Without the odd combination of the minuscule and the grand—both affirmed with absolute seriousness, which is the key to Socratic irony—those who follow Socrates will become either comically self-assured or tragically dissatisfied in their pursuit of philosophical heroism.

Though difficult, imitating Socrates' heroism is not impossible. Plato's own discipleship serves as an example of imitation. In the early dialogues, Plato disappears behind the image of Socrates, but in so doing, he creates a body of writing that is the polestar of Western philosophical reflection. But the gate is narrow. Ironic heroism ups the ante of heroic recognition. Although Achilles exceeds the standard economy of heroic recognition, we feel a commonality with his tragedy. We feel the distance as his life vanishes into the spectral heights of semi-divine achievement. The balance is struck poetically in the final book of the *Iliad:* Achilles wishes to be the greatest among men, not above or beyond men. The dissatisfaction of the hero, however, is not Plato's concern. Socrates expresses no dissatisfaction, and he need give no poetic form to the tragedy of such desire unfulfilled, not even in metaphysical distinctions between inner and outer, or absence and presence, in political distinctions between private and public, or in epistemological distinctions between intuition and speech. Irony gathers into itself all aspects of Socrates' life. His poverty is neither appearance nor reality. The oracle is neither myth nor guarantee of truth. His death is neither irrelevant nor ultimately significant. As a man who examined himself and others, Socrates is a hero whose life was exactly as it ought to have been and who received exactly the public recognition he deserved. He is, in short, a nontragic hero.

In the *Apology,* Plato's primary concern is with the intense pressure that Socrates' enduring irony places on our imitative desire. Achilles' excess and surpassing achievement so overleap our ordinary frame of reference that Achilles becomes an icon, a statue in among the greats, rather than a persistent influence in our lives. In contrast, Socrates never leaves

Athens; his distinctive way of life is on display in the marketplace, unavoidable and persistent. The immediacy of Socrates is literary as well as historical. In Plato's dialogues, Socrates' direct speech and the ordinariness of his way of talking (the talk of tanners and cobblers which Alcibiades finds so inauspicious) makes his discussions immediate and accessible. The difficulties of reading a Platonic dialogue have to do with getting one's mind around what is meant, not with rhetorical overreaching. In just the same way, the difficulty of imitating Socrates does not have to do with his overleaping the standard frames of reference; rather, our imitative desire founders on the difficulty of actually getting one's character around who he is. Socrates stands opposite Achilles: we feel a commonality with Socrates' achievement, but a distance from his existential condition. Such is the difficulty in imitating irony—it so easily becomes comically facile or tragically cynical.

When confronted by Socrates, generations of Plato's readers have felt the intense *eros* of imitative desire that Alcibiades felt. Yet, it is difficult to put a finger on the source of the beauty that fuels Socrates' ability to command such a remarkably personal form of heroic recognition. Everything seems to matter, but always with a wink. We must take the life of the mind with deadly seriousness, even to impoverishment and death. Yet we cannot take it seriously in the wrong way, as if our intellectual virtues qualify us to make laws or to separate ourselves from "the ignorant." We must always remind ourselves that the most important thing is "just a little thing." In the shifting sands of this irony, as Plato knew so well and rendered dramatically in the person of Alcibiades, our desire to imitate Socrates easily fails to find solid footing.

Chapter Four

The Fate of Achilles: Aeneas

Father and fondler of heart thou hast wrung,
Hast thy dark descending and most art merciful then.
    —G. M. Hopkins, *The Wreck of the Deutschland*

Many of Homer's greatest readers wanted, ultimately, to alter his vision of heroic excellence.[1] Vergil, like Plato, is such a reader. Vergil's mastery of the Homeric epics is apparent on every page of the *Aeneid;* the *Iliad* and the *Odyssey* provide the mythic material and the formal structure for the *Aeneid.* Vergil revives and affirms the conventional heroic figure (the warrior) and the conventional heroic frames (quest and war) to examine the role of human greatness. But Vergil incorporates these Homeric paradigms in revisional, largely antithetical ways. For our reading, the most significant antithesis to Homer is the role of powerful and unsatisfied passion. For Vergil, as for Plato, true heroism is more than tragic. The greater heroism is not one in which the hero simultaneously establishes and surpasses the boundaries of excellence, only to run aground on the limitations of a human frame of reference. For Vergil, the proper frame is eternal at the outset. The stage of enactment is ample and the heroic life never suffers from dissatisfied constraint. The Vergilian hero must live up to the magnitude of his destiny. The hero may either fail or succeed, but he is never tragically unrecognized.

In the *Iliad,* Achilles strains against and exceeds the measures of heroic excellence. His wrath and desire for honor are as near perfect as

Homer can envision for mortal man. But Homer also knows well that tripods rust and maidens grow old and die; Poseidon and Apollo shatter and sweep out to sea the mighty Greek rampart, "where so many oxhide shields and crested helmets fell in the dust, and a generation of godlike men" (*Iliad* 12.22–23). Homer can only hint at a frame of reference beyond the vulnerable currency of recognition; but Vergil articulates something more substantial, beyond *tîmê* and *kleos*.

For Vergil, the frame of heroic enactment is as large as the destiny of Rome and incorporates the future and the past; it is defined and maintained by the gods and by fate. As the city of destiny, Rome's founding is preordained by fate and is an event cosmic in scope. Rome embraces the civilized world; it will endure forever, invulnerable to the ravages of time and the limitations of any single generation. As a result, the epic tension shifts. In the *Iliad,* Homer stretches to bring the fullness of Achilles to poetic realization: the way his wrath separates Achilles from the other heroes, his redoubled rage after the death of Patroclus, his overwhelming physical and martial enactment, his expansive range in sadness and magnanimity. In the *Aeneid,* Vergil does not deploy his genius to accommodate the scene of heroic enactment to the grand and ultimately unrecognizable greatness of the hero. Instead, Vergil's poetic task is to depict a man worthy of the preordained scene, a man fit to found Rome. The epic tension, therefore, rests in the relation of the hero to the already recognized, certain achievement of founding Rome. This shift away from the difficulty of recognizing the hero's intrinsic greatness to the difficulty of seeing the hero's proper fit to an already recognized greatness creates a new poetic problem: the problem of participation.

Our question, and the problem of heroism which motivates Vergil's distinctive poetic argument, is whether the magnificent framework of enactment, of founding Rome, dwarfs rather than elevates. Can Aeneas genuinely participate in his heroic destiny? Can the founding of Rome be *his* achievement rather than simply his divinely appointed role? For centuries of readers, the answer to these questions has been yes. In the Christian ages that followed, Vergil was lauded as the height of human reason, the pinnacle of pre-Christian insight. In the *Divine Comedy,* Vergil steps from the shadows of Limbo, where the virtuous pagans reside, to lead Dante wisely through the errors of sin to the very rim of Paradise. Yet the modern American university confines Vergil to a much more restrictive Limbo, to the shelf of authors much praised and little read. This liminal condition, we suggest, is the result of Vergil's depiction of heroism, which is often viewed more with distaste than with disinterest by modern individualists suspicious of empire and eager for a highly personal form of heroism. And perhaps rightly so. The *Aeneid* offers an unsettling vision of human excellence which threatens to depersonalize the hero. Though he comes to embody his mission in an active way, though he blazes with his own anger at the end of the work, he must erase something of himself in order to fulfill his destiny as founder of Rome. Aeneas's goal is not authenticity; it is to rise to the heights of the historical and ultimately divine mission of a great city. To do so, Aeneas must develop into a man fit for the recognition properly accorded the founder of Rome. Unlike the Homeric or Platonic hero, through the expanse of the entire epic, Aeneas must *become* the hero he is destined to be.

Our judgment of the success of Aeneas's participation depends on how we interpret this process of becoming. Vergil is profoundly aware of the importance of this judgment, which is focused on Aeneas. Vergil must bring the man and the event together—and he never equivocates about the event, which for him and for us is a certainty, a historical fact. The man, then, must develop. Vergil must bring the two, Aeneas and the founding of Rome, into a close fit; they are not identical, and Vergil does not make them so. In bringing the man and the event together, Vergil does not clearly make the city a consequence of the man, nor the man a consequence of the city. We argue, rather, that Vergil represents confluence rather than consequence, and conformity rather than priority. This confluence and conformity of man and event are realized in several ways: the personal must take the form of the civic, the human must conform to what is destined, the framework of the temporally enacted must conform to the shape of the eternally fated.

It is possible to see the process of becoming as a continuous perfecting of what Aeneas already is by nature and inclination, or as the acquisition of new qualities, new knowledge, and new passion.[2] We believe that Vergil equivocates between the two, between perfection and change, never suggesting a strong discontinuity in Aeneas's developments.[3] This equivocation is grounded in Vergil's heroic vision and is required by his poetic goals. A discontinuity imposed on Aeneas from outside, by fate or the gods or in any other form it might take, depersonalizes him and makes him a consequence rather than a cause. At the same time, Vergil must insist on some change in the man, otherwise he runs the risk of elevating the hero and turning the consequences of his actions, that is, the founding of Rome, into an extension of Aeneas's heroic qualities, making the man greater than the achievement. In guiding our sense of Aeneas's becoming, the legacy of Achilles is crucial. For our reading, the fate of Achilles in the epic concretizes Vergil's necessary equivocation about change and fulfillment: Achilles must be both fulfilled and destroyed as an heroic ideal.

The *Aeneid* is most commonly, and rightly, read as a diptych. Its first six books, which are the most widely known, correspond to the *Odyssey* in both general and specific ways. Broadly, their theme is one of homecoming. Women detain the heroes in their journeys. An offended deity creates obstacles. Aeneas tells his own story for several books, as does Odysseus. Aeneas, like Odysseus, descends to the Underworld for information and direction. With a second prologue in the seventh book, Vergil initiates the second, Iliadic half, which he calls a "greater task" (*maius opus*, 7.45). The backdrop is war: battles, sieges, lists of troops occur throughout the last six books. Men triumph gloriously and die painfully. Aeneas's armor is lost and divinely replaced. One motivating offense is a woman "wrongly taken," in the eyes of Turnus, Aeneas's greatest foe. A friend, removed from the hero's protection, is cut down; his death spurs furious wrath in the heroes as they take vengeance.

The ways in which the *Aeneid* borrows narrative structure, episode, and imagery from the *Iliad* and *Odyssey* are complex and suggest the difficulty of assessing Vergil's revision of Homeric ideals.[4] For our reading, the most important and richest ambiguity is found in Vergil's use of Achilles. Achilles' heroism is the polestar to which Aeneas's heroism must ultimately stand in relation, whether in harmony or in opposition.[5] Like that of Achilles, Aeneas's heroic achievement must find an animating source in his passion. Yet, unlike Achilles, this passion cannot be presupposed and does not drive Aeneas. Throughout the epic, Aeneas is drawn forward by knowledge that he must found a new Troy on the Italian peninsula. The action does not emerge out a fathomless wrath; rather, events reach toward the momentous founding of Rome. Aeneas is caught in the gravitational pull of this destiny, and Vergil seeks to show us how he emerges with passion sufficient to bind him to this destiny. This complex revision of the Achillean paradigm of heroic passion leads us to approach the *Aeneid* as a triptych.[6] The first four books reveal Aeneas stripped of a nostalgic passion that hinders his destiny; books five through eight present Aeneas as a dispassionate, empty vessel of fate; and books nine through twelve record the kindling of a new passion and his consequent rise to full participation in his destiny.

This threefold reading most effectively reveals the heroic development of Aeneas toward full participation in his destiny. Because we regard Aeneas's heroic development as the replacement of passion—a soft retrospective nostalgia with a hard immediate anger—we view it through the metaphor of palimpsest. In the ancient world, which sometimes used expensive materials like leather or parchment as a writing surface, manuscripts were erased by scraping or washing to make room for another more important or more desired text. A palimpsest is a text thus recycled, and since Vergil is deliberately rewriting his Homeric inheritance, this metaphor is a doubly apt approach to reading the *Aeneid.* The movements of the three parts of the *Aeneid* correspond to their focus on Aeneas as erasable text, erased text, and rewritten text. The first part of the triptych emphasizes the renunciation of the personal: they are the erasure of Aeneas. The second part, especially the visit to the Underworld, focuses on Aeneas as blank, erased, available text. The final part reveals his participation in his destiny: it reveals Aeneas as a new character, a rewritten text. As a vision of heroic achievement, the epic is a vast rewriting of Iliadic heroism away from the problem of recognition and toward that of participation.

ERASING THE PERSONAL: DIDO AND CARTHAGE

Carthage elicits Aeneas's deepest emotions. In its walls, Aeneas sees both his past and his future and feels a yearning for them both. These emotions, his sense of loss for Troy and his longing for a new Troy, fill out the affective portrait of his *pietas.* It is his defining attribute—the prologue calls him the man "singular in his devotion" (*insignem pietate*, 1.10).[7] This quality encompasses far more than its English cognate "piety." *Pietas* is devotion to duty, whether that be duty to family, country, or gods.[8] In Carthage we see the full affective force of that *pietas* in his love of Troy and his desire to reproduce it. Even more, we see the full reach of his human emotion and desire in his personal love for Dido, Carthage's queen. These emotions and desires are normal—we identify closely with them—and not peculiar to the heroic heart. Aeneas feels loss, longing, and love: Vergil develops each at length.

Carthage presents Aeneas with a vivid and literal image of his past. Disguised in a cloud by his mother, Aeneas enters and surveys Carthage unseen. He marvels at the city and its centerpiece, a temple of Juno, and he gazes at the mural painted on the temple walls. It is a depiction of the Trojan War. This ecphrasis is one of Vergil's masterstrokes, as is his "subjective" presentation of it through Aeneas's eyes.[9] The mural presents not just one narrative moment but several discrete ones. Three scenes involve Achilles: his general pursuit of the Trojans; his ambush and murder of Troilus, son of Priam, whose life was prophetically linked to the survival of Troy; and Priam's night visit to Achilles' tent to ransom the body of Hector. The final scenes that Aeneas notices, in which he himself appears, depict moments after Achilles' death.

His response to the representations of his and the Trojans' suffering is to weep—and to hope. "Even here there are appropriate rewards for glory, and tears for human events; they are touched by what humans suffer. No more fear." (1.461–63).[10] This passage recalls and inverts a Homeric moment. Odysseus frequently worries, with good reason, that his name and fame will endanger him; Aeneas believes that their reputation will earn them the safety of a kind reception. Also inverted is the value of Homeric *kleos*. Aeneas is memorialized, as is Troy, thus receiving one form of heroic recognition, but he is remembered as one of the conquered rather than as the victor. Aeneas seems to misread the mural—it *is* painted on Juno's temple and celebrates her victory over Troy. Aeneas's apparent misinterpretation of the mural reveals how powerful, and distorting, is the inclination to read events and people through the loss of Troy. This backward-turned emotion, covering past defeat with a veneer of golden nostalgia, severs Aeneas from the future glory of triumph. Although the epic looks forward, Aeneas seems a character looking over his shoulder.

The second book elaborates and explains this retrospective inclination in detail. Aeneas and the Trojans are recognized and welcomed by the Carthaginians and their queen Dido, who prepares a feast for them. While Aeneas relates his sufferings to the Carthaginians and their spellbound queen, we are made aware of what he feels, what he desires, and what he knows through prophecies. It is but one hallmark of Vergil's genius that he enables us to enter so much into Aeneas's experience in books two and three. Aeneas's tale of the fall of Troy is marked by the extraordinary realism of the events and emotions it recounts. What Aeneas feels is pain: "Your majesty, you bid me to refresh unspeakable grief" (2.3). His first lines are punctuated with words of mourning: sorrow, lamentation, tears, disaster, pain. The "empty" images of the mural are fleshed out from the perspective of an innocent and passionate insider. The guileless Trojans were taken in by the ruse of the horse and the performance of Sinon; Aeneas and his comrades brave the flames to save the city if they can; he watches Achilles' son Neoptolemus slaughter Priam on the altars of his palace. His mother unveils his eyes to reveal the gods Neptune, Juno, and Minerva aiding the Greeks and destroying Troy. Troy is gone; as Panthus declares, "We were Trojans, this was Troy" (2.325). Aeneas's account of the fall of Troy weaves the elements of divine wrath, human grief, and profound nostalgia into a dense, gripping narrative.

Interspersed with the horrors of Troy's ruin, however, are prophecies of the future, prophecies that propel Aeneas toward Italy and a new kingdom. Aeneas tells the Carthaginian assembly of his dream of Hector, long dead, who urges him to flee Troy, taking its hearth-gods and sacred emblems: "Take these as companions of your destiny, seek out the great walls which you will lay for them after you have wandered the wide sea" (2.294–95). He relates a similar instruction given by the shade of his wife Creusa, whom he loses in the darkness in his wild rush to leave the burning city. He leaves his father and son on the shore and returns to seek her, but meets only her ghost. The image of Creusa reproaches him for his "mad grief" (*insano dolori,* 2.776) and then reiterates Hector's command as a prophecy: "Long exile, and the barren stretches of sea lie ahead of you, and you will find the land Hesperia, where the Lydian Tiber waters the fertile fields with its mild stream; there time will bring forth prosperity and a kingdom, and a new queen" (2.780–84). During his wanderings, further prophecies—from Apollo on Delos, from his hearth-gods in a dream, from the harpy Celaeno, and from Helenus in exile in Greece—clarify exactly what he is called to, exactly what he is looking for: "the lands of Ausonia, forever receding . . . the Tiber and its adjacent fields" (3.496, 500).[11]

This constant reminding, this specific reiteration of the goal, focuses the dramatic tension less on the plot and more on Aeneas. We do not wonder what will happen in the next nine books: we are told again and again what will be. Since this reiteration is put in the mouth of Aeneas, we do not ask whether he *knows* what he is supposed to do. Instead, we are uncertain about Aeneas himself. His character is poised between his relentlessly certain destiny, reaching toward the founding of a new Troy, and his backward-turned self-knowledge. Just as his nostalgic perspective colors his reading of the mural, his retrospection shapes his reading of these prophecies. He longed to save Troy; he now longs to reproduce it. This longing for his lost past leads him to false foundings and false admiration.

In his tale of his wanderings in book three he recounts his abortive attempts to found his own walls: first in Thrace (3.16–18) and then in Crete (3.130–39), Aeneas tries to establish a place for his people, whom he calls after himself, the Aeneadae. On Crete, his urge to recreate leads him to name the new town Pergamum after the citadel commanding the plain of Troy; and his people delight in the name (*laetam cognomine gentem,* 3.133). However, a plague shatters their hopes and drives them on, eventually to Chaonia in northwestern Greece, where to their surprise they find Trojans, Helenus and Andromache, ruling over a small kingdom. The vision is vaguely pathetic: the Trojans have rebuilt a "little Troy" complete with miniature citadel and walls; they call a dry trickle the Xanthus after the river in Troy. Aeneas, not surprisingly, is deeply moved by this simulation. After Helenus gives him details of his destiny and Aeneas prepares to leave for Italy, he blesses the Trojans for having completed their destiny (*est fortuna peracta sua,* 3.493), for not having seas to plow or shores to seek, for looking on "an image (*effigiem*) of Xanthus and a Troy which your hands built." Aeneas expresses no awareness of the diminishment of Troy in their replication, and he expresses no sense of the greatness to which he is called. Like the miniature Troy that he sees, Aeneas is diminished by understanding himself only through his association with the past.

Within the epic frame, Aeneas's diminution is clearly visible, but Vergil levels no harsh judgments against him. Vergil is quite capable of the editorial or emotional entry into his narrative,[12] and he avoids comment on Aeneas' nostalgia. Instead, he portrays Aeneas' perspective as natural, almost inevitable. How could Aeneas envision a Troy greater than the one he left? Vergil suggests that he cannot, and for that reason, his nostalgia must be expunged so that his vision can be redirected forward and his aspiration rewritten as a bold commitment to a new Troy rather than futile efforts to recover or recreate the old, defeated Troy. Nevertheless, we are moved by Aeneas's devotion to Troy and understand how the palpable reality of the past exerts a far greater influence over him than the insubstantial and yet to be enacted future. We understand very well why, from a hill above Carthage, Aeneas looks down on the growing city and its active citizens and cries out in admiration: "So fortunate, you whose walls are already rising!" (1.437).

Readers cannot miss the fact that Dido and Carthage provide a very close match to the details of Aeneas's destiny. Here, Aeneas encounters a situation that is a perfect fit for his nostalgic desire to recover Troy. He is in search of a city and a queen; she is a queen and has a city. Her story, told to Aeneas by his mother Venus (1.338–68), also approximates his.[13] Dido flees Tyre after her brother, Pygmalion, murders her beloved husband Sychaeus and hides his crime. Sychaeus's ghost comes to her at night, as Hector's does to Aeneas, reveals the deed, and persuades her to leave her country. With others who hate or fear Pygmalion's tyranny, Dido sails to Africa and founds Carthage on a site indicated by a sign from Juno. All that Carthage is represents her agency: "the woman was the author of the deed" (*dux femina facti,* 1.364). Dido's past resembles Aeneas's, and as founder of a new Tyre, she is doing what he must do.

However closely Dido's story may match Aeneas's, her character seems fundamentally different. She is full of passion. Vergil portrays this passion in two ways, first as a vulnerability, as an impediment to responsible leadership, and second as a dominating and subversive force. The first element is evident in Dido's desire for Aeneas. She is wounded by her love, like a deer struck by a chance arrow from a shepherd who does not realize that he hit her (4.69–73). After she has given in to her passion, Vergil has work in Carthage cease: "Towers begun rise no higher, the young men train no longer, nor build up ports and secure defense walls; all work idles, broken off" (4.86–88). Vergil builds to a crescendo quickly: after Dido and Aeneas consummate their love in a cave, separated from a hunting party by a storm but overseen by goddesses and nymphs, Vergil says that Dido "is no longer moved by appearance or reputation, nor contemplates a secret love: she calls it a marriage, and with this name covers her fault" (*hoc praetexit nomine culpam,* 4.170–72). Her "fault" is apparently the lapse in her meaningful devotion to Sychaeus, whose memory she sets aside to pursue her love for Aeneas. Her passion draws Dido away from the proper course of her life. As Vergil insists, she chooses against her destiny (4.696–97).

Dido's love consumes her and leads her astray, but it is not a weakness. On the contrary, as the reader senses throughout book four, Dido's passion controls. She, and not Aeneas, is the focal point of the narrative. We see the world through her eyes, and Vergil is able to arouse remarkable empathy for her culpable passion. Ancient readers, as well as modern, shed tears over the tragic way in which love's dominance over her leads her to suffering and death.[14] Vergil folds Aeneas into Dido's passion. In her love, as in her city, Dido leads: *dux femina facti.* And Aeneas follows. To signal the subordination of his destiny to Dido's, Vergil portrays Aeneas in Carthaginian clothes, overseeing the construction of *her* city. Vergil may fault Dido, but he does not diminish the power of her passion. She has something Aeneas lacks—the ability to bring others into the orbit of her desire and the confidence to subordinate communal law, past obligations (to Sychaeus), and responsibilities (to Carthage) to her passion.

Dido's power over Aeneas ends instantly with the descent of Mercury, who bears the reproof of Jupiter. Mercury sees a Tyrian Aeneas: he is dressed in clothes woven by Dido, doing her work: "When his winged feet first touched down on the huts, he caught sight of Aeneas laying new foundations for bulwarks and homes" (4.259–61). The god reproaches

Aeneas for his devotion to a woman (*uxorius*) and for his forgetfulness of *his* kingdom (*regni rerumque oblite tuarum!* 4.267) and of his son's inheritance. Mercury's critical perspective cannot obscure what it is, however, that we truly see: a happy and apparently fulfilled Aeneas.[15] Happy is almost insufficient to describe this scene; Aeneas is often described as "happy" (*laetus*) in the *Aeneid*.[16] Vergil gives a picture of Carthage providing Aeneas with a frame that *fits*. It compensates for his loss of Troy and it fulfills his longing to reproduce it. In addition, he appears to fulfill Dido's longing for a husband. She deeply loves him and he loves her, however unequally.[17] All that he knows of himself, both in terms of his past and his understanding of the future, is consistent with what he has in Carthage. But Aeneas offers no resistance to Mercury's condemnation of his absorption into Dido's Carthaginian world, a world which fits him so well. He turns his back on Carthage and closes himself to Dido with a horrible finality.

If Vergil attributes a fault to Dido, modern readers often redirect the fault, much magnified, toward Aeneas, not for his sexual promiscuity, not for failing to understand the fragility of Dido, not for jeopardizing his future (the gods fault him on this last score), but for failing to be "true to himself". Dido appears to have the courage to be true to her passion. Aeneas seems to respond all too compliantly to the commands of the gods. This comparison, however disturbing to modern readers, serves Vergil's purposes. He does not wish us to cast our lot with Dido and our anachronistic ideas of authenticity.[18] Instead, he wishes us to see the future Aeneas, the Aeneas of destiny, as the only real self to which he must be true. When Aeneas is described in foreign, Tyrian clothes, readers are reminded of his account of the night of Troy's fall, when he and other Trojan soldiers donned the armor of fallen Greeks to improve through deception their counterattack. The attempt fails as other Trojans attack them (2.370–430). Aeneas explains that mistake: "We waded in among the Greeks without the protection of our own gods" (*haud numine nostro*, 2.396). There is a pattern of dishonesty in these two pictures of Aeneas, neither malicious, that reveals the importance for him, even the necessity, of identifying himself in terms of his own destiny and his own *numen*.[19] Aeneas fails to do so in both cases, in fighting for Troy in Greek armor and in building Carthage in Tyrian clothes.[20]

Aeneas's false identification with Dido is motivated by his nostalgic passion. He wishes to identify his future with his past, and this cannot be done. But as with his mistaken appropriation of the Greek armor, he escapes. Dido is less fortunate; her passion entraps her. As if to highlight the dangers of a backward-turned desire, Vergil transforms Dido's love into a bitter and ultimately fatal nostalgia. After Aeneas's decision to leave, she builds a pyre simulating the bed which she and Aeneas shared. She lays in it an effigy of Aeneas: "she placed upon the bed remembrances of him, and the sword he had left, and an effigy (*effigiem*) of the man" (4.507–8). Readers may recall the "effigies" (*effigiem*) of Xanthus and Troy which Aeneas admires in Chaonia, mere images, like the murals on Juno's temple. Like Aeneas, Dido misreads the past. She thinks that Aeneas will replace lost Sychaeus, just as Aeneas temporarily imagines that Carthage can replace the loss of his beloved Troy. But the bed of Dido's imagined marriage becomes her pyre, and her love has become her death.[21] Vergil issues a warning as he closes the crucial fourth book with Dido, who breathes out her life breath in the final line, "neither by fate nor by a deserved death, but wretched and before her time" (4.696–97). By following Aeneas, she separates herself from her past, and it is a mistake: in her past are her faithfulness, her reserve, and her reputation for these qualities, all of which she loses for Aeneas.[22] She wishes to replace her past with a new future, and it cannot be done.

Aeneas's diminished, nostalgic persona burns in Carthage with his effigy. Dido and Carthage, as right as they are, as satisfying to Aeneas, as apparently malleable to his destiny, as true to his longings, are not his destiny and must be abandoned. In abandoning Dido and Carthage, Aeneas leaves his past, and in abandoning his past, he renounces the retrospective sources of his character. This renunciation is painful to Aeneas and devastating to Dido. Undone by Mercury's visit, he resolves to leave without even a farewell; when Dido learns and confronts him, he addresses her formally, rhetorically, legally. But the strain breaks out, cruelly. He had never married her, never called it that; "if my fates allowed me to live and tend my own cares as I want, by my wishes, first I would tend to Troy and the sweet ruins of my own people, Priam's high towers would stand, and I would have rebuilt the fallen citadel—for the losers" (4.338–44). The eruption resembles a conversion. Now, it seems, he understands that such longing for Troy is vain, even contrary to his own prophesied greatness. He is not impervious to emotion—he asks Dido not to "set them both aflame" with her sorrow—but he denies it any priority in his decisions to act.[23] The result is more terrifying to the modern reader than other acts of self-sacrifice which emphasize the subordination of the will and the emotions to the greater goal. It is not simply self-discipline that Aeneas lacks.[24] Not only must the source of Aeneas's loves and desires be disciplined or subordinated but his longing for the recovery of Troy (a recovery that Dido and Carthage seem able to allow) must be erased. Aeneas must renounce their love; he must do the erasing.

We may admire Dido for her willfulness, for her Sophoclean passion, for her ability to choose everything, even when to die. Vergil acknowledges her tragic pathos and her human depth, but he denies to her the full reach of heroic greatness. Human greatness may be revealed through tragedy, but it cannot be defined by it. Aeneas sails away from Carthage changed, a greater hero in potential, but in most ways obvious to him and to us, a lesser man. Such is the preparation for his development which will lead to his full participation in his destiny.

KNOWLEDGE IS NOT ENOUGH: THE VISIT TO THE UNDERWORLD

After his depersonalizing choices in Carthage, we feel that his new identity, even if it is the inscription of fate, must become something that Aeneas possesses in equivalent measure to the love and longings he forsakes; this new inscription of destiny must become as clear as his attachment to his past was. If it does not, then he remains emptied and never refilled, and his choice an inhumanly costly one. Many readers of the *Aeneid* see Aeneas in exactly this light: as accepting, passive, uncomprehending. It is hardly possible to read a dissatisfied Aeneas at the end of the work—for he is not so portrayed—but it is quite possible to read his affective relation to his destiny as less than his affective relation to his past. Read this way, the *Aeneid* is a grim text, because the hero shrunk to a facile satisfaction with achieving communal goals does not compare with the hero passionately straining for ethical and societal recognition. Many scholars, and we among them, believe that this reading is contrary to Vergil's vision of Aeneas. Vergil does not minimize what constitutes personal fullness and participation; we want to argue that he intends to enlarge it. Not only is Aeneas satisfied at the end of the work, he is the author of his own fated achievement. Vergil enlarges the personal element by emphasizing the distance and difficulty of traversing the span between the "old life" and the "new life" (to borrow from the analogy of conversion),[25] a span that includes a time when Aeneas is active and yet remains oddly blank.

In our metaphor of palimpsest, Aeneas is erased and blank in the central four books, available for new inscription. In these books, which form the middle of our triptych, Aeneas is between texts, the text of the past and the text of the future. Specifically, Aeneas's enlarged reconstruction of his personal identity, which in books one through four entails his participation in his past, must be filled in by his participation in his future. Just as that participation cannot consist in good luck or divine appointment, Vergil emphasizes throughout this part of the triptych that it cannot be limited to clarity of understanding, or to knowledge. Aeneas's participation in his destiny certainly involves these elements, but Vergil wants him to surpass them and to achieve the same affective involvement in the founding of Rome that he feels for Troy, Carthage, and Dido.

Vergil brilliantly chooses the Underworld to reveal to Aeneas, and to us, a clearer knowledge of destiny, and to indicate that such knowledge is not equivalent to participation in or possession of that destiny. Again his father's ghost comes to him in a dream and tells him to visit him in the Underworld: "then you will learn of your whole people and the walls that destiny grants you" (5.737). Vergil's Underworld, like Homer's, is a pastiche of punishment and nonbeing. Aeneas descends to the Underworld with the Cumaean Sibyl, who gives him more prophecies about Italy. The ones she provides are dark promises of an Iliadic setting. "Wars, I see horrible wars, and the Tiber foaming with rich blood; you will have a Simois here, and a Xanthus, and Greek camps; another Achilles is brought forth in Latium, he, too, born of a goddess" (6.86–90). She tells him what he needs to enter the Underworld, and she serves as his guide, as Vergil himself serves Dante in the similarly stratified *Inferno* and *Purgatorio*. Vergil's Underworld encompasses all the possibilities of afterlife: the static, the punitive, the purgative, and the blessed.

Aeneas is flesh among shades—and Vergil enjoys this, as he imagines Charon's bark nearly sinking under Aeneas's human weight—but the Underworld offers him, like them, a pale image of his own past life. Just past the threshhold, Aeneas and the Sibyl pass through categories of the untimely dead: infants, then the falsely condemned, the suicides, victims of love, and finally casualties of war. Aeneas is shocked and moved by figures from his own past: Palinurus, his helmsman; Dido; and Deiphobus, the Trojan whom Helen weds after Paris' death. These characters are in death as they were in life. His fellow Trojans and enemy Greeks are still armed and wounded, for example, but insubstantial now. But characters from his past, like Dido, refuse to speak with him or, like Palinurus and Deiphobus, are prevented from speaking at length. He begs forgiveness of Dido (a victim of love rather than a suicide) in words reminiscent of her final pleas to him, but she turns away without speaking: "at last, she tore herself away and fled, his enemy, back to the shady grove, where her first love, Sychaeus, tends her cares and matches her love" (6.472–74).[26]

Dido's past comes full circle. In contrast, Aeneas's past becomes spectral. It does not disappear, but his freedom to engage it is constrained by his need and his desire to move forward, to reach his father.

Anchises resides in a different part of the Underworld, one present but undeveloped in Homer.[27] Aeneas and the Sybil travel on a road that forks. One path leads to Tartarus, the city of punishment, and the other to the Elysian fields, where Aeneas finds his father. These fields are full of light and color, populated by poets and priests and "great-souled heroes born in better times" (*magnanimi heroes,* 6.649) who sing and dance and compete in games. Aeneas finds Anchises in a glade, where he is contemplating the souls "about to go to the upper air." The incredible scene that follows incorporates elements of mystic and philosophical thought. Anchises explains that most souls in Elysium participate in reincarnation, which seems completely at variance with the other parts of the Underworld, where existence is grimly final. In Elysium, souls are divine fire that is dimmed by its contact with dull flesh and its fears and desires; even after the death of the body, corporeal stains remain and require purging. After sufficient penance, a thousand years' worth, the souls drink of Lethe, the river of forgetfulness, and prepare to enter their next bodies. What Anchises witnesses in the souls is the future, his and Aeneas's: "he was tallying up the full count of his own descendants, his beloved offspring and the fates, fortunes, characters, and deeds of those men" (6.681–83).

It is significant that at first the thought of the souls returning, of going back, horrifies Aeneas: "What grim lust for daylight is this for these wretches?" (*quae lucis miseris tam dira cupido?* 6.721) The scene of Elysium is Platonic, closely resembling the myth of Er from Plato's *Republic,* and Aeneas's desire seems distantly Platonic as well. He imagines that residence in Elysium and endless contemplation of the forms is superior to a return to earth and bodily limitations. Aeneas views life as suffering, and the thought of returning to life from the Elysian fields is incomprehensible. The epic, however, rejects such a Platonic line. The souls' perfection requires excellence manifested in life, or several lives. Some few, like Anchises, "stay in the happy fields" (6.744), but the rest require rebirth for this perfection. These souls represent unenacted greatness, and Anchises explains that after the stains of their incarnation have been removed, after they have drunk from the river Lethe, "they begin to want to return into bodies" (6.751) in order to progress toward what they will be. It is a profound vision of human identity: somehow timeless in its essence yet existing within time and within lived lives, and requiring the shaping forces of choice and action for fulfillment.

At the risk of oversimplifying this vision, the allegory in Elysium for Aeneas, in terms of our reading, is patent. As the souls in Elysium must drink from the river of forgetfulness, Aeneas must let go of his past as the focus of his *pietas* and as a means of self-definition. Lethe is erasure. The souls awaiting rebirth are conspicuously blank, palimpsests like Aeneas; their former lives are erased and their future lives yet to be written. Their identities are only potential until they live them into being. Aeneas, too, has only a potential relationship to his destiny and its prophecies. He is defined by that potential, just as the shades in Elysium can be called by name, and their "characters and their deeds" (*moresque manusque*, 6.683), as yet undone, can be recounted in a jumble of past, present, and future times. Vergil's vision of heroic potential and realization is brought out in bright detail in his depiction of Elysium.[28] We must keep in mind this parallel for Aeneas, whose heroic excellence, up to this point, seems latent, hidden in the quiet quality of his *pietas*, awaiting enactment.

The long parade of souls is, of course, the history of Rome, from Vergil's perspective, brought down to his present time, to his patron Augustus and his family. It is the future, from the perspective of Aeneas, his destiny spelled out in some detail. Anchises tells Aeneas exactly what he is doing with this survey: "I will teach you your fates" (*te tua fata docebo*, 6.759). The individuals named recall high points of Rome's evolution and serve as paradigms of the final instruction that Anchises gives as much to every Roman as to Aeneas: "Impose your civilizing custom upon peace, spare the submissive and crush the arrogant in war" (*parcere subiectis et debellare superbos* 6.852–53). Aeneas sees in detail what his destiny translates into, and hears the means by which it is realized. Even more, he begins to feel an affective longing for this realization.

Vergil ends the introduction of specific souls on a sad note, with a eulogy for Marcellus, Augustus's nephew and heir, who died young, as will so many in the realization of Rome's founding. But Anchises continues after Marcellus to walk Aeneas through the fields and introduce him to the specific details of his own immediate future: "then he reminded him of the wars that must be waged . . . and he taught him which labors to flee and which to take up, and how he should do this" (6.890–92). In so doing, he "kindles his son's soul with love of his coming fame" (*incenditque animum famae venientis amore*, 6.889). This transition is important, because it reveals Aeneas's first passionate attachment to his own future. This love of his fame, which is already coming, implies more than just acceptance; it betokens a level of affirmation and the transition of the focus of his *pietas,* from Troy to Rome, from his past to his future.

Aeneas sees and hears what his future will be; all that remains is to return. Before their descent, the Sybil indicated that return is far more difficult: "Descent to Avernus is easy—the doors of black Dis are open day and night. But to retrace one's steps and escape to the upper air, this is the task, the real test" (*hoc opus, hic labor est,* 6.126–29). Their return, however, is not difficult at all. Vergil borrows from Homer the myth of the twin gates of sleep, one of horn, one of ivory,[29] and places them within his topography of the Underworld. Through the gate of horn "easy leave is given to true shades," and through the gate of shining ivory, the "spirits below send false dreams to the upper air" (6.894–96). Anchises sends Aeneas and the Sybil out through the ivory gate, the gate of false dreams, and in the following single line Aeneas makes his way back to his ships and his companions.

The scholarship on this passage is extensive: what does Vergil intend by this exit from the Underworld? The ancient commentator Servius suggests that Vergil is implying a falseness to what Aeneas has seen and heard, but this is unlikely. Most scholars see one obvious explanation. Aeneas, as a human, is by definition a "false shade" and cannot exit through the gate of horn.[30] We agree with this reading, but we also read the "falseness" of Aeneas as the limit of the analogy between him and the souls in Elysium. Their erasure, unlike his, is an erasure of memory; their connection with the past is absolutely severed. Aeneas's erasure is one of affect and identification. He shifts the focus of his longing, but his memories remain intact. He does not drink from Lethe. The hearth gods of Troy are with him throughout the epic, signaling the continued role of the past. Aeneas's duty, as he sees more clearly in the Underworld in the figure of his father and the other souls, is to bridge past and future in the right way.

Vergil draws attention to the limits of knowledge explicitly in the final historical digression of the work, and the final ecphrasis, which converge in the shield brought by Venus. In the eighth book, when the Italians have declared war on the Trojans and Aeneas goes inland to ask for aid from the Arcadian king Evander, he receives and understands omens as indications of his impending success. He knows that he is the man "summoned by Olympus" (*ego poscor Olympo,* 8.533). But he is separated from his armor, which he leaves in the colony at the mouth of the Tiber. As Thetis does for Achilles in the *Iliad,* Venus goes to Vulcan and asks for new armor for her son. Vulcan complies, and he inscribes the future of

Rome on the shield. Venus brings the armor and sets it in a "removed glade"; just as in the sixth book, Aeneas meets a parent in such a glade and "is once more shown the future under parental auspices."[31] Aeneas cannot get his fill of gazing at the god's work, and for a hundred lines Vergil revisits Rome's past, rehearsing the famous paradigms of Roman *pietas* and scruple. Aeneas knows only delight: "he marvels at these things; ignorant of the events he rejoices in their image, lifting to his shoulder the fame and destiny of his progeny" (*rerumque ignarus imagine gaudet,* 8.729–31). The import is clear. Precise knowledge of destiny is at the same time unnecessary and not enough. The status of the future's "reality" is one of the chief concerns of the entire epic and the special focus of book six. Aeneas's destiny is real but potential, true but insubstantial. There is something about Aeneas's exit through the gate of *falsa insomnia* that focuses on the gap between his substantiality and the insubstantiality of his destiny and of his knowledge. It is significant for our reading, and for Vergil's definition of heroism, that Aeneas's new identity is not established with his knowledge of the future. Knowledge is not enough. Heroism, so different in the *Aeneid,* still requires performance and enactment.

THE NEW WRATH

At the end of the eighth book, when Aeneas is equipped with the divine armor, we are invited to ask exactly what it is that he still lacks. He has turned away from his past as it was reflected in Carthage; he has received all knowledge necessary from his father in the Underworld; he has found the Tiber and met Latinus, with whom he made peace; he has visited the site of Rome, where Evander now reigns, and received the divine imprimatur of the armor. The sum of these things, however, does not equal a clear and convincing heroism that rivals Achilles. Aeneas must still emerge recognizably from his blank state to a new, rewritten state. Vergil cannot tell us how this transformation happens, because it does not exist in moments of realization or epiphany. He can only show us the transformation by presenting moments of its emergence through enactment.

The crucial tenth book introduces most clearly how action determines the shape of one's life, not only for Aeneas but for all. The book begins with a council of the gods. Jupiter forbids all divine intervention in the human affairs, just as Homer's Zeus does in the eighth book of the *Iliad.* Zeus, however, anchors his decree in threats of violence, and he is later seduced by Hera; in his postcoital slumber the gods again enter the fray.

Vergil's Jupiter is unavailable to seduction and secures obedience by his authority. Far from relinquishing control over the events, he insists that destiny be allowed to work itself out. It will do this, Jupiter says, through the actions of the men involved. "Each man's undertakings will bring him grief or good fortune (*laborem fortunamque*). King Jupiter will be the same to all. And the fates will find a way" (*fata viam invenient*, 10.111–13). Men's decisions and their actions are the vehicle for destiny, but not determinative of it. By their actions men determine their *labor* and *fortuna*, a hard road or an easy one. And of course, their actions also determine their fame, their *kleos,* as Jupiter acknowledges; the battle-field retains its Iliadic economy. Before battling Turnus, Pallas prays for success to Heracles, his divinized familial patron; and Heracles weeps because fate does not allow him to save the young man. Jupiter consoles him: mortals die, their time is short, and many of the gods lost sons at Troy; but "to magnify fame with deeds, that is the hero's work" (*famam extendere factis, hoc virtutis opus*, 10.468–69).[32] Enactment brings fame to the humans, as it brings destiny into the temporal world.

Aeneas understands this as a personal need as well as a cosmic one. Just before he meets Turnus in single combat, in a surprisingly dark leave-taking of Ascanius, Aeneas offers a view of his past actions that is more than the realization of destiny; his vision is reflective, personal, focused on himself, a premonition of the union between self and destiny. In this farewell, Aeneas offers himself, or part of himself, to his son as *exemplum:* "Son, from me learn what it is to be heroic and to truly toil. Learn what it is to be fortunate from others" (12.435–36). What he exemplifies he names *virtus* and *verus labor,* which we translate as verbs, as active states. Aeneas also tells Ascanius that he is a negative paradigm of *fortuna.* This self-description comes somewhat as a surprise. His knowledge of fate is specific. He is able to console his son and companions by "teaching them their destiny" (*fata docens,* 12.111), just as his father's shade taught him. His knowledge of his role in that destiny is also specific. And yet Aeneas claims not to be an example of *fortuna,* good luck, pleasant results, the easy way. He is a model of *labor.* For Aeneas, *labor* is ambivalent: it encompasses both the enactment of his destiny and the difficulties that attend that enactment. He exemplifies both. Aeneas has come to know that he is ultimately responsible only for the enactment of his duty, not for the circumstances in which he enacts it nor the recognition he receives for it. He judges the circumstances and the consequences to have been negative. They have amounted thus far to *labor,* the antithesis of *fortuna.* At the same time, Aeneas understands that his duty exists for him independent of the circumstantial ease or difficulty of accomplishing it, and it must be enacted.[33]

Enactment, for Aeneas as for Achilles, requires a return to battle. Aeneas is absent, for the most part, in books nine and eleven, and present in books ten and twelve. Like Achilles, his absence serves as a foil for his importance, and reveals the distance between him and the others who toil in battle on both sides. Turnus appears as the clear champion to oppose Aeneas, cast in the Iliadic role of Hector, whose success enjoys free rein as long as Aeneas is elsewhere. Aeneas's absence, however, is not due to any dissatisfaction or wrath. In book nine, he is still returning from Evander's town; book eleven begins with Pallas's funeral and a truce, and the inevitable meeting of Aeneas and Turnus is delayed.

Aeneas's return to battle reaches two points of crescendo, both of which connect Aeneas, through passion, to his deeds. After Turnus kills Pallas, rejoicing in the grief he has caused to Evander, and takes his swordbelt as spoil, Aeneas assumes an Achillean rage and invincibility on the field. He slaughters men as if he had "a hundred arms and a hundred hands" (10.565–66) and humiliates them in his fury. Turnus is deceived and led from the battle by Juno, and Aeneas eventually turns his attention to Mezentius, the exiled and apostate king of Etruria. Mezentius is quickly wounded in the thigh by Aeneas, but as he moves in to kill him, Mezentius's son Lausus intervenes and fights Aeneas off, allowing his father to retreat. The mismatch is too great, and Aeneas's warning to the boy—"your *pietas* is deceiving you into rashness" (*fallit te incautum pietas tua,* 10.812)—is unheeded. Aeneas's anger is piqued and he kills Lausus, then immediately pities him: "the mirror image of his own *pietas* for his father came into his mind" (*et mentem patriae subiit pietatis imago,* 10.824). This is also an Achillean moment, but from the *Iliad*'s final book. As Achilles sees in Priam his own father's grief, Aeneas sees in Lausus his own devotion for his father. This, however, is not a development or a return to humanity in Aeneas; it is the manifestation of his most characteristic feature even in the most extreme circumstance.[34] Aeneas's pity prevents him from despoiling Lausus as Turnus despoils Pallas. He recognizes Lausus's excellence and honors it. Aeneas lifts Lausus's body and returns it to the enemy.

The killing of Lausus is meant to contrast with Turnus's killing of Pallas. Vergil sets up the contrast early in the book, when he has Pallas and Lausus pass each other in the field by Jupiter's decree, "but soon each one's fate awaits, to fall under a greater enemy" (10.438). In Aeneas's act we are far from any Christian sense of mercy, which does not belong.

Aeneas feels pity for Lausus now dead, but that pity is based not on Lausus's wretchedness but on his virtuous enactment of his *pietas*. It is exactly the quality that Turnus holds in contempt and ignores in his treatment of Pallas. "I wish that his father were present" (10.443), Turnus says before he kills Pallas; and afterward, to Pallas's comrades, "Arcadians, remember these words of mine and carry them back to Evander. I send Pallas back to him just as he deserved him" (10.491–92). Turnus is able to enact his martial excellence, as able as Aeneas is, but his moral isolation in doing so violates the communal and divine standards that govern the world of Vergil's epic. Turnus's passion does not link him to the purposes of Jupiter or to the cosmic pattern of fate.

Turnus's death has received more scholarly attention than any part of the *Aeneid* except book four and Dido.[35] These two parts are consonant, of course. Dido and Turnus provide the greatest obstacles to Aeneas and his destiny, and both are characterized by their *furor,* their passion. This parallel does not apply to Turnus's death, however. Aeneas chooses to kill Turnus, withholding from Turnus the pity that Lausus's death evokes from Aeneas in book ten. Turnus is wounded, abandoned by his protecting gods, and aware of Aeneas's complete victory. In this state of defeat, he calls upon Aeneas's *pietas*. "Please pity the old age of my father Daunus (for you had such a father in Anchises) and pity me; or if you prefer to banish me from life's light, return me to my people" (12.933–36). Aeneas hesitates. This appeal to *pietas* is supported (though Turnus does not know this) by Anchises' instruction in the Underworld to "spare the conquered" (6.853). Turnus seems to use Aeneas's *pietas* against him, to turn Aeneas away from action. At that moment it appears that Aeneas's final enactment will be characteristic of him but as far from the Iliadic world as possible: a passion encompassed and constrained by something greater than the hero.

After Turnus's appeal, Aeneas wavers until he sees the swordbelt of Pallas, which Turnus has taken as a spoil of war. The sight of it infuriates Aeneas; he becomes "inflamed with fury and terrible with anger" (*furiis accensus et ira terribilis,* 12.946–47), and invoking vengeance for that crime, Aeneas stabs the helpless Turnus, whose "disdained life flees to the shadows below" (12.952). The act seems uncharacteristic of Aeneas, but it identifies him with Achilles. Achillean passion is wed to his now-prospective *pietas*, his dutiful submission to that which is greater than any man, the founding of Rome. This passion is the final element necessary for Aeneas to inhabit his destiny. He acts, both as a man animated by the inner urgency of passion, and as a man destined for glory.

Aeneas's passion is Achillean in measure but not in consequence. Aeneas rages as personally but less narrowly than does Achilles. From the perspective of Aeneas, Turnus is criminal: the blow is struck in the name of Pallas, who exacts his penalty in Turnus's "wicked blood" (*scelerato ex sanguine,* 12.949). Aeneas feels multiple obligations of *pietas,* not only to parental devotion (a concept that Turnus invokes to save his life but violates in killing Pallas) but also to the bonds of guest-friendship.[36] Aeneas wavers because *pietas* both demands Turnus's death and urges against it, as affective *pietas* had both urged him to leave and yet stay with Dido. The resolution of this dilemma is the identifiable moment of Aeneas's change. The moment of his apparent repudiation of *pietas* is in fact the transformation of his *pietas.* From the perspective of the epic, Aeneas's *pietas* is now enlarged, more expansive and "fate-full." It has become, like Achilles' will, a moral law, but one consonant with the rhythms of fate and the judgment of Jupiter.[37] Aeneas's act cannot be analyzed into a divine framework, a personal framework, or a communal framework. It is uniquely his, personal in affect, communal in obligation, cosmic in scope. Unlike Achilles' (or Turnus's) will, Aeneas's *pietas* is not limited to himself or to the narrow confines of his particular circumstances. It is the vehicle for his heroic enactment, but also the vehicle for his realization of destiny; it is both his character and his action, both terrible and morally right.

There is no dissatisfaction; there is no disproportionate wrath; there is no violation of communal or divine sanctions. Aeneas, through enactment, becomes the hero that he is destined to be, incorporating all of his innate excellence (summed up in *pietas, virtus,* and *labor*) into his heroic participation. Fate enlarges him without invalidating him; his participation in his destiny is his achievement.

THE FATE OF ACHILLES

Achilles is present in the *Aeneid* even in the prologue, where he earns special mention as a murderer of Trojans and the threat that the survivors escaped. The Trojans are "the survivors of the Greeks and of pitiless Achilles" (*reliquias Danaum atque immitis Achilli,* 1.30). This strikes the right note for the *Aeneid*: Achilles was the greatest warrior at Troy on either side, the culmination of physical and martial excellence, but he had a limit. He killed as many as he could, but he could not kill more than fate allowed, and fate is the governing force behind the actions of this epic. Fate is clearly invoked throughout the prologue, something greater even than Juno's wrath. The *Iliad* invokes "the will of Zeus" in its prologue, but views it as an indiscernible, and therefore irrelevant, frame for meaningful human action. The *Aeneid* must disagree: fate provides the only meaningful and relevant frame for heroic action. Achilles functions in the *Aeneid* as the contradictory symbol of that essential judgment. Achilles provides the positive paradigm for passionate action; but he also provides a negative paradigm, albeit an innocent one, for finding a meaningful frame for his excellence.

In the *Aeneid*, Achilles is understood as more than a historical figure— a symbol of human excellence and an emblem for heroic and victorious antagonism against Troy and its descendants. As such, Turnus serves as the Italian Achilles. The Sybil seems unequivocal in her analogy between the two: "another Achilles is brought forth in Latium, he, too, born of a goddess" (*alius Latio iam partus Achilles, natus et ipse dea,* 6.89–90). Like Achilles, Turnus has a nymph for a mother, Venilia (10.76). And Turnus understands himself in terms of the analogy. As he taunts the Trojan Pandarus in combat, Turnus predicts, "You will tell Priam that even here you have found an Achilles" (9.742), then kills him. Symbolically, however, Vergil also assimilates Aeneas to Achilles with numerous parallels of image and action. The divine armor is but one example. Aeneas's similarities to Achilles congregate in books ten and twelve, where Aeneas's rampage on the battlefield is reminiscent of Achilles. After Pallas's death, Aeneas takes captives to sacrifice on the funeral pyre (10.517–20); he refuses ransom (10.530–34); finally, like a hunting dog he chases Turnus who flees like a deer (12.749–58). All of these scenes have clear Iliadic precedents. It is significant that the parallels between Aeneas and Achilles come from the later books of both epics, as both heroes approach their very different achievements.

It is not surprising that, as both Turnus and Aeneas share parallels to Achilles, they are also assimilated to each other in description, action, and simile: both are most handsome, their martial valor equal, their rage deadly.[38] We are reminded of Achilles and Hector. Hector is dressed in the armor of Achilles, who secures his own death by killing his own image in Hector. The similarities between Turnus and Aeneas, however, involve their appearances and their enactments, but obviously not their deaths. In fact, they move in opposite directions toward and away from death. This movement is reflected in a verbal echo: when Aeneas first appears in the midst of the storm, "his limbs go slack with a chill" (*Aeneae solvuntur frigore membra,* 1.92); and when Turnus receives Aeneas's sword in his chest, "his limbs go slack with a chill" (*illi solvuntur frigore membra,* 12.951). Aeneas's relationship to Turnus, like his relationship to

Achilles, is one of both similarity and difference, and his transformation at the end of the *Aeneid*—or our realization of it—makes him both more like and more unlike them.

The similarity to Achilles is more obvious in the end: Aeneas blazes with anger and kills Turnus, rejecting his plea for mercy in doing so. This is an Achillean moment, not the first that we see from Aeneas, but the most thorough, because it blends the killing of Hector with the supplication of Priam. Turnus's appeal is inconsistent with his character and his enactment, and Aeneas does not recognize any resemblance between himself and his victim. All resemblances are past; Turnus represents what Aeneas was, and in rendering the future substantial, Aeneas makes the past insubstantial. Turnus becomes a shade at the moment Aeneas fully occupies the Achillean center of gravity.

What are we to make of Turnus, since he is given such development in the text, as a second Achilles? Is Vergil suggesting that one Achilles kills another? Two diverse readings present themselves, one emphasizing disjunction and change, the other conjunction and fulfillment. The emphasis on disjunction invokes tragedy and the Iliadic hero, and such an interpretation might run thus. Insofar as fate is universal and progressive, human destiny is not, as in the *Iliad,* a matter of numbered days and choices. Human destiny is simply a subset of the larger movement, which lies behind substantial, lasting institutions that are engendered through human achievement. The *Aeneid* documents one realization of fate that amounts to a new order of things, an order that Aeneas represents, and that new order does not allow for Homeric heroism. The Homeric vision of excellence is too limited, the *kleos* won by such heroes, too small, too personal. That heroic economy suffers from a myopic understanding of the broader scope of greatness. So far from true heroism, the indignant, honor-based excellence may actually impede the activity of fate, though it cannot divert it. Eventually, whatever stands in the way of this new order will be crushed. Turnus, then, is a representative of that individualized vision of heroism, of an honor that can be gathered about the great man in the form of golden tripods, swift horses, and the armor of defeated adversaries. As such, he has no place in the community of Rome. Like Achilles at the end of the *Iliad,* Turnus is "a man out of all season."[39]

An alternative reading focuses on conjunction, where the Achillean dimension is not destroyed by Turnus's death, but absorbed. Beginning in the seventh book with three references to Circe and her magical powers of hybridization, this thread of transformation and incorporation runs through to the final conversation of Jupiter and Juno. When her time for interference is up, Juno makes a stunning request: that the name, language, and clothing of Troy be suppressed, that the Latins remain as they are. Jupiter concedes all these things, and adds that Trojan custom and rituals will be added but submerged under Latin guise. Many readers view this negatively, and it does appear that Juno wins, even though the degree of her victory is not completely clear.[40] We maintain that Vergil views this positively, and that the theme of incorporation extends to the very end of the epic. Turnus is not "out of season"; Aeneas is the man for all seasons. Turnus is both Hector *and* Achilles; Aeneas incorporates and appropriates Achilles.[41]

Both of these readings have merit, but neither captures fully the scope of the epic. It seems wrong to suggest that Vergil intends no sympathy, or worse, for Turnus.[42] If so, then Vergil fails miserably, for his accounts of Turnus do win our affection. But our sympathy for Turnus cannot overturn our sense of Aeneas's rightness. Turnus is a tragic hero, but Vergil sees a heroism beyond tragic. He dramatizes that priority by having his hero of destiny, who is not immune to sorrow, kill the hero of tragedy. Turnus realizes his error, although too late, and his realization allows us to point to a moment when Turnus apparently transcends himself, sheds his fury and attempts a reintegration by appealing to Aeneas's *pietas*.[43] Turnus is profoundly human at that moment in his fallibility, his fear, and his recognition of error, and he offers Aeneas an opportunity to display his own humanity by recognizing a resemblance in his enemy, to erase another passionate bond to the past by forsaking revenge. Aeneas refuses the opportunity and promptly ends Turnus's life, and Vergil the epic.

In ending the epic in this way, Vergil drives home both the necessity and danger of Achillean passion. To ignore Achilles is impossible; to absorb him is dangerous. Achillean passion is necessary in the narrative of the *Aeneid* to weld the man to the event, to depict the destined founding of Rome to Aeneas as a personal achievement, as both a fulfillment of Aeneas and the realization of destiny. Without this passion, Aeneas cannot fill his role with the distinctiveness of his character. However, Vergil cannot overemphasize this passion, for the danger of Achillean passion lies in the isolation and tragedy that follows in its wake. The founding act cannot be too personal, too inscrutably passionate; otherwise, Aeneas begins to supersede his achievement, just as Achilles' passion supersedes both his military triumphs and his magnanimous acts. The man becomes the measure. In order to fill Aeneas's founding achievement with a genuinely personal dimension, and yet to avoid making the glory of Rome somehow relative or subordinate to the personal potency of the founder, Vergil carefully holds the passion of the man and his preordained role in tension. Neither is to gain the upper hand in the reader's mind.

Vergil never releases us from the tension, but as readers, we tend to find the final flash of Aeneas's passion but a thin thread that links his character to his achievement. Vergil's depiction of genuine heroic participation is extraordinarily artful. He sees very clearly how difficult is the poetic task of joining a man's character to the greater glory of Eternal Rome. His account of an emergent hero of independent action—erased of retrospective passion, guided forward by knowledge of his destiny, and then rewritten in the labors of battle, culminating in explosive anger—always takes place against the horizon of destiny and under the watchful eye of Jupiter. The effect he seeks is to show us a hero enlarged rather than diminished by the larger measures of glory. Yet it is impossible not to feel the distance between the egoism of Achilles and the obedience of Aeneas as a diminishment. Rome and Aeneas are not identical, and Aeneas's civic accomplishment, however great, cannot simply be weighed against its personal costs as if in a "double-entry ledger."[44] Aeneas's quest for a new Troy involves more renunciation than our sense of individuality seems to allow. He must leave Dido, and does so with an abruptness that Vergil affirms as necessary. He must give up his nostalgia and most of all he must allow the defining feature of his character, *pietas*, to be redirected and joined, if for only a moment, to his burning passion. No final accounting reconciles the columns of loss and gain, and many of Vergil's readers consider it the ultimate sign of his humanity and his vision that he could embrace both light and dark in a single work.[45]

But the *Aeneid* is much more a shrine to Aeneas than the *Iliad* is to Achilles, whose dissatisfaction precludes that sort of admiration. Paradoxically, it is that very dissatisfaction that allows us to stand beside Achilles in a way that we cannot stand beside Aeneas. If we cannot match Achilles' pain, we can at least identify it as being like our own, rooted in ambition, unrecognized and unfulfilled. But Aeneas stands apart, more than ever in the final moment as he becomes fully identified with destiny and satisfied. His significance partakes of the symbolic at the expense of the literal: Aeneas is not just an excellent man but also the triumph of Rome and Augustus, and the realization of fate.[46] Our unease at Aeneas's distance lies at the heart of this study. Our sense of Aeneas's alienation from the human condition is neither a "modern" nor a "Christian" response.[47] A readerly unease is not to misread Vergil but to read him

well. At the same time, to read the work only with unease, without recognizing the possibility of enlargement by participating in a greatness
that exceeds the human frame of reference, constitutes a failure and an
unwillingness to entertain Vergil's poetic ambition. For Vergil's goal is to
bring us to consider a greatness that is not essentially tragic, to consider
a heroism in which the man does not exceed the measure, but rather, participates in a greatness that we can recognize and glorify.

The problem of heroic participation does not solve the problems of
imitation and recognition: it subsumes them. Who in Vergil's putative
audience, then or now, is to recognize whom, and who is to imitate
whom?[48] Neither recognition nor imitation comes to the fore within the
Aeneid, for there is no counterpart to the Greek army nor to the Athenian jury. Whether the Latins or Trojans recognize Aeneas appropriately,
or even whether the reader does, is unimportant. Nor is imitation intro-
duced as a goal for the other characters or for the general reader. Imitation, such as it is, is guaranteed by the constant reference to the future
and the successors of Aeneas's *pietas.* The Rome of Vergil's day exists as
evidence of some type of imitation. Both of these concerns, for recognition and imitation, are subsumed in the problem of participation. Imitation becomes legacy; recognition becomes citizenship.

Christianity provides a similarly antitragic model for human greatness,
and our reading of the *Aeneid* helps to train us to see how the New Testament links Jesus to the greatest heroic measure of all, the divine. The
literary argument of the gospel stories of Jesus is very different, but the
effect sought is similar. The individuality of the man must be inseparable from his destiny. Further, more than any other ancient hero, Aeneas's
self-erasing acceptance of his destiny provides parallels for the Christian
understanding of the life of faith.[49] Aeneas provides a model for subsequent Christian theologians; his destiny resembles Christian goals. The
concepts of self-denial, dying in Christ, and the belief that "all things
have become new" emphasize complete change and a severance from the
past. No less horrible choices than Aeneas's are issued by Jesus: "No one
who puts a hand to the plow and looks back is fit for the kingdom of God"
(Luke 9:62); or even more terribly, "Whoever comes to me and does not
hate father and mother, wife and children, brothers and sisters, yes, and
even life itself, cannot be my disciple" (Luke 14:26). Vergil depicts the
horror of such a call by portraying the essential costs to the individual.
But Vergil is not writing allegory. Vergil does not suggest that Aeneas is
participating generically in a universal destiny, and therefore reveals a
general pattern. The founding and ruling of Rome will involve others, to

be sure, but Aeneas's relation to it, and his responsibility to it, are singular. Nonetheless, to the extent that we, as readers, can see Aeneas's grappling with his destiny, and can feel the tension between the personal element of independent passion and the supra-personal horizon of greatness, then we can be more articulate about the distinctive project of Christian heroism. For Christian writers struggle with the same literary challenges that animate Vergil, even as they propose a radically different kind of heroism.

Chapter Five

Messianic Triumph: Jesus

If one says no more of Christ than that he is a teacher of humanity, a martyr to the truth, one is not adopting the religious standpoint; one says no more of him than of Socrates.
—Hegel, *Lectures on the Philosophy of Religion*

Recognition, imitation, and participation: our thesis has been that these three notions guide us to see certain difficulties in the human engagement with greatness. Across their heterogeneity, the three classical depictions of heroes we have considered signal these difficulties. Achilles' greatness exceeds the theater of the Trojan conflict and its standard economy of recognition. It is not at all clear how, or even whether, others can offer Achilles the communal praise and acknowledgment that are his due. In his final isolation at the conclusion of the *Iliad*, even the reader, privileged over Achilles' comrades with knowledge of Achilles' final magnanimity, is left without obvious response. How are we to characterize the man, whose passion exceeds his achievements? How can we give proper form to our acknowledgment of his greatness? In short, how can we recognize Achilles? Homer, as we have argued, builds the tragedy of Achilles around the difficulty of answering these questions and placing Achilles in a stable and secure spot in our pantheon of virtue.

Plato intends us to feel the magnetic attraction of the hidden beauty of Socrates. The currency of recognition appropriate to this golden-souled Silen is, finally, imitation, a currency all the more valuable because the irony of Socratic greatness raises the stakes of devoted discipleship. His way neither conforms to nor rebels against standard Athenian ideals; the divine horsefly raises more questions than he answers, and to become his disciple requires one to follow him personally and intimately rather than ideally and at a distance. The upshot is a final Socratic irony. The uncertainty of his virtue increases rather than diminishes his attractive power. One feels the pull of his greatness. "Yes, it's all about thinking clearly!" or "Of course, the whole thing is about intellectual honesty." But platitudes melt and are reshaped by the particular form of Socrates' questioning and the constant undercurrent of his piety. Unable to grasp Socratic virtue as a maxim or generalization, we either fall away from imitation, or we redouble our attention to the sheer uniqueness of his way of living. Yet, what kind of heroism can this be? Should the hero not achieve or embody a greatness that is more than sheer individuality? How can Socrates be worthy of imitation without being a certain kind of person, an identifiable and enviable archetype? But Socrates never points beyond himself, and as a result, his heroic gestalt is strangely immediate, but inimitable.

Vergil is no less preoccupied than Homer or Plato with the enigmas of greatness. No longer unrecognizable in unbounded expansiveness of passion made effective in action, or shrouded in ironic ambiguity as a conqueror who speaks and acts in ordinary ways, the greatness Vergil envisions is palpable and immediate because it is realized in a civilization. Excellence is found but not exhausted in Roman practice and encoded into Roman law. Neither recognition nor imitation prove difficulties for Vergil's readers. One attends sacrifices before the temples. One enters into the disciplines of Roman citizenship. However, precisely because this greatness is so vivid and available, for Vergil the problem of participation emerges with a special potency. Senators meet in the Forum; priests make offering to maintain the favor of the gods. Each has his or her role within the organism of Roman greatness. Yet how can anyone rise to inhabit the full form of this greatness? Who can take on the weight of the entirety of Rome and make that greatness coextensive with his identity as a heroic agent? How can one man *be* great, as Rome *is* great? These questions shape Vergil's epic account of the founding of Rome, an event written into the code of all time and affirmed by Jupiter. Aeneas rises to inhabit that fate-driven moment, not as a pawn of fate, not as a cog in a machine already in motion, but as a man of surpassing *pietas* and passion.

Although we seek to see these classical texts in relation to one another, we do not imagine that they are related "dialectically." As we have shown, Plato certainly depicts Socrates against a Homeric background, and

Vergil even more so. Yet the influence of literary texts does not reduce to "themes" or "motifs" or "problems" that define, somehow, the real commerce of the poetic imagination. The penetrative force of poetic inheritance is rarely thematic and never a matter of "problems," seen or solved. Instead that influence is more nearly primitive, sensual, literal, and unconscious, as inherited form and content define the boundaries of imagination and constitute the reflex responses of creativity. Our purpose, then, has been to highlight themes of recognition, imitation, and participation in order to guide our reading. Homer wished to render Achilles in his greatness, a greatness necessarily embedded in the standard communal forms of recognition that governed the lives of Greek warriors. He did not wish to bring to consciousness "the problem of recognition." Our claim has been that a certain articulateness about recognition as a textual and social dynamic, like imitation and participation, concentrates our attention as readers, and does so in a way that we are drawn more closely to, rather than abstracted away from, the literary strategies deployed by the authors to depict their heroes.

Why, then, would Homer seem to order his account of Achilles according to a problem of recognition, while Vergil attends so exclusively to participation? This is not a question we have set out to answer. Still less have we intended to suggest a developmental scheme, as if the problem of recognition is sublated, through imitation, into the problem of participation. The change from Homer, through Plato, to Vergil admits of interesting speculation about the social and historical conditions that shape our conceptions of and aspirations toward greatness. However, dialectical schemes treat literary texts as transparent media for the putatively real content of thought and culture—"problems" or "ideas" or "concepts"—the interaction of which gives texts their meaning and import. Nothing could be further from our intention. To treat poems as literary husks surrounding a conceptual kernel, and then to interpret with the goal of liberating the idea from its sensual, verbal, and literary form, strikes us as pernicious. We have not sought to supersede the texts with our readings. We have not substituted a conceptual argument—for example, "Because Achilles surpasses the standard economy of recognition, he cannot be integrated into communal understanding"—for the texts' more effective poetic arguments. Our goal has been illuminative, to chart the patterns of poetic preoccupation that are deeply connected to the kinds of concerns appropriate to interest in and desire for greatness. How can I recognize excellence? How can I imitate greatness? How can I participate in surpassing achievement? Homer and Plato and Vergil answer these questions with their depictions of their heroes. Of that we are sure. But we have not distilled the essence of these answers for transport elsewhere. Their literary efforts constitute their answers, and our notions of recognition, imitation, and participation help us read those answers well, or they serve no valuable purpose at all.

As we turn to Christian writings, we want to emphasize these notions. Far less than in our treatment of classical literature do we offer hypotheses about historical development or influence in Christian works. Homer provides the horizon for Vergil's epic imagination. Achilles is a ready figure for Socrates to use in his ironic self-description. Although classical literature comes to have a profound role in the history of Christian thought, and Hellenistic and Roman culture influenced life throughout the eastern Mediterranean, the first Christian writers did not regard Homer, Plato, or Vergil as their primary frames of reference.[1] The Jews who authored the various Gospels, letters, and visions that constitute the New Testament wrote under the saturating influence of another, quite different body of literature, itself preoccupied with glory and greatness. It is now called the Old Testament, but for the writers of the New Testament, it was simply "the scriptures." If our purpose were to identify the antecedents to New Testament accounts, we would delve into these scriptures. However, our objective is literary, not historical. Thus, as the problems of recognition, imitation, and participation guide our reading of the New Testament, we do nothing more than carry over to Christian writings a trained interpretive sensibility. Why the author of the Gospel of Mark is preoccupied with recognition is not a question we think our reading of Homer in chapter 2 will answer. We only wish to see his preoccupation more clearly, along with concerns about imitation and participation, and to feel these preoccupations as intrinsic to the kind of greatness the New Testament wishes to bring to our attention.

Our approach to the New Testament will not have the sustained unity of our first three chapters. Authorship, style, and genre vary across the New Testament, and we cannot provide a close reading that approaches this heterogeneous body of literature as a single literary effort. Nonetheless we do not intend to be any more distant from the texts of early Christianity than we have been from the texts of Homer, Plato, and Vergil. We shall use the themes of recognition, imitation, and participation to guide our engagement with portions of the New Testament. We wish to read what has been written, not to search the texts for examples and evidence, as if the problems of recognition or participation required the assembly of "recognition passages" or "participation passages." Recognition, imitation, and participation indicate foci for interpretation; they mark a differentiation of readerly sensitivity, and this differentiation either brings us closer to what the New Testament undertakes as a literary artifact, or it does not. Our thesis is that, trained by close readings of the *Iliad, The Apology of Socrates* and the *Aeneid,* we can read the New Testament well. Classical literature has tuned our ear. Now we are prepared to hear the distinctive ways in which the fundamental Christian texts speak about greatness.

We could press Jesus into classical patterns of heroism. His contest with Satan in the wilderness can be manipulated to parallel Homeric heroism. Milton, as we shall see, does just that. Jesus' parabolic teaching and oracular pronouncements, combined with the Gospel accounts of his confused followers, can suggest Socrates. The New Testament emphasis on Jesus' role as founder of the kingdom of God can lead to parallels with Aeneas and the founding of Rome. Each of these parallels seems plausible, but none illuminates. They confuse material convergence with common patterns of literary difficulty and poetic solution.

For our reading, Christian literature grapples with the enigmas of human greatness, and although the Christian view is often at odds with the classical views, concerns about recognition, imitation, and participation do emerge. The Homeric parallel serves to illustrate. For different reasons and in a different way, Jesus cannot be recognized in the standard economy. The author of Mark, like Homer, wishes us to see this impossibility, but unlike Homer, this Gospel writer does propose a solution. The Gospel of Mark is enigmatic, but not tragic, and the upshot is a radical literary argument: we can only recognize the crucified Jesus if we believe in him as the Son of God. Thus, the parallel rests with a shared difficulty—seeing and responding appropriately to the greatness of the hero—not in parallel action or characterization or resolution. The same holds true for a link between the *Aeneid* and the Gospel of Matthew. The nature of the kingdom founded is worlds apart. The destiny appointed differs dramatically, and the character of the two heroes bears no resemblance. Yet, like Vergil, the author of Matthew is concerned to join the man to the greatness, to link the carpenter's son to King David and the messianic hope of divine blessing consummated. This messianic greatness is materially different, even at odds with the Vergilian ideal of Roman greatness. But both are surpassing, and both seem untethered from the limitations of a human life. On just this point, the author of Matthew shares a common literary project with Vergil. Both strain to tell a story in which their hero is wedded to the unquestioned horizon of greatness that they each, in their vastly different ways, presuppose.[2]

The New Testament pushes the limits of the heroic; its project is, to use Milton's phrase, "Above Heroic." Jesus participates to the point of converging with the very source and essence of greatness, God himself, and the Gospels understand our recognition in the heightened religious terms of worship and obedience. In order to flush out the Christian understanding of Jesus' heroism, his relation to greatness, and the form in which we are to honor him, we will consider the Gospel of Matthew's treatment of the problem of participation, and then, more extensively, we will analyze the Gospel of Mark's approach to the problem of recognition. Against a background of messianic expectation, the author of Matthew seeks to persuade his readers that Jesus of Nazareth does not just teach about holy things and perform wonders. He is joined to the eternal purposes of God in the very particularity of his life. Convincing readers that Jesus participates in something so transcendent as the maker of heaven and earth intensifies the problem of recognition. We know how to admire sages, even to devote our lives to their teachings, but Jesus is more than an oracle, more than a source of wisdom. He is the Son of God, and the Gospel of Mark crafts a story about Jesus that forces us to repudiate as inadequate our standard expectations about how to recognize Jesus. With remarkable ambition, even aggression, the Gospel of Mark seeks to guide us toward the unexpected fittingness of worship as the proper recognition of Jesus.

THAT THE SCRIPTURES MIGHT BE FULFILLED

The Gospel stories are not the credulous stumblings of second-generation Christians trying to preserve a record of the life and teachings of their rabbi. They are not compendia of oral fragments stitched together by scribes and copyists. Quite the contrary, whether or not one thinks Christianity the product of a disappointed apocalyptic imagination, or the consequence of Paul's will-to-power, or the work of the Holy Spirit, one must admit that the Gospel stories are profoundly premeditated acts of literary ambition. They have a demonstrated potency, and centuries of Christian devotion testify to their power.

Precisely because the Gospels are so plain, so inattentive to the pleasures of well-wrought phrases and lovely description, they give little aesthetic pleasure, little of the sheer poetic joy so ubiquitous in the *Aeneid*. The evangelists focus their ambition, and they set out to produce a singular effect in the minds of their readers: to acknowledge the divine greatness of Jesus and the consequent vocation of discipleship. The Gospels seek to command our destinies, and the literary execution of that desire yields the sophisticated constructions of the story of Jesus. These Gospel stories bring us to see Jesus in all his greatness, for in so seeing, the writers of the Gospels are convinced that we cannot help but follow. His heroic greatness compels an obedient recognition.

The final verses of the Gospel of Matthew portray the commanding authority of Jesus, and in so doing, point directly to the conclusion that all the Gospel writers presuppose. After Jesus' death and burial, Mary Magdalene and "the other Mary" go to the tomb. When they arrive, they find the stone rolled away and encounter an angel. The angel tells them that the crucified Jesus has risen from the dead and goes before them to Galilee. The women tell the disciples what the angel has told them, and the disciples go to Galilee. On a mountaintop, the risen Jesus declares his universal reign, for he has "all authority in heaven and earth." On the basis of this authority, Jesus then commands his disciples to go and "make disciples of all nations." This mission involves incorporating the nations into Jesus' kingdom through the sign of new citizenship, "baptizing them in the name of the Father and of the Son and of the Holy Spirit." Lord of this new nation, Jesus tells his disciples to teach these new followers "to obey everything that I have commanded you" (Matt. 28:1–20). This finale to the Gospel pictures Jesus as a commanding king, gathering his vassals to lay battle plans for conquering all that lies before them. He has all authority; it remains only to exercise it through his disciples.

The literary ambition of the Gospel of Matthew does not rest in persuading its readers that there exists a divine authority over heaven and earth. The author of Matthew presupposes the backdrop of Jewish faith in the God who created heaven and earth. Still less does the Gospel of Matthew wish to convince us that this God can (metaphysically) or should (morally) involve himself in worldly affairs. The Jewish faith presupposed has no difficulty linking the Creator with the God of Israel, the LORD who established a covenant with Abraham, brought Israel out of Egypt, and delivered the faithless nation into exile. There is a God, and he issues commands. The possibility of such a God and such commands may preoccupy ancient and modern philosophers and skeptics, but they are alien to the Gospel of Matthew. In this Gospel, the focus is on linking the man Jesus to the final scene of regal authority, and by implication, to the God who has all power and who rightly commands. The urgency of literary argument parallels Vergil's imperative in the *Aeneid*: to describe a hero who participates in the greatness for which he is destined. Thus, the Gospel of Matthew wishes to convince us, through the first twenty-seven chapters about Jesus of Nazareth, who was born in Bethlehem, lived in Nazareth, and died outside of Jerusalem, that he rightfully ascends, in the final chapter, to the mountain top and assumes all authority in heaven and earth.

For the Gospel of Matthew, the criteria by which to judge whether or not Jesus "properly ascends" is contained in the messianic expectation encoded into the scriptures of Israel. Unlike Vergil, the author of Matthew is not interested in Jesus' character, his *pietas*. Instead, emphasis falls on an enacted conformity to a pattern of life. This different approach to showing participation is important. Vergil places little emphasis on Aeneas's outward conformity to his destiny because his destiny dictates no specific order of events. Events are in the hands of the fates, and Vergil is concerned to show that Aeneas's character fits with his destined role. In contrast, the author of Matthew must show that Jesus is just that man who fulfills all the relevant qualifications for the role of the anointed one who consummates the vocation of Israel. Just as Aeneas is not an accidental founder of Rome, so also Jesus is not an accidental messiah. He is not the placeholder for a divine exercise of power, any more than Aeneas is a pawn of the gods. Rather, Jesus fittingly and rightfully inhabits the messianic role.

The criteria of messianic expectation are very different from those assumed by Vergil, not only in content, but also in form. For the author of Matthew, Jesus ascends the mountain in Galilee *because* of what he has said and done and finally what is done to him. Here, something like "character" or "identity" seems relevant, and a certain parallel between Matthew's Gospel and Vergil's treatment of Aeneas obtains. The hero must be linked to his destiny in an essential way. But the Gospel swings away from the logic of the *Aeneid* in how it establishes that link. Aeneas fits; Jesus fulfills. Aeneas's status as patient rather than agent, as one pressed forward by events rather than the unique and personal source of action, presents Vergil with a problem. The epic seeks to overcome this passivity and purely fated sequence of action by welding Aeneas's passion to his destiny. The Gospel story moves in the opposite direction. Jesus' independent agency must be subsumed into his messianic role. The narrative builds toward his suffering and death, in which Jesus is ever more passive, ever more at the mercy of the will of others. But at just this point, the author of Matthew sees the greatest conformity to the messianic pattern. Rather than passion and inscrutable personal decisions, what *happens to* Jesus is, in the end, the most decisive reason for thinking that he is the messiah. In passion endured rather than passion expressed and enacted, Jesus fully participates in his role as the one who possesses "all authority," commanding his followers from the mountaintop at the end of the Gospel.

The literary strategies for persuading his readers that this passive and obedient Jesus participates in the surpassing greatness of his role are many. Although we cannot engage in a close reading of the gospel as a whole, we can sum up the essence of these diverse strategies in a single phrase: these things happened that the scriptures of the prophets might be fulfilled. The idea is simple. In the history of Israel and the writings of the prophets, the author discerns a pattern of expectation.[3] God will use Israel to bring his plans for all creation to completion, and he will do so through the work of a single man, a Son of David, a Son of Man, a Son of God, an Anointed One. We need not worry about the semantic variance between these titles. The central point is that God, the source of all power and the consummation of all greatness, establishes a pattern in which the power and greatness will be exercised, and His purposes achieved. Jesus of Nazareth, the Gospel of Matthew relentlessly argues, fulfills that anticipated pattern.

The Gospel of Matthew is dominated by the work of showing this fulfillment. The most obvious cases are when the author cites scripture, guiding his reader by the nose. The literary effect of this citation of scriptural fulfillment is a convergence of divine foreordination and human agency and motivation. The opening chapters of the Gospel provide the most sustained illustration of this technique. Matthew described Mary's pregnancy and her husband's altogether reasonable concern. An angel of the Lord intervenes and tells Joseph not to divorce Mary. The angel tells him the name of the child to be born is Jesus, which is a modification of Joshua and means "deliverer." This compact episode ends with the crucial tag line: "All this took place to fulfill what had been spoken by the Lord through the prophet" (1:22). The active and future-oriented potency of God is bound up with Jesus.

This strategy of linking particular details of Jesus' life to messianic expectation is repeated again and again. Jesus' place of birth, Bethlehem, is anticipated by the prophets (2:5). Joseph takes his family and flees to Egypt, not only to avoid the murderous intentions of Herod but also "to fulfill what had been spoken by the Lord through the prophet" (2:15). So, also, does Herod's subsequent rage have more than human significance. He is furious that he has been tricked by the wise men, who have gone home by another way, but this very plausible intra-narrative motivation for the horrifying episode of the slaughter of the male children of Bethlehem is layered with supra-narrative significance. It fulfills the prophecy of Jeremiah. In the same way, Jesus' return to the land of Israel and subsequent residence in Nazareth takes place according to a correspondence of prophetic necessity and ordinary prudence. Herod's son is a threat, and keeping a good distance from Jerusalem seems wise, but all the same, the turn of events occurred "so that what had been spoken by the prophets might be fulfilled" (2:23).

In each instance of fulfillment, the divinely ordained template is not imposed upon recalcitrant human events. Rather, the template of messianic fulfillment coheres with human events that are intrinsically plausible on their own terms. Events occur because of ordinary human motivations of fear, prudence, and deception. The Gospel of Matthew combines these narrative rationales but does not force the reader to choose between them. Unlike Vergil's approach, where the larger purposes of the epic intervene through oracle, divine interference, the relentlessly turning wheels of fate that Jupiter is pledged to uphold, and finally, by the spark of Aeneas's passion, the author of Matthew draws both elements together from the outset and reinforces the conjunction throughout. With the recurring claim that events occur so that the scriptures might be fulfilled, the horizon of greatness is near and intimate to the action. Patterns of fulfillment create a seamless conjunction of a pre-ordained pattern and human action, not just in the episodes that tell of Jesus' birth but throughout the Gospel. In each instance, the man Jesus is welded to messianic enactment so thoroughly that the one becomes identified by the other. To know the messianic role is to know Jesus; to know Jesus is to know the messianic role.

In one episode, the author of Matthew gives readers a direct view of this convergence. As Jesus approaches his death, he retreats with his disciples to the garden at Gethsemane. Anticipating his trials and suffering, he throws himself on the ground and prays, "My Father, if it is possible, let this cup pass from me" (26:39). Jesus seems, for a moment, alienated from his fate, wishing that he might be someone other than the messiah, other than the one who must suffer so that the scriptures might be fulfilled. His active agency and personal passion seem to run in a direction different from the messianic pattern. Yet the Gospel of Matthew immediately records a shift to internal assent, and in so doing, closes the gap between Jesus and his role. Jesus follows his petition with a qualification: "Yet not what I want but what you want." He prays again a second and third time, narrowing his petition. "My Father, if this cannot pass unless I drink it, your will be done" (26:42). The contrast with Aeneas is telling. Jesus' personal link to his role takes the form of obedient submission rather than independent action. He is not enlarged by action to fulfill his role; rather, he empties himself of will and purpose in order to be absorbed into his role. No longer drawing back from the pattern of messianic expectation, Jesus is prepared to endure all.

As Jesus makes his final prayer, his hour is at hand. As prophesied, one of his disciples betrays him. A large crowd with swords and clubs arrives. One disciple resists, seeming to offer a route of escape, a way to allow the cup to pass from Jesus' lips. However much his prayers in the garden might suggest hesitation and doubt, in this moment of arrest, Jesus emphatically affirms his fate. He upbraids his disciple. "Do you think that I cannot appeal to my Father, and he will at once send me more than twelve legions of angels?" he asks (26:53). The point of this rhetorical question is not to claim a special status or to brag of divine favor. He is not trying to put down the feeble efforts of his disciple by contrast to his vast resources and power of action. Rather, the effect of this declaration of power is to completely close the gap between Jesus and his messianic role. Tellingly, the reason Jesus gives for refusing to call for the twelve legions of angels recapitulates the central device of Matthew's literary argument. He could escape—even triumph on the spot—"but how then," asks Jesus, "would the scriptures be fulfilled?" (26:54). He does not choose to be the messiah; he has been chosen, and because he *is* the messiah, he must drink the bitter cup of suffering and death. The convergence of reasons for the culminating fulfillment of Jesus' messianic role is complete. The Father wills it; the scriptures say it must happen; Jesus insists that it must be so.

The literary genius of the Gospel of Matthew rests in the fact that readers are not forced to choose among the power of the Father, the prophetic veracity of scripture, or the identity of Jesus as the "real" force that animates the action. Quite the contrary, the patterns of fulfillment in the story of Jesus push together the divine, the messianic, and the human frames of reference. The will of the Father does not contest with the will of the Son. The prophecies of scripture do not supersede human agency and motivation. The Old Testament horizon of greatness—the Father of Abraham and his promised messiah—do not eclipse the limited scope of the life and action of the young man from Nazareth. Far from conflict, the Gospel of Matthew's relentless theme of fulfillment brings each dimension into fruitful, and finally indispensable, relation.

The messianic background is so woven into the story of Jesus that he has no textual identity outside expectation and the fulfillment of scripture.

The pressures of convergence that characterize Matthew's narrative of fulfillment encourage an intensification of the convergence of divine, messianic, and human. We are brought to anticipate fulfillment, even when none is explicit. To read otherwise requires us to read against rather than with the text. For example, the Gospel of Matthew tells that Jesus leads Peter, James, and his brother John to a high mountain where he is transfigured "and his face shone like the sun" (17:2). Here, the reader trained in patterns of fulfillment thinks of Moses, who ascended Mount Sinai, and whose face shone from his conversation with the Lord (Ex. 34:29). The thought of Moses is reinforced by the Gospel's report that Peter wishes to cover the shining face of Jesus, just as Moses veiled his face (compare Matt. 17:4 with Ex. 34:33). Nothing rests on the plausibility of this isolated link between the author of Matthew's account of the transfiguration and the Old Testament background of God's revelation on Sinai and Moses' heroic role as leader and lawgiver. Instead, the crucial point is that the driving force of the Gospel of Matthew—"that the scriptures might be fulfilled"—encourages just such a reading. The reader can never see Jesus as too closely connected to the divine glory that Israel's history records and messianic prophecies foretell. In this way, the literary argument of the Gospel of Matthew merges the man with the horizon of his greatness.

In their creedal formulations, Christians identify Jesus as the Son of God, and they do so with precision. Jesus is the incarnate Son of God, very God from very God, begotten not made, of one substance with the Father. In saying this, Christians make a clear statement about Jesus' participation in greatness. God is Almighty, the maker of heaven and earth—to use a later, medieval formulation, God is that which nothing greater can be conceived—and Jesus participates in that greatness in the fullest possible sense. He is that greatness; he is God. We can wrestle with the plausibility of such a thought. A finite man is God? A crucified first-century Palestinian Jesus is that which nothing greater can be conceived? Such questions are as ancient as they are legitimate, but they are beyond the scope of our inquiry. We only wish the reader to see that Matthew's literary argument leads to exactly the radical proposals of the Nicene Creed. The more Jesus fulfills the scriptures, the more his life enacts the will of the Father whose promises constitute the core of these scriptures, and the more Jesus participates in divine glory and triumph.

The author of the Gospel of Matthew need not construct a perfect argument, need not write a narrative of complete convergence. His guiding pattern of fulfillment triggers an ambition in his readers. Anyone who thinks, with the author of Matthew, that Jesus is the messiah, will search the scriptures for ever more detailed, ever more multilayered patterns of fulfillment. In this search, whatever gaps remain in the Gospel of Matthew will be closed, if only by the force of exegetical effort. The pressure of the literary argument—that the scriptures might be fulfilled— joins Jesus to the one who gives messianic expectation such urgency, the Lord God of hosts, maker of heaven and earth. The creedal tradition of Christianity testifies to the success of this literary argument.[4] To say that Jesus is God joins greatness to the very center of Jesus' identity. He does not participate in greatness through a choice, a passion, or an achievement; he *is* the source and font of greatness. No one who accepts the literary argument of the Gospel of Matthew can question the authority of such a man—the God-man—as he ascends to the mountaintop in the final chapter to command his disciples. The man fits the role because he writes the script.

PREPARE THE WAY OF THE LORD

Reading historical criticism of the New Testament is like eating sand: it neither offers pleasure nor provides nutrition. This is especially true of many historical-critical treatments of the Gospel of Mark. Designated a primitive Gospel, it has often been treated as a source document, providing nuggets of episode and teaching for the putatively more sophisticated authors of the Gospels of Matthew and Luke. To the extent that scholars have tired of this crossword puzzle approach, efforts have been directed toward discerning the "Markan community," and the text is treated as a sociocultural bathtub ring that must be analyzed for clues about a context now drained away. Lost is the striking unity and ambition of the gospel story itself.

The Gospel of Mark is relentless in its strategies of literary manipulation. The focus and manipulation of the author of Mark are best understood, for our purposes, as a sequel to Matthew. If one accepts, as does the author of Mark, that Jesus really does participate in the greatness of the divine plan for all things, then how ought we to dispose ourselves to this man? The more successful the author of Matthew, the more difficult and pressing this question. As our reading of the *Iliad* highlighted, a surpassing hero is the measure but cannot be measured. As such, he exceeds the ordinary reciprocity of heroic recognition. The standard currency of honor seems insufficient, and the greatness of the hero demands more. The peculiar demands that Jesus puts upon heroic recognition constitute the almost singular focus of the Gospel of Mark, and the author undertakes to illuminate the difficulty of recognizing the greatness of Jesus. His argument is radical. We should adopt the way of repentance, baptism, and faith as the proper, doxological currency with which to honor Jesus. To recognize him, we must glorify him as did his disciples.

The Gospel of Mark begins as if recognition were not a problem at all. This story, writes the author in the first line, is "the beginning of the good news of Jesus Christ, the Son of God" (1:1). For the Gospel of Mark, then, the subject of the story is straightforward and ready at hand. Jesus is the anointed one, the beloved son, as the voice from heaven says only a few lines later (1:11). What the author of Matthew sets out to show, the author of Mark assumes and simply declares. Moreover, this introduction not only identifies Jesus but instructs the reader how to respond to him. In this way, the introduction tells us how to recognize Jesus in the full sense of acknowledging him in word and deed. A messenger, John the baptizer, goes ahead of Jesus, telling the Gospel readers what to do. They should "prepare the way of the Lord" and do so by making "his paths straight" through "a baptism of repentance for the forgiveness of sins" (1:3–4). John's words are reinforced with the first words from Jesus' mouth in this Gospel account. "The time is fulfilled," the author of Mark has Jesus say, "and the kingdom of God has come near; repent, and believe in the good news" (1:15). The pattern of recognition is set out. See Jesus as he truly is, the anointed one, the Son of the Most High, and in seeing him, go before him under the sign of baptism, believing in the good news of his coming.

Everything seems clear at the outset; something very much like standard Christian practice is indicated. Recognition of Jesus involves repenting, or turning to him, receiving the mark of baptism and believing in him. Of course, notions such as "christ" and "son of God" are semantically deep, suggesting a number of different patterns of messianic expectation that run through the Old Testament and the extra-canonical literature of Judaism. Moreover, just how we should understand the task of straightening the paths of the Lord is uncertain. Historical scholars often emphasize these ambiguities, but miss the literary effect of the opening lines of the Gospel of Mark. The point is not the specific meaning of the divine titles or content of recognition. Jesus' greatness is that which has been promised Israel (however that might be understood), and his recognition requires us to consummate the covenant observance of Israel through baptism and faith (however they are understood ritually, morally, and personally). The function of these opening declarations, within the Gospel, is to stimulate consent in the mind of the reader. "Quite right, Jesus is the Son of God," thinks the sympathetic reader, "we are to repent, accept the mark of citizenship in his kingdom, and believe in his lordship." The story as whole, however, does not rest satisfied in this consent. Rather, the direct and open proclamation of the first verses is followed by an account of the indirect and ambiguous world of Jesus' teaching and action. The larger narrative is shaped by the contrast between the opening declarations of Jesus' identity and the subsequent shadowy skein of parable and episode. The effect is to call into question the sincerity and depth of the reader's initial, uncomplicated consent to Jesus' greatness.

This contrast between the opening clarity and the ensuing opacity signals a general pattern of blindness and vision, veiling and unveiling, that dominates the Gospel, both in textual detail and overall effect. Jesus heals both in secrecy and openly; he commands a silence that, paradoxically, heightens rather than diminishes publicity. He reveals the secrets of his teachings to his disciples, yet they remain in the dark. His glory is exposed on the Mount of Transfiguration, but it is misperceived by Peter. His glory is veiled in humiliation on the cross, yet he is rightly recognized in the clarity of his identity, by the centurion. In these, and many other ways, the secrecy theme is part of the larger textual dynamic of the Gospel of Mark that both conceals and reveals. The moments when we think we see greatness—a man who has the power to heal, cleanse, and even raise the dead to life—the text presents as moments of blindness. Moments when we cannot see greatness—the dead man on the cross—the text presents as the ultimate moment of clear vision. What begins as so lucid and obvious ("Oh, of course, the sacred account of the Son of God in whom we believe") becomes a dark forest in which we are easily lost.

The author of Mark builds blindness into the characters in his story. The crowd, the learned men of Israel, the neutral Roman judge, even the disciples, fail to recognize Jesus. They see him as a power to be reckoned with, but they do not follow the clear pattern of recognition outlined at the outset of the Gospel—repentance, baptism, and belief. Like a man who claims to see a fire in the next room but has settled down to read the evening paper, what the characters in the Gospel of Mark say and do suggest a seeing that is blind, a recognition that is so inappropriate to the man encountered that we are led to doubt that they can see at all. The reader, however, does not enjoy omniscience. Like the pull of scriptural fulfillment in the Gospel of Matthew, this Gospel draws the reader into an intra-textual dynamic. However, the text works on us in a very different way. Instead of enticing us to see ever-greater layers of messianic fulfillment, the Gospel of Mark plays tricks on the reader. The literary force of this story of mis-recognition absorbs the reader into the blindness—and the strange insights of the blind—that dominate this narrative.[5]

At every turn, the author of Mark reinforces the play of blindness and insight. In the opening chapters, Jesus encounters demons who possess unfortunate souls. These demons have a clarity of vision. They see Jesus in his greatness, giving him obeisance by speaking his name of honor, "Son of God," and they flee from his superior power. But this recognition is only partial. The demons know Jesus and no longer impede his work, but they do not go before him to prepare his way. The demons are incapable of rendering to Jesus that which is proper to his greatness: repentance, baptism, and belief. The demons clearly fail to offer this recognition. They see the fire but rush into the flames. However, here as elsewhere the failure of recognition is not empty. The genius of the Gospel of Mark is to bring readers to see within the blindness narrated in the text. The blind seeing of the demons brings the reader to see that awe at the power of Jesus, even knowledge of his true identity, does not signal proper recognition.[6]

Whereas the demons see but do not believe, the crowds that follow Jesus around the Galilean countryside evidence a nearly complete blindness. These crowds are made up of people who see a miracle worker and seer, a man who can heal, cast out demons, cleanse defilement, and teach with authority. He has the power to make things happen. He can speak in such a way as to make men drop their nets; he can cause demons to flee, and weight his words with the authority of scripture itself. This power attracts crowds. After recounting just a few episodes of powerful speech and action, the author of Mark portrays harried disciples hunting for Jesus, finding him, and breathlessly telling him, almost in the spirit of urgent warning, "Everyone is searching for you" (1:37). Jesus is a man who has an immediate, public, and attractive effect. However hidden might be his true identity, he does not pass through Galilee unnoticed.

To search for Jesus is not to follow him, at least not in the manner declared at the outset of the Gospel. The crowds flock to Jesus, but far from offering him their services as ones who would go out before him to make his way straight, they impede his work. Only ingenious methods overcome the suffocating mob, as the author describes a scene in which a paralytic is lowered through the roof of a house to receive Jesus' blessing (2:1–5). Indeed, Jesus must make plans to avoid being overwhelmed by the crowds, perhaps killed by the sheer weight of their pressing humanity. Preparing to preach by the Sea of Galilee, "he told his disciples to have a boat ready for him because of the crowd, so that they would not crush him" (3:9). By the time he teaches a second time by the seaside, this contingency becomes a necessity. The narrative effect is subtle, but direct. By following Jesus in this way, the crowds drive him away just as they seek to draw near. With Jesus removed to a boat, the crowd has created a distance by their lust for nearness.

The crowds foreshadow subsequent, more direct accounts of the difficulty of recognizing Jesus. The Gospel presents him as a man with the power to give us what we want: deliverance from suffering and sickness, shame and defilement. The crowds come precisely because they see this power. But their seeing is utterly blind. Proximity is not the same as "believing in." Pursuit of his benefits is not the same as advancing to prepare others to receive his gifts. Tellingly, at the apex of his public popularity, Jesus is in a boat at sea, ready to sail away from the crowds. Moreover, in this scene Mark does not have Jesus outlining a new law for his kingdom. Instead, Jesus teaches the gathered multitudes the parable of the sower, a parable that seems as obvious as his power in word and deed, but which, he tells his disciples, is designed to deceive those who hear. Not only has Jesus retreated to a boat, but he has distanced himself from the crowd with words that he states cannot be understood.

Jesus sails away from this odd scene of anti-teaching, of speaking that deliberately obscures. Although he will, for a brief moment, return to teach and feed (see 6:30–44), thereafter the crowds in this Gospel story appear more and more clearly as a threatening mob. In the final scene, the crowd will shout "Crucify him!" (15:14). This final role, so striking in its antithesis to the pattern of recognition articulated at the outset of the Gospel, does not represent a shift in the character of the crowd. They always see Jesus, but blindly. Just so, when Pilate presents Jesus and a robber, the crowd in Jerusalem chooses Barabbas. His name means "son of the father," so in a perverse play on the true identity of Jesus, the author of Mark portrays blindness in Jerusalem. Earlier in the story, the crowds chased after him as supplicants rather than advancing before him as servants. Now, at the end, the crowd gives life to one condemned to death for his sins, and in so doing condemns to death one who is innocent, but who will give life to others.

Patterns of reversal in which blindness has encoded within it a reversal of insight feature prominently in the account of Jesus' transfiguration.

Immediately after the healing of a blind man,[7] Jesus goes to Caesarea Philippi, and he asks his disciples what they "see" in him. After evading the question by reporting what others see, Peter ventures an answer: "You are the Christ." Peter seems to see clearly. Yet, hot on the heels of Peter's answer, Jesus teaches the way of the Son of Man. Peter will have nothing of this. He rebukes Jesus, and Jesus immediately rebukes Peter in return. "Get behind me, Satan!" exclaims Jesus (8:33). Peter sees as do the demons. He sees Jesus' power, but not the narrowness of his way. Peter, then, sees but does not see.

Just as Peter can see that Jesus *is* the Christ but cannot see the way of Jesus *as* the Christ, he also sees but fails to recognize the transfigured Lord in the full sense of rendering to Jesus that which is due him. When Jesus takes Peter and James and John up a high mountain, they see Jesus transfigured. They do, indeed, see, but the disciples do not see clearly. They do not know what to say. Peter in particular fails to see the purpose and fate of the power of transfiguration. He thinks that the glory of the transfigured Jesus calls for a booth or sanctuary on the mountaintop. By proposing that he build a booth or tent, Peter echoes the Exodus commandments to build a tabernacle for the divine presence. He thinks that the power of Jesus, a power he thinks he sees clearly, requires a veil. It must be hidden. But within the larger narrative, Peter fails to see. The Christ does not have an awesome and overwhelming power that must be hidden. He has a hidden power that must be revealed, and in order to do so, he must descend from the mountain and enter the city of Jerusalem. And in Jerusalem, he will die naked on a cross rather than dwell clothed in the veils and curtains of the Temple sanctuary. To recognize him entails following him to the cross as a disciple.

Peter's blindness is paradigmatic. He sees, but does not recognize, and in his failure, the reader sees more clearly, both who Jesus is, and the way in which he calls for the recognition already announced by John the Baptist. This literary strategy of depicting a revealing blindness is central to the literary ambition of Mark. Everything is false and dark, but somehow the very pattern of the error casts light, anticipates the truth, and drives the reader toward discipleship. The words of Jesus in explanation of the parable of the sower announce just this effect. "There is nothing hidden" says Jesus, "except to be disclosed; nor is anything secret, except to come to light" (4:22). The blindness found in this story serves a purpose. It discloses even in its hiding. Jesus concludes his strange teaching on hiddenness and disclosure with an imperative that turns out toward the reader. Since hiddenness reveals, Jesus admonishes his disciples to "pay attention to what you hear!" (4:24). Even stories of blindness bring insight, and the reader must beware of ignoring the opaque and obscure as he or she searches the Gospel story for moments of clarity. There is nothing hidden in this story, except to disclose and bring to light.

We must not be naive at this point. In these words of Jesus, the author of Mark offers the hermeneutic key to his Gospel of secrecy and hiddenness, and the upshot is an intensely ambitious literary claim on our attention. Like the Gospel of Matthew, no textual detail or narrative episode is innocent. The reader has been warned. If a parable or episode seems clear, then the sustained pattern of false perception and shallow clarity that dominates the Gospel of Mark makes the reader hesitate. "Have I really seen the point of this passage," we must ask ourselves, "or am I seeing as do the demons, as does the crowd, with a superficial and false clarity?" The same holds true for the passages that seem obscure, ill conceived, and mute. Nothing, warns the voice of Jesus in this Gospel, is hidden except to be revealed. As such, no aspect of the text may be set aside as peripheral, uninteresting, or irrelevant. Just as we should beware of complacent clarity, so also should we not trust our own blindness. By questioning our presumptive understanding and our misunderstanding, then, the author of Mark absorbs the reader into his story. Nothing is simple. Everything must be read and reread and reread, for every seeing conceals a blindness, and every blindness a seeing. If we see how the text functions, then we can never look away. The more deeply we grasp the literary strategy of blindness and insight, the more we find ourselves paying attention, again and again, to what is said, the more we find ourselves paying attention to the hero of the story: Jesus.

Paying Attention to One Episode

The story of the fate of John the baptizer (Mark 6:14–29) is an extraordinarily concentrated instance of narrated blindness that prepares the attentive reader for sight. The account of John's death is a developed flashback that breaks the forward action of the Gospel. At first glance, this passage seems like the Gospel writer's attempt to tie up some loose ends. Since John the Baptist is so prominent at the outset of the Gospel, surely we need to know what became of him. Moreover, in 3:6 we have already learned that the "Herodians" have joined the Pharisees to plan to destroy Jesus, and so at this juncture of the narrative, the author might well be giving macabre seriousness to that doom which, at this point, hangs mostly in the background.[8] Or, perhaps the immediate purpose of the narrative of John's death is to explain Herod's anxiety about Jesus' identity. Herod fears that Jesus is the beheaded John raised from the dead. So we might readily explain this narrative digression as the author's attempt to report on the fate of one of his key characters and to reinforce the theme of Jesus' hidden identity.

However apt these suggestions might be, this digression is much more than a tying up of loose ends or a reinforcement of general themes. As readers, we need to remember that the Gospel of Mark ends without resurrection appearances (here we accept both the ancient and modern consensus that Mark ends at 16:8). In view of this ending, it is significant that, other than Jesus and the messenger in the empty tomb, only Herod mentions the possibility of resurrection in this Gospel story. No other characters, disciples or otherwise, can see this triumphant possibility in Jesus. Such an anomaly should warn us that this artful digression concerns matters basic to the "good news" that the author of Mark sets out to tell. The warning should be heeded, for as we turn to the peculiar details of Herod's worries and John's death, we can see that this digression is a crucial foreshadowing of Mark's deepest concerns. All things are hidden in order to be revealed.

The account of John the Baptist's death affirms Herod's worries but reverses his (and perhaps our own) assumptions about the greatness of one who possesses great power. The elements of John's demise are narrated in compact form: arrest, binding, venial conspiring in the court for John's death, an unwitting agent of destruction, an unwilling authority who gives in to the demand for death, a gruesome death, burial. Given the basic pattern of John's death, we can see Herodias as the high priest. Like Caiaphas with respect to Jesus, she is utterly determined to seal the fate of John. Herodias's daughter parallels the unwitting crowd in Jerusalem. She is easily manipulated by Herodias to do that which Herodias knows Herod cannot refuse. Further, like the crowd in Jerusalem that surprised Pilate by choosing the thief Barabbas, the girl asks not for the trinkets or adornments of youth, as Herod might have expected, but for the head of John the Baptist. Herod anticipates Pilate. He does not want to condemn John to his death, but is unable to resist the pressure of events. John's death takes place amidst the festal celebration of Herod's birthday and he magnanimously offers his daughter her pleasure, just as Pilate offers the crowd their pleasure with the prisoners before them. Both Herod and Pilate are trapped by their promises. Both are troubled by the consequences, but they execute nonetheless.

We seem, then, to be reading a foreshadowing of Jesus' passion in

John's own arrest and execution.[9] In this sense, Herod *is* right about Jesus' identity and power, even as he mistakenly identifies Jesus as John returned to life. However, Jesus is not the risen John now teaching. Jesus, whom Herod worries might be John, is not a man who, killed, can exercise the power of self-resurrection so as to return to life and resume his active ministry. Instead, the suffering and now dead John foreshadows the fate of the man Jesus. John's pattern of death, not his power over death, is the key link between him and Jesus. Herod sees the link, but the true nature of the relationship is hidden, and he is blind, both to the significance of John and the true power of Jesus.

How are we to read the significance of this foreshadowing and Herod's odd combination of sight and blindness? Is Mark simply preparing the readerly soil, so to speak? Is Mark just giving us a dress rehearsal of the passion drama? Or does this peculiar digression yield clues about the Gospel's use of blindness as a whole and its preoccupation with seeing rightly? We have been warned that all things are hidden in order to be revealed, so we should assume that this digression is fully loaded with textual significance. Consider Herod's preoccupation with power. Herod, unlike the disciples, is deeply concerned about the possibility of resurrection, the power of life over death. Herod is willing to entertain the possibility of such power, and in his anxiety about Jesus, he senses that such power must be recognized. This stands in striking contrast to the terrified response of Jesus' followers at the end of Mark's Gospel, for whom death seems final. Yet Herod's assumptions about resurrection, like his assumptions about Jesus' identity as the risen John, are mistaken. Herod reverses the actual form of Jesus' greatness, as well as the proper form of recognition outlined in the introductory verses of the Gospel. Herod worries that Jesus has power over death, and he is anxious to accommodate himself to that power. This is a reasonable conjecture, since one who can save himself surely has power over others. A deathless man fears no other, and with such power he can attract the loyalty of all in the hope that they might share in such power. Perhaps, then, Herod is anxious and wishes to know exactly who Jesus is so that he can petition Jesus to share his power with him. Yet Herod is wrong: about John, about Jesus, and about the power he has. As the reader knows, Jesus is not the risen John. John prefigures the crucified Jesus. Jesus does not manifest John's power; rather, John goes before Jesus and anticipates, in the pattern of his death, the power of Jesus.

Herod's mistaken reversal of the relationship between John and Jesus signals many layers of mistaken reading of the gospel story as a whole.

The author of Mark warns us against being wrongly impressed by Jesus' own miraculous power over sickness and death in the healing and reviving stories. We are not to be like the crowds who chase Jesus around the countryside, seeking to be close to a great power of wisdom and life. We are not to imagine that Jesus is an oracle, a magician, or a divinity who is deathless. Herod, like so many readers of the Gospel, confuses the signs of Jesus' greatness with its true source and essence, thinking Jesus a great power to be sought and measured. His mistake, embedded in an account of John's death, which prefigures Jesus' death, is telling, and it guides the reader. We should see that Jesus' power is in and not over death, and that we should recognize him by going before him in discipleship rather than following after him in order to get a piece of his power.

This reading of Jesus' passion into the death of John the Baptist exemplifies the literary force of this Gospel. Things are veiled so that they might be unveiled, and the text is forever enticing its readers into a pattern of seeing and not seeing. This occurs across the text. At the conclusion of this story of Jesus, he dies amid much mockery. This culminates in the strongest possible argument against Jesus' claim to be the Christ, and that recapitulates Herod's assumptions about power and greatness. "He saved others; he cannot save himself. Let the Christ, the King of Israel, come down now from the cross, that we may see and believe." "Save yourself! Come down and show your power!" (15:30–32). This mockery articulates entirely sensible objections to any claim on behalf of Jesus' heroism. What possible messianic hope might there be in the poor man, suffering a humiliating fate, mocked even by common thieves who die with him? But can the reader see Jesus differently? What heroic achievement *are* we to see in the dying man?

Our claim is that the strange parallel between John's death and Jesus' death is part of the author's overall literary strategy: to prepare the reader to see the Jerusalem scene with new vision. The crowd in Jerusalem has the same inverted vision that characterized Herod's speculations about the power of Jesus as John. A man who can save himself from death surely has a power to be feared, respected, even propitiated. However, seeing power in this way is *the* central blindness of Mark's Gospel. For a power of self-salvation is not the power of Jesus. His power is in dying to save others. The author of Mark shows the way toward seeing just this. To see Jesus requires us to see his greatness *in,* and *not in spite of,* his suffering and death. Only in the hiddenness of such greatness is it revealed. To the extent that we can see Jesus in just this way, then and only then, argues the Gospel as a whole, are we able to escape the false recognition of

Herod, the crowds in Galilee, and even the demons—a false recognition all too easily assimilated to a faith that seeks supernatural power and gnostic wisdom.

WATCH!

The clarity of Mark never extends beyond the formal outlines of faithful recognition stated by John the baptizer at the outset: repent, be baptized, and believe. The text is constructed to bring the reader to exactly this turn toward Jesus. Pay attention to what you hear. Keep looking at what you see. Not only does the author of Mark achieve this effect through episodes such as the death of John, but he also uses more direct methods. The end of the so-called little apocalypse of Mark (chapter 13) dramatically reinforces the relentless drive toward the centurion's sight. When asked for signs of the things that are to happen, Jesus begins with a long list of specific warnings, all of which are just as urgent as the rest of Mark's Gospel. These signs and warnings begin with false signs. "Many will come in my name and say, 'I am he!' and they will lead many astray" (13:6). These signs build from war, to a brother's betrayal of a brother, to scenes of desolation in which those caught unawares will wish they had never been born, to the very darkening of the sun. But the author of Mark knows that, for the reader, such signs are useless. The wisdom of the parables, the moral directives of the teaching, even knowledge of the end of times: these matters leave us still vulnerable, still blind. Indeed, Jesus warns of the futility of knowledge. Not even the angels who presumably enjoy a great deal of spiritual vision, or the Son, who is the very teacher of the parables we have heard, know the future. They are blind as well. Only the Father has the eyes to see.

Thus, the warnings end with a final exhortation. "Take heed, *watch*; for you do not know when the time will come. It is like a man going on a journey, when he leaves home and puts his servants in charge, each with his work, and commands the doorkeeper to be on the *watch*. *Watch* therefore—for you do not know when the master of the house will come, in the evening, or at midnight, or at cockcrow, or in the morning—lest he come suddenly and find you asleep. And what I say to you I say to all: *Watch*" (13:33–37, RSV). The effect on the reader is powerful; one must open one's eyes and pay attention. One should not imagine that one has grasped the kernel of truth, the essence of the idea, the primary datum that allows one to look up and then elsewhere. Once again, the author of Mark has constructed the scene in order to reach out and grab the reader.

The future is hidden, but all things are hidden only in order to be disclosed, so the agenda is set: Watch!

But pay attention to what? The exhortation looks forward in the narrative rather than backward across the various specific signs Jesus has recounted. The exhortation to watch follows a sequence. We do not know when the master will come: in the evening, at midnight, at cockcrow, or in the morning. These divisions map directly onto the action ahead. Jesus will sit with the disciples for supper in the evening. At midnight, the eyes of the disciples will flutter shut while Jesus prays in the garden at Gethsemane, awakened only by a crowd with swords and clubs. At cockcrow, Jesus will confess his identity before the high priest while Peter denies him in the courtyard below. In the morning, Christ will be delivered over to Pilate. And what of the final act in the passion drama, the "third hour" of the day when Jesus is crucified? In the third hour, the Temple is destroyed and the Holy One is uncovered in His nakedness. Just as the story of John's death and the episode of transfiguration prepare the reader to see Jesus' power disclosed in death, so also does the formal structure of the conclusion of the apocalyptic warnings anticipate the temporal sequence of Jesus' death.[10]

After the exhortation to watch, the text shifts from obscurity to clarity. The Markan Gospel of disjunctive and often enigmatic action is transformed into a tight drama of extended and continuous action. Mark's narrative sheds whatever secrecy and opacity it cultivated in the previous thirteen chapters. From now until the end of the Gospel, the narrative is highly realistic. The author's rhetorical strategy seems clear: now the "facts" will be so radiantly clear that even our faulty vision will not deceive us. The clutter of parable and miracle gives way to a form of exposition that is so direct and simple we cannot help but see. And this seeing culminates in a reiteration of the divine title that opens the Gospel. The centurion, a character who does not judge, deny, deceive, or mock, watches Jesus die, and in this watching, he says, "Truly, this man was God's Son" (15:39). The centurion is obeying the signal commandment of the Gospel of Mark. He is watching. In so doing, the centurion embodies the formal pattern of recognition. As Jesus dies, the centurion turns toward him rather than away. In pronouncing him the Son of God, he goes before the crucified man to prepare his way. The centurion recognizes Jesus with words that both identify and glorify him.

The New Testament is a wellspring of radical solutions. Like the member that sins and must be cut off, barriers to ascribing all greatness to

Jesus are rooted out by the Gospel writers. The contrast with Vergil is telling. The problem of Aeneas's participation in his destiny as the founder of Rome is central to the *Aeneid.* Vergil shows Aeneas's human inadequacy, he describes a purification or erasure of Aeneas's backward-looking *pietas,* and then he concludes the epic by telling the story of Aeneas's *labor et virtus,* culminating in the sword thrust into the breast of Turnus. Yet, so seriously does Vergil take the gap between the founding act and the great city of Rome that the *Aeneid*'s conclusion is not unequivocal. In the clearest moment of our discernment of Aeneas's participation in his destiny, he does so by the thinnest threads of inscrutable passion, a flash of anger and thrust of the sword. Many readers have remained unconvinced, and for them, Aeneas remains a pawn of fate rather than the agent of his destiny. The Gospel of Matthew treats Jesus' participation in his messianic role as a truth to be repeated rather than a possibility to be artfully suggested. The Gospel begins with scene after scene of fulfilled prophecy, and even the briefest moment of doubt in Jesus' prayers in the garden of Gethsemane seems suggested only to be answered with the compounded force of necessity. Jesus is his role, and must be so by the Father's will, the words of scripture, and Jesus' own choices. In this sense, the author of Matthew never entertains participation as a "problem"; he never opens a gap between man and deed, between character and greatness, between passion and necessity, for more than a moment. Jesus is the messiah, and the literary argument does not seek a thin thread to link Jesus to his greatness. Instead, the text winds coil after coil of heavy cable around Jesus and Israel's expectations. The upshot is remarkable. In a way alien to Vergil's assumptions about the distance between the greatest of all things—Rome—and any particular man, even one ordained by Jupiter as Rome's founder, the Gospel of Matthew presses toward convergence. Participation is intensified to the point of simple equation. Jesus simply is that which is greatest.

As Christianity follows the Matthean argument to its end, the currency of recognition must change. Jesus is not a hero; he does not embody or manifest greatness, power, or virtue. He is the messiah, a role so intimate to the glory of God that subsequent Christian generations will describe this messiah as God incarnate. This radical participation in greatness ups the ante of recognition, shifting the focus away from honor and admiration, and toward worship and obedience.[11] Unlike Achilles, then, Jesus does not exceed the standard economy of heroic recognition. He is not a surpassingly superior man, a profound teacher, or a powerful miracle worker. The New Testament presents Jesus as transcending human weights and measures. Yet in so doing, he does not recede from view; he does not retreat to the veiled realm of his tents, as does Achilles. The hidden is disclosed. Jesus' culminating scene in the Gospel of Mark is not private; it is public, and rather than tragically unrecognized, veiled in the excess of surpassing greatness, the pronouncement of the centurion testifies to the simplicity of a recognition paid in the currency of faith. Jesus discloses divine glory, and far from speechless, the centurion finds words that the Gospel readers already have on their lips as those who have repented, been baptized and believe—the crucified Jesus is the Son of God. As a consequence, Christianity may be perverse, irrational, and wrong-headed, but in its account of Jesus, his participation in greatness, and our recognition of his greatness, of one thing we can be certain: it is not tragic.

Transparency and Imitation: Paul and Early Christianity

"Thou seemest human and divine.
The highest, holiest manhood, thou:
Our wills are ours, we know not how,
Our will are ours, to make them thine."
                    Alfred, Lord Tennyson,
                        In Memoriam A.H.H.

"**B**ehold, the Lamb of God who takes away the sins of the world!"
(John 1:29, RSV). With these words, John the Baptist proclaims
the cosmic and definitive scope of Jesus' action. The writer of the Letter
to the Hebrews expands on the Baptist's point, emphasizing the singularity and finality of Jesus' role. "Every priest stands daily ministering and
offering time after time the same sacrifices, which can never take away
sins." The economy of ritual sacrifice is unending and lacks decisive consequence. "But he," continues the writer, "having offered one sacrifice for
sins for all time, sat down at the right hand of God, waiting from that time
onward until his enemies be made a footstool for his feet. For by one
offering he has perfected for all time those who are sanctified" (10:11–14).
In his death, Jesus completes the drama of salvation. The crucified messiah is a "fragrant offering and sacrifice to God" (Eph. 5:1), and this sacrifice is sufficient. On the cross, Jesus' greatness is complete and
triumphant. Thus, the Christian disciple must value Jesus' actions as all-
encompassing; they need never be repeated; they can never be surpassed.

The more the New Testament succeeds in persuading its readers that
Jesus is this kind of hero, the Son of God who dies that others might live,
the less room appears to be left for our greatness, our achievement and

accomplishment. Since he is the founder of the kingdom of God and perfect sacrificial victim, what is left for us to do? The pinnacle of God's dealings with humanity, Jesus accomplishes all, leaving no residual space to fill, no mopping up exercises, no peripheral sacrifices to perform. Jesus commands from the mountaintop, and the disciples need only hear and obey. Recognition of Jesus' greatness and achievement does not involve offering him the admiration, awe, and respect that we give those greater than ourselves. The Gospel stories explicitly repudiate forms of recognition that exalt Jesus as the wisest of men, deserving our respect and attention as philosophical seekers, just as those stories reject the attempts to fit Jesus in a human hierarchy of power. For the Gospel of Mark, the centurion points to the only pattern of recognition appropriate for Jesus: we must proclaim him the Son of God, and thus offer him the recognition of worship and obedience that befits the God of Israel.

In this sense, Jesus is like Socrates. Both are absorptive in their singularity. Socrates' absorptive power rests in his irony. He attracts disciples because of his wisdom, but he has no teachings on particular subjects, no expertise to communicate. As a consequence, his disciples have no basis on which to rival him. They cannot possess him; they cannot hold him closely enough to measure him, and themselves against him. Alcibiades tells of his night with Socrates. He had hopes of seducing the older man, and in so doing, fixing Socrates in an identifiable social role of attraction and reciprocity. Yet Socrates is insensitive to the beauty of the young Alcibiades, and he remains remote, receding from his grasp rather than drawing closer. Alcibiades must reach toward him in the vain effort to capture his beauty, to draw near to the golden soul within the Silen figure. But with a wink and a smile, Socrates always recedes, and in receding, invites redoubled imitative effort. We never find Socrates advancing toward us, and as a consequence, we can never engage him in rivalry. Are we better mathematicians? Are we less superstitious? Are we more pious? Do we have a greater independence from civic institutions? Do we have as great a love for civic institutions? Do we know, even more deeply and profoundly, that we do not know—or are we just posturing in a cheap skepticism or convenient relativism? Irony is the wedge we drive between ourselves and the grasping claims of everyday life; Socratic irony is the wedge Socrates drives between himself and the heroic desires of his followers.

Jesus' absorptive power is very different, but no less effective. Jesus does not recede in ironic self-distancing. Instead, Jesus absorbs by advancing and filling the frame of reference with his greatness. Unlike

Vergil, who sought only to link Aeneas to the eternal greatness of Rome with individualized labor and personal passion, the Gospels drive Jesus together with divinity with compressive force. The messianic pattern is so fully inhabited by Jesus in the Gospel of Matthew that he comes to define that pattern. He is depicted as so apt to the horizon of divine glory that he is identified as God. The saving arm of God that had brought out the Israelites from Egypt is manifested with full and final potency in the saving death of Jesus. This literary push toward convergence of person with the very idea of greatness sets the terms for recognition. As the Gospel of Mark works so hard to bring the readers to see, one comes to Jesus either in worship or rejection.

Where Socrates resists rivalry with an ironic wink, Jesus' enlarged achievement makes him so far from us that we can not measure him, or ourselves against him. Jesus is the messiah, the New Testament insists, and we are not. He does something for us that we can not do for ourselves. He is the Son of God, the alpha and omega, who encompasses our very existence. As a result, within the Christian frame of reference, any thought of rivaling Jesus' messianic achievement is simple insanity. His greatness is beyond the reach of our character and agency. Yet, impossibly distant, Jesus is also intimate, for unlike Socrates, he does not recede from view; he does not wink with irony. As Paul preached in Athens, the greatness of God is not beyond us, but is, rather, close to each one of us. Just so, for the author of the Gospel of Mark, the centurion is not speechless; he is not confused and uncertain. He sees and proclaims. In this sense, Jesus' messianic enactment is ready at hand, unveiled and public, open and accessible. So close at hand, Jesus absorbs. No part of the life of the Christian may be held in reserve as a potential basis for mounting an independent claim to greatness. Every knee shall bow to Christ Jesus, says Paul in the Letter to the Philippians (2:10), and this omnipotent triumph includes all that we, as individuals, have and possess. Recognition offered in worship is total and all-encompassing. However unrivaled and divine is Jesus' heroism, we do not follow at a distance. His heroism makes an ever greater claim on our own desire for heroic achievement.

Our modern ideals of personal achievement may rebel against this absorption of all things into the glory of God in Christ. We may value self-possession, fierce independence, having one's own voice. We may insist that absorptive worship is a self-denying destruction of any distinctively human achievement, a form of self-evacuation. This is not just a modern problem. On the face of it, the Christian ideal of discipleship seems like a renunciation of heroism. Even Vergil, knowing that the greatness of Rome could never be simply equated with the character of any man, sought to find the pattern of action and affect that, uniquely part of one man's life, made him fit to found the great city. He did not want Aeneas to be nothing more than a personal version of his shield, which depicts the great triumphs, a mere emblem or symbol of Roman greatness, a poetic vessel into which he might pour the essentially communal achievement of Rome. Christian literature has no such worries. Jesus issues direct commands. He calls his disciples with the simple words, "Come and follow me." They put down their nets and follow him, and the Gospel writers offer no clues to why the disciples obeyed. Jesus called, and into those who follow, he pours his own purposes and power. To the extent that the New Testament as a whole echoes this pattern of following, Jesus' power supersedes and replaces all other human projects for achieving greatness and glory. As later Christian theology so forthrightly announces, the followers of Christ are not to seek their own labor and passion in order to forge a link to Jesus and his kingdom; disciples are to become icons of their master.

Where we might see a problem in Jesus' absorption of all heroic endeavor, the writers of ancient Christian literature saw none. For the followers of Jesus, the singularity of Jesus' messianic achievement empowered; his greatness gave life and power to his followers, and did so precisely as an absorptive power. Believers repented, were baptized, and believed. The New Testament does not indicate that this discipleship is a distant and passive obedience. Instead the New Testament presents this form of recognition as leading to our immediate and active participation in the greatness of Christ. The Acts of the Apostles is archetypical. The day of Pentecost brings power to the disciples. They have the ability to speak other languages (2:4), and they possess the power to heal (3:7). In both cases, however, the narrative is clear that this power comes from Jesus and must serve to glorify him. The power of tongues spreads the message of Jesus' saving death; the disciples speak his message, not their own. Questioned by the authorities, Peter explicitly denies that he healed the lame man with his own power. He is but a vessel for the power of Christ. Thus, however active and effective, for the faithful, all power comes from Christ, and any achievement is his alone. The disciples, then, are instruments of his will, mouthpieces for his word, vehicles for achieving his purposes. They participate in a drama of Jesus' triumph, but not as independent actors. They have been taken captive to Christ, bound to him as strongly as he is bound to his own messianic role. They repent, are baptized, and believe, and in so doing, they receive the power of the Spirit and become incandescent with the greatness of Jesus.

The opening chapters of the Acts of the Apostles offer an idealized story of Christian triumph, a romance of the early church. For just this reason, the logic of the Christian view of heroic discipleship is especially clear; it is a heroism of transparency. As they offer themselves to Jesus in baptism and faith, the disciples make themselves transparent to his power. This turn to Jesus is evacuative and, in this sense, seems the end of any possibility for human greatness. Yet, as we shall see again and again in this chapter, the distinctive Christian claim is that the empty soul offered to Jesus is filled with a power and glory greater than any human possibility. The self, evacuated of heroic ambition by repentance, is filled, in baptism, with the greatness of Jesus himself. In that sense, even as Christianity utterly renounces any rivalry to Jesus—indeed, rivalry becomes idolatry—the ideal of discipleship, at its most ambitious, allows for a recapitulation of Jesus, a mimesis of divinity in the life of the believer. The life of the believer, devoid of independent purpose and achievement, participates in divine greatness. Precisely as transparent, then, loss becomes gain. Renunciation of the heroic ambition that characterizes the Homeric, Platonic, and Vergilian quests for greatness creates a new, obedient Christian heroism.

Our goal in this chapter is to understand the logic of this heroism by analyzing the ways in which early Christian literature depicts the participation of the believer in Christ. How is the empty vessel of faith filled with the glory of God? In this literature, everything rises and falls on faith in Jesus as the Son of God; it is the first principle of transparency. This literature is not insensitive, however, to the need to persuade believers that they can participate in Christ, and through him, in the power and glory of God. And the goal of this persuasion is not to reassure readers concerned to preserve this or that area of life for a specifically human achievement, unabsorbed into Christ. The heroism of transparency is not a heroism of leftovers, not a matter of tasks and projects that, somehow, remain outside of Jesus like crumbs under the table. Instead, in the literature we will consider, heroic discipleship is as ambitious as it is self-effacing. Transparency to Christ must be complete, and because complete, entirely filled with the power and potency of Jesus' heroism.

We will proceed by snapshot rather than close study or panorama, considering four literary presentations of the Christian ideal of discipleship, each of which is keyed to the theme of imitative transparency to Jesus. The first and most difficult is Paul's correspondence with the Corinthians. As letters of exhortation, explanation, and reprimand, these literary artifacts are complex in rhetoric and substance. Our goal, however, is rather simple. We wish to discern the pattern of life Paul advocates, the way of life that Paul thinks the Corinthians should strive toward in order to grow from children in the faith into adults who dwell more fully in the truth and power of Jesus. In short, we want to discern the outlines of Paul's ideal of Christian excellence, his vision of heroic discipleship.

The other three texts are more straightforward. Ignatius's letter to the Romans and the anonymous *Martyrdom of Polycarp* offer clear instances of early Christian patterns of imitative desire (Ignatius) and enactment (Polycarp). Transparency takes on the set pattern of mimicking Jesus' passion, and both texts emphatically reaffirm the central assumption that animates the opening chapters of the Acts of the Apostles: transparency to Christ makes the believer incandescent as the disciple participates in the greatness of Jesus. The final text is Athanasius's *Life of Anthony*. This account of saintly achievement represents a crucial modification of the heroism of transparency we find in the Acts of the Apostles. A human pattern of ascetic discipline mediates between Christ and the believer. Absent the condition for explicit recapitulation of Jesus in the details of his saving death, Athanasius attempts to articulate a pattern of sanctity that connects the believer to Jesus. The Pauline ideal of transparency, then, takes on a structured form that can be the object of a faithful quest that culminates in the achievement of a Christ-like form of holiness.

"Not I, But Christ in Me"—
The Ambition of Transparency

The total change of conversion, from old to new, as Paul preached, was something that the Corinthians found difficult to accept. Christianity brought with it a new life in its turning from sin and its obedience to Christ, and this basic reorientation seemed to pose no problem. However, the totality of the disjunction between old man and new apparently did pose a problem. The Corinthians, naturally enough, were interested in the connective joints between their human gifts and capacities, their very selves, and their participation in their destiny as children of God in Christ. The joints that they cherished we can reconstruct from Paul's letters: they valued, along with faith, their wisdom, power, and nobility, among other things. Paul addresses these very properties in order to dismiss them as contributions to participation in Christ in any way: "Consider your own call, brothers and sisters: not many of you were wise by human standards, not many powerful, not many were of noble birth. . . . [God] is the source of your life in Christ Jesus, who became for us wisdom from God, and righteousness and sanctification and redemption" (1 Cor. 1:26, 30). Jesus has become all things for those who believe in him, and the only contributions the Corinthians could make are repentance, baptism, and belief. To these believers, Jesus then becomes their properties: their wisdom, their power, their nobility. Thus, the goal of the believer, Paul maintains, is to live lives transparent to this wisdom, power, and nobility, lives transparent to the Christ who transforms them and makes them new.

This is the essence of Paul's letters to the Corinthians. And we can easily concur that in superficial and communal ways, the newness that Paul promotes is liberating and an improvement. From his letters we can identify harmful differences, both social and practical, which divided the Corinthians, and which Paul attempts to sweep away. The Corinthians were apt to view each other still "according to the flesh," in terms of social standing and birth; they were divided in their ritual observances, in terms of marriage and the eating of meat sacrificed to idols; they chose to resolve certain differences with each other legally, in court before a judge; and they apparently practiced the sacrament of communion in cliques and factions, leaving poorer believers uninvolved while others overindulged. The patterns of prerogative and privilege that structure our recognition of human status and achievement seem to have held sway.

Paul works to eliminate these differences from the Corinthian church, sometimes with encouragement, sometimes with condemnation, always promoting unity and submission. Paul sees all of these attitudes and practices as impediments to unity. There is much more, however, that Paul seeks to sweep away. These practices and beliefs of the Corinthians are more importantly impediments to transparency to Christ, and Paul seeks to remove them in that they obscure Christ in us. The most familiar example is his polemic against wisdom. Paul reminds the Corinthians, "For I determined to know nothing among you but Jesus Christ, and him crucified." Jesus was the entirety of his knowledge, and Paul emphasizes his own relative emptiness: "And I came to you in weakness and in fear and in much trembling. My speech and my proclamation were not with plausible words of wisdom, but with a demonstration of the Spirit and of power, so that your faith might rest not on human wisdom but on the power of God" (1 Cor. 2:2–5). Wisdom is obviously not in and of itself the problem; it is a problem insofar as it becomes the focus of attention and a distraction from the power of God.

Therefore Paul focuses the Corinthians relentlessly on Christ, who alone is not only salvation but sanctification, and who is the only source of status and prerogative. Christ is power, and Paul points the Corinthians to Christ for wisdom, for strength, for honor, for all sources of boasting. In terms of the ambition for transparency to Christ, the personal properties of the Corinthians, or of any Christians, are of no objective importance. Paul subordinates all Christian action to obedience to Christ, even at the level of thought: "But we have the mind of Christ" (1 Cor. 2:16); "we take every thought captive to obey Christ" (2 Cor. 10:5). In fact, Paul suggests, when one places emphasis on one's personal properties, those properties become impediments to transparency to Christ. They impose limitations where there are none: all things belong to the Corinthians, and they "belong to Christ, and Christ belongs to God" (1 Cor. 3:22–23).

This extraordinary availability of divine excellence, this power in Christ, is not somehow merely theoretical for Paul—it is practically realized in him. As a visible example of this transparency, Paul offers himself to the Corinthians. He is transparent to Christ as Christ is transparent to God. Paul denies his own wisdom and power and claims only the power and authority given him by Jesus, and in so doing claims an unsurpassable power and authority. His transparency to Christ is most manifest in his exhortations to the Corinthians to imitate him, Paul: "I appeal to you, then, be imitators of me" (1 Cor. 4:16) and "Be imitators of me, as I am of Christ" (1 Cor. 11:1). Transparency becomes heroic in this exhortation: Paul recognizes himself, but as Christ-like and not as himself, as a standard of excellence. Paul's transparency to Jesus is the sole ground on which he can offer himself to the Corinthians for imitation.

Paul's imitation of Jesus comes very close to identification with Jesus. Theologically, this is exactly what Paul wants to imply: one died for all, therefore all died; those who live again should live not for themselves but for Jesus; he became our sin, therefore we should become his righteousness (2 Cor. 5:14–15, 21). That all believers died in Christ and were risen with him is imitated in the actions of repentance and baptism; that we should become transparent to his righteousness involves every aspect of us in the newness of conversion. We have no interest in questioning Paul's sincerity in merging himself with Christ. For the Corinthian church, recipients of the exhortation, Paul was available for imitation in a more immediate way than Jesus was. Jesus was the message, the redeemer, the source of the power—but he was not available as a visible pattern for the Christian life. Of course, he had not been for Paul, either; but Paul felt himself shaped with grace, informed with vision, and endowed with authority,[1] and these qualities, extrinsic but real, made him worthy of imitation. Practically, however, the result of such an identification with Jesus heightens the confusion of imitative discipleship and Jesus' own unique status, even in Paul's own self-presentation. He toggles back and forth between his own worthiness (through Christ) and his own unworthiness, between his inferiority and his equality with the most eminent apostles (2 Cor. 11:5; 12:11). He cites his "leastness" and then claims to have labored more than all (1 Cor. 15:10). Why does he not elaborate on those labors? Because like the events of his life, there is "nothing to be gained by it" (2 Cor. 12:1). His life is empty, filled only by Christ. In place of such a narrative of labors, Paul provides an inimitable account of his own history, his own unique call, his own revelations and requirements, all of which constitute his identity. The transparency he claims both evacuates and fills.

What can we learn from Paul about the nature of our imitation of Jesus? When Paul speaks about acts to perform, he attempts answers that take a partly liturgical form when he speaks of spiritual gifts (1 Cor. 12–14), distributed unevenly by the Spirit to each believer as God wills. This emphasis on spiritual gifts recapitulates the same dynamic of transparency, one which evacuates and fills. The gifts do not matter objectively: Teaching has no intrinsic value, nor prophecy, nor speaking in tongues, except in that these gifts are transparent to Christ and made valuable by him. The spiritual gifts do matter, however, in that they are the modes of the Corinthians' transparency to Christ: If one has the gift of teaching, one should teach; if one has the gift of healing, one should heal. The gifts matter functionally as means of building and unifying the church as Christ's form in the world. Paul never suggests an imitation that follows the narrative form of his life. In fact, Paul gives contrary evidence about the form that his life took. He has a definite history, both a Jewish one and an apostolic one, which he "boasts" of (2 Cor. 11:21–33), but in his delivery of the gospel, he became "all things to all men" (1 Cor. 9:19–23) in order to demonstrate the malleability, the applicability, of salvation to all. It seems significant that Paul suppresses any account of his life that emphasizes what we might consider an imitable pattern. Instead, we hear of calls and ministries and gifts. How then does one imitate Paul? And how was he imitating Jesus? It seems clear that for Paul, discipleship does not require imitation in any specific sense. He imitated Jesus by emptying himself and obeying; the Corinthians were to learn from Paul, even imitate Paul, by doing the same.

Paul, for all his didacticism, does not offer a specific pattern to the Corinthians. There is of course a formal entry into the faith, and a form to its observance. Christians are those who have repented, been baptized and believed, forsake immorality, gather to share communion and worship, shun fellowship with professing believers whose lives do not conform to these basic practices. But when pressed for the pattern of transparency, Paul offers no more than himself, a patternless pattern. Should one marry or remain unmarried? Remain as you were when God called you. Should one eat meat or not? Do not cause your brother to stumble. Should one seek prophecy, seek faith to move mountains, give away all possessions, give one's body to be burned? Seek to love and to give, like Christ, and like Paul himself, for without love, we are nothing. Paul's own specific activity in his transparency to Christ is not the content of his exhortation to imitate him. It is not important for the Corinthians to do as Paul *does,* in any particular sequence of action, but to be transparent to Christ as he *is.*

We should therefore read Paul's exhortations to the Corinthians as primarily evacuative in order to prepare for a filling with God's glory. Paul attempts to sweep away anything that would serve as an impediment to their transparency to Christ, even those personal properties which seem valuable not only in the world but also in service to God. Eloquence is such a property in the rhetorically charged world of the Corinthians. Apollos, the Alexandrian Jewish convert who followed Paul in ministry in Corinth, is described in Acts as an "eloquent man" and "fervent in spirit" (18:24–25), and he seems to have won the admiration of the Corinthians, who noted Paul's relative lack of skill in comparison. For himself, Paul eschews the use of eloquence in preaching the gospel: he proclaimed not "in persuasive words of wisdom" (1 Cor. 2:4). But Paul does not condemn eloquence or Apollos for using it. Instead he renounces its intrinsic value. Nothing has value except through Christ; all must be renounced to be regained in newness. For Paul, to measure power and value apart from Christ is living and regarding "according to the flesh," by human standards. Paul values the human only when it is made incandescent by the divine, only when it is transparent to the power of God through Jesus Christ. This is the heroism of transparency, and it is the greatest power.

Paul's approach to discipleship has the elegance of the perfect solution. How much greater a power can one have than Christ within? The Corinthians, however, needed to be persuaded. It is possible to view the Corinthian Christians as jaded refugees from a sin-sick cosmopolitan culture at the crossroads of Greece and Rome, confused about basic elements of morality and faith, and to see their questions in that light;[2] but we see in the questions of the Corinthian church concerns that are similar to Vergil's, and to ours. Theirs are questions of participation. How should I think of all that I am, which I bring to God? How should I think of my wisdom, my power, my noble birth, my marital status, my scruples? These are no longer only issues of church unity but of personal significance. The Corinthians wonder what exactly survives the change from old to new, what participates in the power of Christ. As we have argued, Paul does not view transparency as a problem of any sort: one must evacuate oneself to be filled, as he himself exemplifies. But the Corinthians appear troubled by questions of transparency and imitation, both in terms of their own properties and in terms of the specific actions that they should follow. The Corinthians stumble over the dynamic of evacuation, wishing to hold parts of themselves and their communal relations in reserve, abandoning themselves, in part, but not in whole. Paul urges them to understand the dynamic of filling and the glory to be found in transparency to Christ. Paul's goal for the Corinthians can be understood as a heightening of their ambition: he views their ambition on behalf of themselves and on behalf of Christ as too small, and he wants to increase it.

One central subject of Paul's letters to the Corinthians which reveals his concern for heightened ambition is his attention to the factions of the Corinthian church. Their focus on "the things of the flesh" led to a tendency toward the elevation of individual Christians, and this places a screen of human achievement between them and Christ. It is this tendency, with its resulting disparagement of his authority, that motivates much of what appears as rhetorical bullying in his letters to the Corinthians. But Paul was placed in a bind by this "fleshly" valuation of the Corinthians: he must attempt to efface himself and his coworkers (though with what success we cannot know) without becoming faceless. He never considers the total evacuation of renouncing any authority over the Corinthians, and so he must exercise that authority without claiming it as his own. He must exert power over the Corinthians and guide them toward the proper form of Christian life, but do so in such a way that success would not be *his* achievement.

Paul's careful negotiation of this difficulty characterizes his most trenchant passages. The Corinthian church was particularly fractious and divided itself under various leaders who had taught them or whose words they had read. The first quarter of Paul's first letter to the Corinthians addresses these divisions directly. "What I mean is that each of you says, 'I belong to Paul,' and 'I belong to Apollos,' and 'I belong to Cephas,' and 'I belong to Christ.' Has Christ been divided? Was Paul crucified for you? Or were you baptized in the name of Paul?" (1:12–13). These factions apparently arose after both Paul and Apollos had left Corinth and were primarily in connection with them through correspondence.[3] Apollos's influence must have been considerable, to judge from Paul's letter, and Paul approves of him. But Paul and Apollos had very different methods of presentation: Apollos was an "eloquent man" and "fervent in spirit," while Paul describes himself above as weak and with no superiority of speech or wisdom. The Corinthians themselves were sometimes even harsher in their opinion of Paul: "For they [some opponents of Paul] say, 'His letters are strong and weighty, but his personal presence is unimpressive, and his speech contemptible'" (2 Cor. 10:10). The allegiances of the Corinthians were made not for reasons of doctrine, as we might suppose. Apollos was teaching nothing that Paul disagreed with, as far as his letter reveals, nor was Peter (Cephas), nor, obviously, had Christ. What, then, was the basis for divisions in Corinth? There have been many suggestions for the causes of these factions.[4] We argue that the Corinthian factions had a personal rather than a social or historical basis. Paul's words suggest that the Corinthians were aligning themselves under these various men on the basis of their actions and personal properties, either observed, in the case of Paul and Apollos, or reported, in the cases of Peter and Jesus. Thus, Paul is not chastising the Corinthians for their misunderstanding of teaching but for their adulation of the teachers. Paul, like all other evangelists, has but one message, and neither he, nor any other witness to the gospel, is the message: "For we do not proclaim ourselves; we proclaim Jesus Christ as Lord, and ourselves as your slaves for Jesus' sake" (2 Cor. 4:5). The "personalization" of the gospel and of its exegesis lies at the root of the problem that Paul addresses.

It is central to Paul's ambition of transparency that the problem is compounded and not solved by the presence of a group who were "of Christ" (1 Cor. 1:12).[5] What must this group have thought or done to identify themselves? Paul does not mention them specifically again. But it is significant for our reading that Paul criticizes the presence of a faction of Christ along with those aligning themselves with the apostles. One gathers that in the evolution of the church in Corinth, some of the believers felt that they had outgrown Paul in some way or that his instantiation of the gospel was less authoritative than that of Peter, the foremost disciple, or less eloquent than that of Apollos, the persuasive Alexandrian personality; and some apparently rejected all affiliations and adhered only to Jesus in an exclusive way. Some Christians in Corinth clearly questioned Paul's very ministry, which he defends in the ninth chapter of 1 Corinthians and the eleventh of 2 Corinthians. For Paul, no matter how much he proclaimed that he was not the message, such a rejection of him was a rejection of the Christ he preached. He makes virtually no distinction between what Christ has done in him and what he has done in Christ: "But by the grace of God I am what I am, and his grace toward me has not been in vain. On the contrary, I worked harder than any of them—yet it was not I, but the grace of God that is with me" (1 Cor. 15:10). This equivocation between grace and labor closes the gap between what is Christ and what is Paul, and therefore between presentation of the gospel and its representation in a Christ-like life. In fact, Paul identifies himself so strongly with Christ that, as we discuss above, he is able to urge the Corinthians to imitate *him,* as he does twice (1 Cor. 4:16; 11:1). Paul is very present in his letters to the Corinthians, though he never presents only himself. He presents Christ and represents Christ with almost no distinction. Paul does not want there to be a faction "of Paul," but he also does not want there to be one "of Christ" which would exclude his authority as a representative of Christ.

The issue of Paul's authority is the point at which his ambition of transparency converges with his message. Paul asserts his authority and he does so with supreme confidence. But this seems to contradict all passages from the two letters that emphasize submission to Christ and to other Christians. If he were willing to allow his own authority, but not the eating of meat, to be a stumbling block to Corinthian believers, then his words seem to violate his own principle of love. It is much more likely, rather, that Paul believes that his authority as an icon of Christ benefits the Corinthians. It is on the behalf of Christ that Paul asserts his authority, because he is a testament to Christ's transformative power, and it is on behalf of the Corinthians that he asserts it, because his example, like his teachings of unity and submission, removes impediments to transparency. When the Corinthians denigrate his authority, Paul views it as an example of their lack of ambition, both for themselves and for Christ, since they do not recognize that it is Christ who has filled Paul and is the source of his power, nor that Christ will do the same with them, once they enter into the dynamic of transparency. If the Corinthians cannot see that he is a mirror of the glory of Christ, then they deny the reality of Christian transparency, which is finally to deny Christ's saving and transformative power. Paul's ambition is neither self-promoting nor self-denying, and it reveals the degree to which Paul views his incandescence in Christ as possible, and actual.

In his assertion of heroic transparency Paul expresses vividly what it looks like to deny oneself in obedience and yet to possess completely all of one's attributes, now charged with divine power.[6]

> Indeed, we live as human beings, but we do not wage war according to human standards; for the weapons of our warfare are not merely human, but they have divine power to destroy strongholds. We destroy arguments and every proud obstacle raised up against the knowledge of God, and we take every thought captive to obey Christ. (2 Cor. 10:3–5)[7]

With the metaphor of battle, Paul imports the image of heroism into the Christian life. In Paul's language of victory, Jesus triumphed over sin and death and gave his followers a paradigm of triumphant living. But his triumph, according to the Gospels and to Pauline theology, is more than paradigmatic—it literally becomes ours.[8] With this convergence of human and divine, Paul is able to venture into the world of Homeric confidence: "Anyone I face I have the weapons to defeat." But the excellence that supports and undergirds that confidence is completely antitragic. Since it comes from God, there is no possibility that God will not recognize that power which is his own. Moreover, because the power to be Christ-like does not stem from our imitative efforts, but from the potency of grace, our participation is secured. Thus, Paul's confidence is not based on his own properties or merits, but on Christ's power and glory. His confidence that faith makes us transparent to Jesus relaxes the problems of heroic achievement. When one is transparent to Christ, God's glory and greatness shine through that believer.

IGNATIUS OF ANTIOCH: DYING TO IMITATE

Imitating Christ is a not a multistep program. The New Testament, for all of its clarity about the foundation of discipleship, does not prescribe a clear path of discipleship, and the lives of disciples, the original twelve and those coming after, reveal a variety of forms of imitation. In the absence of definitive direction, of course, the lives of disciples themselves could be taken as prescriptive, and they often were. But some of the most distinguished—and distinct—disciples were those who lived the most unscripted lives, whose imitation of Christ in many ways resembled him very little. Paul serves as a premier example. Not only do the facts of his life differ, but even the energy and direction of Paul's centrifugal efforts on behalf of the gospel stand in sharp contrast to the singular and finally passive centripetal movement of Jesus toward Jerusalem. Paul takes the message of that central event and spreads it across the eastern Mediterranean. Even though early Christianity had no difficulty accepting Paul's claim to be Christ-like, other more mimetic forms of following were sought. One such form of imitating Christ, and perhaps the most authoritative, was to die at the hands of persecutors.

First-person narratives are sometimes tinged with an enthusiasm for suffering that betrays a self-conscious sense of action, a drastic need for something like conventional heroism. This note is sounded in the letters of some martyrs, who beg not to be spared, not to have their suffering lessened, not to mitigate the torment of their deaths. Nowhere is this more clear than in the letter of Ignatius, bishop of Antioch, to the Romans. Ignatius was condemned around 107 C.E., during the reign of Trajan. Somehow he was able to receive visitors and to write while being transported by armed guard to Rome to be killed. He writes to certain churches or groups of Christians, including those Christians at Rome. In his letter to the Romans, Ignatius bids them not to interfere or intercede on his behalf, which would be to do him "an unseasonable kindness" (4.1). He is fascinated with the prospect of being eaten by animals, and longs for it: "Let me be fodder for wild beasts—that is how I can get to God" (4.1). "What a thrill I shall have from the wild beasts that are ready for me! I hope they will make short work of me. I shall coax them on to eat me up at once and not to hold off, as sometimes happens, through fear. And if they are reluctant, I shall force them to it" (5.2).

The letter is full of the paradoxes of physical death and eternal life, of dying and being born. Ignatius knows that in dying he will "get to Jesus Christ," and having committed himself to this, he believes that staying alive would impede true living. He writes the letter, in his own words, "with a passion for death" (7.2). What is striking is that Ignatius does not articulate his desires against a background of courage or fortitude, sounding the notes of a conventional heroic *persona*, or even in the language of power. He speaks in the language of desire and purpose; his desire for death is his "godly purpose."[9] His desire and purpose are evacuative and mapped entirely onto the passion of Christ, but as an enacted event rather than a spiritual truth. Because Ignatius understands that this form of transparency *will* erase him completely, he does not join his evacuative desire with a corresponding desire for filling. To be sure, Ignatius anticipates an ultimate and total fulfillment in which he will be with Jesus more perfectly. But in his letter there is only evacuation for Ignatius, a complete transformation from an imperfect living to an eternal, perfect death.

Unlike Paul, Ignatius wants to blend two ideas of discipleship, that is, transparency to Jesus and the recapitulation of Jesus' passion. Jesus' death provides a pattern for Ignatius, so that Ignatius's understanding of the Christian life transparent to Christ is envisioned through the details of Jesus' death, both as historically detailed in the Gospels and as liturgically remembered in the bread and wine. For Ignatius, there is a pattern for heroic discipleship. Ignatius says that he knows that his martyrdom is best for him, because "now I am beginning to be a disciple" (5.3); and when he is dead and consumed, "then I will truly be a disciple when the world will not even see my body" (4.2). The discipleship Ignatius desires exists in following the pattern: "Allow me to be an imitator of the suffering of my God" (6.3). Ignatius imagines excellence, in fact, human perfection, in one form: Jesus. And because of this he defines the status of disciple in terms of patterned imitation: the disciple (*mathétés*) is most perfectly a mimic (*mimétés*). This is not the extent of the ethical program that he taught to other Christians, for whom martyrdom existed only as a general possibility. He emphasizes faith and love and spiritual gifts in his other letters, but for himself he expresses a narrow, singular vision of a Christian life, and it involves a close, and horrible, *imitatio Christi*—horrible to us but joyfully anticipated by him. Ignatius sees only glory and never shame in his mimicry.

Unlike Pauline transparency, the extreme compression of Ignatius's desire and God's will into a specific form of death, with no visible consequence, signals the potential for the imitation of the martyr to approach rivalry or replacement. The martyr, as the word itself implies, is a witness to Christ, and Ignatius means to re-present Christ. The distance between re-presentation and representation can grow quite large, and it is in the gap that the tendency toward heroism, both self-conscious and attributed, grows. What is so important about Ignatius's account of his own fate is that he never allows room for his own heroism. At no point does Ignatius glorify himself, nor is his letter didactic; he does not generally speak of himself as a martyr or a teacher or someone to be imitated in his imitation of Christ.[10] He understands transparency and evacuation in precisely one way, and he understands it personally.

In the eyes of the audience, however, such a representation becomes a thing worthy of admiration in itself, and the act of the martyr becomes more than a representation of Christ; it becomes an interposing form available for imitation. A more obvious example will reveal the process at work. Traditionally it is believed that the apostle Peter was crucified in Rome under the persecutions of Nero. According to his legend, he asked to be crucified upside down, because he was not worthy to die as his master did. But why? Peter seems to have understood that imitation invites rivalry, and he asks, in this instance, not to be made to imitate in the same precise way. The irony, of course, is that crucifixion upside-down seems to be a greater suffering than crucifixion rightside-up—a worse way to go, if you will. Certainly Peter's intention, whatever the truth of his death, was never to outdo—for his master had frequently clarified the relative status of the disciple beneath the teacher—but Peter was not in control of the receptors and transmitters of his own tradition. Throughout the history of the church, the danger of attributing heroism to the imitators of Christ is especially strong. Where Christ should be the hero, the sufferings of the martyrs are assimilated to the sufferings of Christ, and those who intend to serve as a witness to Christ become nearly a replacement of him.[11] The martyrs must walk a precarious line, knowing both that transparency is the proper form of Christian discipleship and that imitative desire tends toward rivalry. For this reason, the church has traditionally taught that martyrdom is a glorious witness, but that death is not to be sought. The shaping forces of transparency must be God's, both in grace and providence. One is made a martyr; one cannot make oneself a martyr.

RECAPITULATION IN THE *MARTYRDOM OF POLYCARP*

In the *Martyrdom of Polycarp* we see none of the anxiety of Peter in his crucifixion; for the author of the letter, Polycarp can never be *too* close to Christ.[12] Polycarp's closeness is the essence of his greatness, and the author wants to show that greatness in terms of the patterned recapitulation of Jesus' passion in Polycarp's death. The anonymous *Martyrdom of Polycarp* tells briefly, in the form of a letter, of the auto-da-fé in which Polycarp, the aged bishop of Smyrna, lost his life. He was arrested and burned to death in 155 C.E. In his relatively direct account, the author clearly sets forth the details that link Polycarp to Christ, and in so doing steers the reader toward a particular interpretation of the event and of Polycarp's Christ-like identity.

The anonymous author draws explicit parallels between the martyrdom of Polycarp and events of Jesus' life, especially the crucifixion. In his first chapter he asserts that everything took place as it did "in order that the Lord might reveal to us from above a martyrdom in accordance with the gospel" (1.1). This accord is one of form. The details are spelled out:

Polycarp is outside the city when they come to arrest him (5.1); the police chief, Polycarp's chief persecutor, is named Herod (6.2); they came against him at night, with an armed crowd, "as against a robber," and found him in an upper room (7.1); Polycarp then asked for time to pray (7.2–3); some repented that they had come after him (7.3); his captors led him into the city seated on a donkey (8.1); he was largely silent before officials who tried to persuade him to comply and save his life (8.2); the crowds clamored for his destruction (12.2); to ensure his death he was stabbed by a guard (16.1); and with the blood from his wound, a dove appeared (16.1).[13] There is no attempt to synchronize completely the sequence of events between the two lives: Polycarp enters on a donkey after his arrest, not triumphally; the dove appears at Polycarp's death but at Jesus' baptism. The shared details of the two lives are brought out and the differences are suppressed. The author merely draws our attention to the parallels obvious to him, which he wants to be obvious to us.

Like Ignatius, the author of the *Martyrdom of Polycarp* joins discipleship and patterned imitation. The anonymous author wants to stress the identity between these two concepts, even using them together as virtual synonyms, "disciples (*mathétai*) and imitators (*mimétai*) of the Lord" (17.3). In this narrative, however, the identity between discipleship and pattern has a reductive effect. In the account of his martyrdom, Polycarp becomes an example of pure mimetic participation in the glory of Jesus. The author of the *Martyrdom of Polycarp* does not, however, animate Polycarp with the desire of Ignatius, so that the participation of Polycarp is, in terms of his passion, even thinner than the participation of Aeneas in his destiny. Polycarp is neither evacuated nor filled; the author presents a convergence of Polycarp and Christ in which the reader is not encouraged to distinguish some "authentic" Polycarp from the pattern that he imitates. It is clear that Polycarp is *not* Jesus, but exactly how he differs is a matter of indifference.

This convergence of Polycarp and Jesus in pure mimetic participation results in a remarkable transfer. Polycarp's unobstructed imitation of Jesus allows for the divine power of Christ to flow objectively into him. Polycarp was the recipient of reverence and honor in the Christian community during his life (13.2), and some of his captors recognized his piety and repented of their participation in his arrest on that very night (7.2). After Polycarp's death, one Nicetes proposed to the Roman governor that he not allow the Christians to have the body, as they wanted, "so that they not abandon the crucified one and begin to worship this man" (17.2). That the author included this fear is interesting: he presumably intended to reveal the depths of Jewish animosity and of Greek and Roman misunderstandings of Christianity. But his reply to that fear is stunning: they are ignorant of the fact, he says, that we can never abandon Jesus, who died for our salvation and for all sinners, in order to worship someone else; "for we worship him as the Son of God, but the disciples and imitators of the Lord we love, and they are worthy of our love *because of* their unsurpassable devotion (*eunoia*) for their king and teacher" (17.3). The author clearly presumes that Polycarp's glory is reflective and not personal. It leads those who see him to worship Christ, not Polycarp, or any other worthy martyr. The author then closes the chapter with the prayer that he and the others who witnessed Polycarp's death become "sharers and fellow disciples" with the imitators of Christ (17.3), as Polycarp's appointed fate was to become a "sharer of Christ," that is, a sharer of his sufferings (6.2). There is no heroic achievement other than a recapitulation of Christ's achievement.

Nonetheless, despite the author's relentless emphasis on convergence, Polycarp becomes, in one sense, an independent object of worship after his death. After his body is burnt, he gives off the fragrance that alludes to the sweet offering of Jesus; and Christians gathered up the bones that remained, valued now "more highly than precious stones, more refined than gold," and put them in a fitting space; then they celebrated the anniversary of his martyrdom (or, as the text says, the "birthday") both "for the remembrance of those who have already fought the fight, and for the practice and preparation of those who are about to" (18.3). The holy bones are a tangible receptacle of the divine power that Polycarp's unobstructed imitation makes visible.

Such mimetic participation, unmediated by fulfillment, desire, or purpose, can easily become a rival paradigm of human greatness. The objective force of God's glory *in* Polycarp allows his witness to take on an independent weight and gravity, symbolized in the enduring power of sanctity in his bones. In this way, Polycarp's imitation of Jesus became a thing itself worthy of remembrance and imitation: "all desire to imitate his martyrdom, which happened according the gospel of Christ" (19.1). The author is able to assimilate the desire to be "like Polycarp" to the desire to be Christ-like. The effect is to make Christian heroism more available, more immediate as a possibility in the life of the believer. Perhaps this is an example of perfect transparency, because Polycarp does not take credit for himself, nor is there any confusion about the grounds for his persecution and death. He so little obstructs Jesus that his loving disciples scarcely express a distinction in their definition of greatness.

Unlike Paul, whose correspondence with the Corinthians suggests that others distinguished between *his* witness and Christ's power, to the detriment of the former, the author of the *Martyrdom of Polycarp* signals an uncomplicated unity. Polycarp's witness is powerful because it is so transparently Christ-like in suffering and death.

THE QUEST FOR HOLINESS:
THE LIFE OF ANTHONY

The persecutions that shaped the fates of Ignatius and Polycarp into a visible recapitulation of Jesus' passion did not endure. The author of the *Martyrdom of Polycarp* was confident that the manifest glory of Polycarp's death would triumph over unbelief. Events proved his confidence just, for by the fourth century, the Roman Empire embraced Christianity. No longer did the local magistrate play the role of Pilate, and the local citizenry assume the part of the Jerusalem mob. The world would not cooperate in fulfilling a desire for a martyr's death, and as a result, the desire to imitate Christ had to find other, less immediate and objectively transparent patterns. In this environment, the quest for holiness emerged as the successor to the way of martyrdom. Ascetical discipline replaced arrest, trial, suffering, and death as the agonistic stage on which the Christ within was made public, visible, and effective.

One of the most important expressions of this new form of transparency to Christ was the *Life of Anthony*, the story of a holy man who sought after sanctity in the deserts of Egypt in the mid–fourth century. Written by Athanasius, the great theologian and bishop of Alexandria, this account of Anthony's life came to exert remarkable influence, not only in the fourth century, but in subsequent centuries as well.[14] Augustine's *Confessions* testify to the influence of Anthony's story. On the day of his own conversion, a friend tells Augustine of an acquaintance who had read the *Life of Anthony*, and was so inspired by Anthony's remarkable life he abandoned his lucrative career, canceled his planned wedding, and devoted his life to the rigors of holiness.[15] It is against the background of this report of the decisive influence of Anthony's example that Augustine decides to undertake his own renunciations and to enter the strict path of ascetical disciplines. In the same way, generations of monastic readers after Augustine have treated the *Life of Anthony* as a font of inspiration and a guide to the unique heroism of the Christian quest for holiness.

The key to the influence of the story of Anthony is Athanasius's assimilation of heroic ideals to the Pauline commitment to Christ-like transparency. Athanasius is able to describe Anthony's life as an ongoing personal project that brings into play a wide range of human powers and energy. Anthony's life is a quest involving tests and triumphs that are visible for us to see and at which we marvel. He defeats demons; he confutes heretics and pagan philosophers; he founds a veritable kingdom of monks in the desert; he foresees the future and counsels emperors. Without doubt, the Anthony depicted by Athanasius is a man enlarged by his successful quest for sanctity. Yet, for all the room and scope that Athanasius gives to the remarkably strenuous project of self-discipline, he preserves the Pauline ideal. Athanasius consistently attributes Anthony's greatness to God. "It was clear," writes Athanasius of some of Anthony's particularly glorious achievements, "that it was not he who did this, but the Lord bringing his benevolence to effect through Anthony" (para. 84). Just as Paul claims his own authority, yet not his own, but Christ's in him, so does Athanasius depict Anthony's glory, yet not his own, but Christ's in him. Thus, for Anthanasius, Anthony does not recapitulate Jesus with the brute objectivity that characterizes the death of Polycarp; nonetheless, Anthony does manifest, in word and deed, the power of Christ that Paul insists is the inward glory of the faithful.

As Athanasius begins the story, he describes a young Anthony who enjoys the most auspicious of circumstances for solid piety and respectable citizenship. He is born into a devout and well-to-do Christian family. Serious and sensitive as a youth, he takes very naturally to Christian instruction and practice. However, when his parents die, Anthony is bitten by the desire to live more strictly in the way of Jesus. Heeding Jesus' commandments and the example set by the apostles, he sells his inheritance and gives the proceeds to the poor. Yet this is still not enough. Ever desiring to conform himself to Christ, Anthony submits himself to the instruction of "men of zeal" who live in solitude and simplicity, apart from the community (para. 4). In this way, Anthony enters into the strenuous path of holiness, taking on the role of an "athlete" who would compete for the prize of sanctity.

To both ancient and modern readers this renunciation of possessions and the adoption of solitude can seem a dramatic display of spiritual conviction. For Athanasius, however, such acts simply set the stage for the coming action. Anthony's initial self-denial initiates rather than ends his labors. The way of asceticism, for Anthony, will not be placid, his solitude not contemplative but full of action and contest. Far from escaping the trials of ordinary life—the daily round of obligations, the distracting activities of maintaining a household, the mundane matters of normal social intercourse—Anthony's withdrawal from everyday life intensifies his struggles. His retreat is only apparent; it is, in truth, an advance toward the more severe tests of spiritual endurance.[16]

Athanasius immediately turns to these severe tests, for they mark the beginning of Anthony's many conquests. Echoing Christ's temptation in the wilderness, Anthony is tempted by the devil. The temptation is three-fold, and, taken together, this series of tests provides the first of many tri-als that Anthony must endure throughout his life. In the first temptation, the devil appears as a beautiful woman, testing Anthony's restraint of lustful desires. The second temptation involves beating and lashing, test-ing Anthony's ability to endure pain and suffering on behalf of faith. The third and final temptation subjects Anthony to visions of wild beasts who would tear him apart, testing his fear of death. In each temptation, Anthony resists, drawing on the wisdom of Jesus, whose example he fol-lows, and depending on the strength of grace that he knows God provides to the faithful. Successful in this test, Anthony is triumphant, and this first scene of spiritual victory provides Athanasius with the opportunity to articulate the fundamental logic of Anthony's spiritual achievement.

As Athanasius describes the scene, the voice of God comes down to the exhausted but victorious Anthony: "I was here, Anthony, but I waited to watch you struggle. And now, since you persevered and were not defeated, I will be your helper forever, and I will make you famous every-where" (para. 10). This divine address has three components, each of which is indispensable to Athanasius's account of Anthony's heroism. First, God is always present in Anthony's struggles; Christ is with us in our time of trial, and the ascetical athlete never endures or acts without Christ's power. Second, the triumph of God's grace has room for human enactment; God waits and watches even as he undergirds and supports the faithful. However immediate the presence of Christ, that presence does not overwhelm or replace human agency. Third and finally, the tri-umph of grace in which the disciple participates merits recognition. The saint shares in the glory of God. We need to look at each component of Anthony's heroism in detail.

"I was here, Anthony" signals the persistent theme of divine presence. At every juncture, Athanasius is clear that Anthony acts on the basis of an inner, divine power. It is not Anthony who triumphs—or more precisely, not Anthony alone who triumphs—but God within Anthony. In the brief account of Anthony's youth, Athanasius shows him as a child of the church, baptized and catechized, nurtured within a family of pious con-viction. Such a man does not enter the desert to contest with the devil as a *tabula rasa,* drawing on innate human powers. From the very outset, Anthony has been formed in Christ. Athanasius is, therefore, quick to draw on Paul's description of his labors in order to underline the significance of Anthony's victory. "Working with Anthony," observes Athanasius with a certainty born of his commitment to the New Testament's description of discipleship, "was the Lord, who bore flesh for us, and gave to the body the victory over the devil, so that each of those who truly struggle can say, It is not I, but the grace of God which is in me" (para. 5). Later, as Anthony describes his own achievement in a long discourse to his ascetical followers, he strikes the same note. Speaking of his victory over demons, Anthony says, "I was not the one who stopped them and nullified their actions—it was the Lord" (para. 40). The warrior saint wins no independent victories; rather, he recapitulates the victories won by Jesus and, in so doing, does not attain any purely personal achievements but comes to participate in Jesus' saving achievement. Here, the Pauline heroism of transparency holds sway.

The distinctive genius of the *Life of Anthony,* however, rests in Athanasius's ability to add the second, enacted element to this Pauline heroism. The divine power in Anthony has personal weight, even if it has no independence from Christ's heroism. God has already triumphed over Satan in Christ. Anthony is very clear that Jesus' victory is universal and complete (para. 42). Nonetheless, God stands back and allows Anthony to struggle with temptation. The voice says to Anthony, "I waited to watch your struggle." God allows Anthony to undergo his own, personal test, and does not intervene from without, *deus ex machina,* in order to directly control the outcome with his surpassing and always triumphant power. Just as Jesus' triumph still allowed for Ignatius and Polycarp to be subjected to a pattern of arrest, suffering, and death that recapitulated his passion, so now, in a time after martyrdom, the ascetical hero is allowed room to exercise faith and undergo tests that will manifest the Christ who dwells within. The heroism of Jesus is absolute, for Athanasius, but it allows for human reenactment, as Anthony's example illustrates.

Anthony enjoys many opportunities to exercise his faith, and the *Life of Anthony* might easily have been titled "The Many Triumphs of Anthony." His contest with demons is ongoing, providing further occasions for victory. He leaves his isolated hermitage in order to go to the city, where he contends on behalf of orthodoxy against heretics (para. 46). He enters into debates with pagan philosophers and defeats them with the force of his words in a contest of wisdom (para. 72). He even struggles against the arid fruitlessness of the desert and the threatening destructiveness of wild beasts, emerging victorious as he plants crops and commands the animals (para. 50). The reader, then, has ample opportunity to watch Anthony struggle and triumph. To be sure, God's grace is triumphant, but it triumphs in a way that opens up space for a human endeavor, and as Athanasius insists, Anthony was "daily being martyred by conscience, and doing battle in contests of faith" (para. 47). This consistent depiction of internal and external human action makes Anthony appear to the reader as a warrior in his own right, exercised by constant conflict and ever victorious over his foes. This is the case no matter how often Athanasius, both as narrator and through the voice of Anthony, reiterates the prior and continuing dependence on grace, no matter how much he points to the surpassing glory of Christ. So central is the image of the triumphant spiritual warrior that Athanasius suggests that the contest and victories are not simply permitted by God, but are arranged by providence in order to train this exemplary "athlete" of the spirit (para. 12). God's grace, it seems, includes a pedagogy of spiritual achievement, and for Athanasius the agonies of faith are positively constitutive of the divine plan of salvation. The Christ-like identity of the disciple becomes thick with personal enactment.

This heroic persona is reinforced by the third and final component of the divine address to Anthony at the conclusion of his first great victory over temptation. "Since you persevered," says God, "I will make you famous." To the victor goes honor and glory, and God promises that this standard heroic expectation will be upheld. Without doubt, Athanasius's conviction that glory remains a real possibility for the heroic disciple is the key to the immediate success and enduring influence of the *Life of Anthony*. The human desire for excellence and the attendant expectations that excellence will be rewarded with appropriate recognition need not be renounced by the heroic disciple. Quite the contrary, for Athanasius, such desires and expectation are fulfilled and redoubled, for Anthony's glory is not human, but divine.

As the *Life of Anthony* unfolds, the divine promise is fulfilled. Anthony's victories manifest his spiritual power, and that power attracts attention. Although he has embraced solitude, and he moves ever more deeply into the isolation of the Egyptian desert, retreating to the "inner mountain" (para. 49), people seek him out for advice about spiritual discipline, and he eventually becomes the leader of a desert community of monks. As his triumphs increase, his fame grows and, sensible of his power, petitioners come. Some ask to be healed by his spiritual power.

Judges come to ask him to resolve, Solomon-like, difficult cases (para. 84). His public influence is so great that Athanasius observes that "it was as if he were a physician given to Egypt by God" (para. 87). His fame extends even beyond Egypt. The emperor writes Anthony "as to a father and beg[s] to receive responses from him" (para. 81). Finally, Athanasius concludes his *Life of Anthony* by appealing to the glory that Anthony has accumulated. "Proof of his virtue and that his soul was loved by God," Athanasius writes, "is found in the fact that he is famous everywhere and is marveled at by everyone" (para. 93). Anthony's name is praised at the four corners of the earth, and to him every knee is bowed.

With such a fulsome picture of Anthony's spiritual heroism, we can easily imagine that the Pauline ideal of transparency, however often affirmed in passing, is eclipsed by a pattern of human achievement that rivals Jesus' heroism. The Christian warrior, we might think, carves out a kingdom of personal sanctity and acquires a degree of spiritual power that, although always in the service of God, remains independent, and as such, must be recognized and honored by God. Yet such an impression is contrary to Athanasius's intention. He wishes to assimilate heroic images and vocabulary to the Pauline ideal of transparency; he does not wish to propose an alternative account of Christian heroism. We fail to grasp Athanasius's literary and theological ambition if we confuse Anthony's participation in Christ's heroism with a claim to a separate heroism, and we must resist this confusion if we are to understand the larger project of incorporating accomplishment and endeavor into the Christian vision of discipleship.

In order to guard against this misinterpretation of Christian heroism, Athanasius emphasizes two aspects of Anthony's heroism: first, the exclusively evacuative logic of Anthony's struggles with temptation, and second, the convergence of Anthony's achievements with the heroism of God in Christ. In his discourse to his followers, the voice of Anthony undercuts his victory over demonic temptation. He warns those who wish to embark on the ascetical life that "we ought not to boast about expelling demons, nor become proud on account of healings performed" (para. 38). However real the experience of temptation—and for Athanasius's readers, both ancient and modern, such experiences are as real as any personal dimension of life—Anthony insists that the power of evil is an illusion. Speaking of the demons who assault him, he insists that "it is evident that they possess no strength!" (para. 28). In Christ, God has triumphed over evil and has stripped the demons of their power. Thus, for Anthony, victory in temptation takes a simple form: one must trust in the triumph of God and announce to the demons their powerlessness. To be sure, such a simple technique must overcome severe obstacles, but such obstacles are internal; they are self-created. We lack trust in God, and therefore we invest demons with the power of our fear, our anxiety, our lusts, so that in falling to temptation, we become victims of none other than ourselves. For this reason, the ascetical struggle is always evacuative; it involves a renunciation of those parts of ourselves that give power to temptation. Thus, one can never boast of victory over temptation, for the defeated enemy is oneself.

In view of Anthony's description of his own self as the enemy of sanctity, the Christian hero, however radiant with the glory of spiritual attainment, is antithetical to the Homeric hero. "Some glory in chariots, and some in horses," Athanasius has Anthony say in a particularly pointed passage, "but we glory in the name of the Lord our God" (para. 39). The ascetical warrior, vigorous in conflict and triumphant in the many tests of temptation, has no basis on which to claim the glory of victory. It is Anthony's armor—*his* passions and desire—that are stripped off the defeated foe (himself), and *that* armor is to be discarded, and the armor of God put on. Thus, Athanasius's summation of Anthony's discourse is fitting: "The ones who were cured were taught not to give thanks to Anthony, but to God alone" (para. 56). This is not a vain attempt by Athanasius to counteract a heroic vanity that his fulsome description of Anthony's achievements stirs up in the reader. It follows from the logic of Anthony's victories, for he defeated himself, and no other enemy.

For Athanasius, spiritual heroism is not simply evacuative. The second, glorifying aspect of Anthony's heroism is just as important as the first, ascetical aspect. Anthony's life is characterized by positive achievements: he heals, foresees the future, counsels with wisdom, guides monks with paternal love. These positive achievements are crucial, for they testify to the trustworthy promises of God. The spiritual warrior has confidence that God will put his power and passion into the place of that which has been defeated by self-denial. However, the divine potency is not generic. In each achievement, Anthony imitates Christ. He is a prophet in his ability to foresee the future. He is a physician in his power to heal the ailments, both bodily and spiritual, of petitioners. He is a king in his counsel to the emperor, Solomonic in his wise adjudication of difficult cases. Thus, although Anthony does not mirror Christ as directly as the martyrs, when he manifests spiritual power, he does so as one formed in the image of Christ. Just so, again and again, Anthony announces that it is not he who triumphs and achieves, but Christ in him. "The performance of signs," he tells the other monks, "does not belong to us—this is the savior's work" (para. 38)

Here, Athanasius is utterly confident. He wishes us to see the glory of Anthony's spiritual achievement, a glory that will stimulate imitative ambition in us. As Athanasius announces in his introduction, "I know that even in hearing along with marveling at the man, you will want also to emulate his purpose." So potent is his image, thinks Athanasius, that just the outlines of his life presented in this brief story will spark imitative desire. Yet Athanasius does not think that in so stimulating our desire to imitate Anthony we will be distracted from the Christian goal of becoming Christ-like. Anthony never seeks his own glory—indeed, to renounce such a desire is central to the ascetical quest. Instead he seeks to serve the glory of God in Christ. In this aspiration, Anthony is successful. For Athanasius, and for generations of readers, Anthony is so transparent to Christ that a desire to share in the glory of his ascetical triumphs does not lead to a cult of "Anthonians." Rather, his example intensifies the desire, in others, to glorify Christ in his supreme and all-encompassing triumph. Thus, Athanasius concludes the *Life of Anthony* with an exhortation to his readers that sums up his view of Anthony's heroism: "Read these things to the other brothers so that they may learn what the life of the monks ought to be, and so that they may believe that our Lord and Savior Jesus Christ glorifies those who glorify him" (para. 94). Those who give up their lives, for Jesus' sake, will find life in him, because he pours himself into those who pour out their lives for him. When we see and marvel at the glory of Anthony, we do nothing other than see and marvel at the glory of God in the divine heroism of Jesus Christ.

Athanasius was confident that Anthony's heroism was transparent to the surpassing heroism of Jesus, and he commends his *Life of Anthony* accordingly. However, his marriage of Pauline transparency to the very human need for heroic action and recognition is difficult to sustain. As Athanasius describes Anthony's final days, he focuses attention on the conditions of Anthony's burial. "The Egyptians," Athanasius reports, "love to honor with burial rites and to wrap in linens the bodies of their worthy dead, and especially holy martyrs, not burying them in the earth, but placing them on low beds and keeping them inside, and they intend by this practice to honor the deceased" (para. 90). Anthony renounces this honor and is concerned that his followers will venerate his dead body; he retreats to his "inner mountain" in order to forestall such an outcome. There, before his few intimates, he makes his farewell. He concludes this discourse with strict instructions to keep his place of burial secret, for he is worried that his corpse will become the object of devotion (para. 91). Anthony knows that his glory is Christ's alone, a glory he shares only insofar as his life is Christ-like. He possesses no glory that is his own, and with death his life ends, and his transparency to Christ ceases, living on only in the memory of his example, not in the bones of his body.

This careful treatment of Anthony's death suggests that Athanasius knew very well how easily we are tempted to parse the divine and human, separating the heroism of Jesus from the heroism of exemplary disciples, and in so doing, raise up a glory of sanctity that can begin to rival the glory of God in Christ. Athanasius may have been confident that Anthony points beyond himself to God, but he is not so confident that the reader will look *through* Anthony to the true source of his glory. It is difficult to affirm a distinctively personal scope for human achievement within the life of the obedient disciple which does not, somehow, take on independent weight. If Christ penetrates into the words and actions of Anthony, then we might well imagine that he penetrates into his bones as well, bones that we might possess as a source of sanctity and power separate from the particular pattern of his Christ-like life. In so doing, we begin to conceive of an excellence and achievement, a heroism and a glory that float free from the glory of God in Christ. Athanasius, like Paul, repudiates such a thought; for both, and for the Christian vision of heroism, there is no glory outside of Christ.

Yet, even as Athanasius warns against venerating Anthony's bones, he cherishes Anthony's cloak and sheepskin, given to him after his death, as "great treasure." He describes their value in a way that restates his vision of Christian heroism. The talismans of Anthony's life are priceless, "for even seeing these is like beholding Anthony, and wearing them is like bearing his admonitions with joy" (para. 92). For Athanasius, Anthony's disciplines, trial, and triumphs shaped him into an icon of Christ, and to behold him and marvel at his glory is to behold and marvel at the glory of God in Christ. The cloak and sheepskin, like the *Life of Anthony* itself, rekindle the memory of Anthony's Christ-like life and vivifies his pattern of holiness. They are then great treasures, pointing to the surpassing glory of God.

With this combination of a strict Pauline commitment to transparency, and an equally strong commitment to a real and personal participation in the glory of Jesus' singular and universal achievement, Athanasius establishes the poetic task of Christian heroism. One must describe a heroic disciple fleshly enough to wear cloaks and sleep on sheepskins, yet translucent and spiritual enough to mirror Christ rather than himself. The early medieval poem the *Song of Roland* offers a useful illustration of how weighty heroes are so often opaque to Christ. The heroes of the *Song of Roland* are vivid and their action full of pathos. But Christ and the power of grace function in a purely external manner. Charlemagne has pieces of Jesus' cross embedded in the hilt of his sword, and the poet conceives of the conflict against the Islamic invaders as a defense of the honor of Christ against the shame of pagan infidelity. However, none of the characters takes on Christ-like form, either in motive or action. The heroes are real and the glory tangible, but the greater glory of God in Christ functions only as the distant horizon for the dramatic action. The reader cannot cherish Roland, his courage and his devotion, and in so doing be confident, as Athanasius was of his glorification of Anthony, that Roland will bring one closer to Christ.

Our interest, however, is not to analyze a heroism that is only nominally Christian. We do not intend to understand Christian heroism through its failed and partial expression. Instead, we wish to enter into the complex nuances of successful depictions of heroic transparency to Christ. To that end, we now turn to Edmund Spenser and John Milton, two early modern poets who embraced Athanasius's difficult task: to describe a human undertaking and achievement that yields an entirely Christian heroism.

Chapter Seven

The Poets of Christian Heroism:
Spenser and Milton

Then I saw heaven opened, and there was a white horse! Its
rider is called Faithful and True, and in righteousness he
judges and makes war.

Revelation 19:11

Put on the whole armor of God, so that you may be able to
stand against the wiles of the devil.

Ephesians 6:11

In the atmosphere of persecution, whether expulsion from the syna-
gogue or death in the Roman arena, imitative participation in the glory
of Jesus was obvious and visible. The subtle and internal conformity to
Christ that Paul so vigorously advocates is clarified in the deaths suffered
by Ignatius and Polycarp. The outward trial or test reveals—and in the
case of Polycarp, nearly surpasses—inward faith. Christians can offer the
palm of heroic recognition to someone other than Jesus, because in glorifying the martyrs, the form of Christ himself is glorified. The pattern of
imitation brings Jesus to the fore, and in glorifying the martyr, Jesus is
magnified as the faithful disciple is assimilated to the pattern of Christ.
The church presents the lives of the martyrs for admiration and imitation, but always under Paul's description: not them, but Christ in them.

Not all enjoy opportunities for martyrdom. As the classical world
became the Christian world, temptation superseded persecution as the
testing arena in which faith becomes visible. In the deserts of Egypt or
the villas of Cassiciacum, new saints created new orders. Monastic and
communal patterns of devotion were modeled on Anthony and his quest
for holiness, and a pattern of sanctity emerged which, though serving
Christ, was not strictly and transparently Christ-like. In this new pattern

the heroes of sanctity slide away from a straightforward recapitulation of Jesus' passion, and they take on an independent significance as founders and exemplars of a new way of life. The literary challenge of hagiography rests in drawing this independence into the orbit of the Pauline vision. However different the outward pattern, the inward path of faith must recapitulate rather than replace Jesus' heroism.

Because the Pauline vision of transparency defines the ideal toward which monastic sanctity strives, the most important pattern for the medieval world was Francis of Assisi. His achievement was renunciation: of social standing, wealth, family, even clothing and shelter. This crucifixion of self marks his participation in divine glory, and it leads to one of the most striking images of the medieval period: the beggar conqueror. Museums are full of art representing Francis's triumphs: casting demons from a city, taking the gospel to the sultan, preaching to the birds of the wild. As important as these manifestations of heroic potency are, Francis's triumphs culminate in his absorption into Jesus, so much so that he was honored with the marks of Jesus' wounds. The inward transparency was so complete that an outward transparency followed, as both consummation and culmination. With the stigmata, Francis achieved his quest for a purely Christ-like sanctity. The poverty he chose made his conformity to Jesus visible, and the monastic quest for holiness folded back into the martyr's way of transparency.

Dante was a great proponent of this Franciscan ideal, and he offers a remarkable assessment of Francis's achievement. Francis is the highest saint in the *Paradiso.* Guided by Aquinas, Dante hears the story of Francis, but as allegory, not as realistic description. Francis's life is presented as a marriage to Lady Poverty. The allegorical form, which merges the real and the symbolic, erases the distinction between inward and outward forms of poverty. Lady Poverty is not only outwardly poor, as her name suggests, but inwardly. She has been abandoned and unloved, "despised and scorned" (11.65). To marry Lady Poverty, Francis embraces self-scorn. Moreover, under the plasticity of allegory, Francis can be both himself and a figure of Christ. His marriage echoes the union of the Son of God with sinful flesh, as well as Christ's marriage to his church (cf. Eph. 5:22–33). The allegory expresses his complete participation in Christ. Franciscan poverty is finally spiritual, an evacuation of one's self to make room for Christ within. For Dante, then, Francis represents the fulfillment of the Pauline ideal: "Not I, but Christ in me."[1]

With Protestantism, the Pauline ideal becomes systematically central.[2] The very name "Protestantism" comes from a protest against and rejection of "works righteousness," a form of Christian ambition that depends on the distinctive acts and achievements of the believer. Luther built his message on Paul's unequivocal emphasis on the prevenient love of God: "By grace you have been saved through faith, and this is not your doing; it is the gift of God" (Eph. 2:8). We are justified by faith, not by works. Calvin expresses this same dependence on God with a stark message of predestination. Before the foundation of the world, some were chosen for salvation, some for perdition. Calvin warns against probing the mystery of God's choice, but the doctrine of predestination clearly guards against the illusion that we achieve our own salvation. It is not our doing, and as such, the glory of the elect is God's alone. In this way, whether with an emphasis on justification by faith, or through a belief in predestination, Protestant theologies affirm the heroic priority of God.

In such a system of thought, the role of human participation can be minimized by the singular emphasis on grace. For example, in classical doctrines of atonement, grace is understood as the divine forgiveness of sin won in Jesus' sacrifice on the cross. We can see how this is grace; it is an unmerited deliverance from a just punishment. And we can see how such an obedient sacrifice wins Jesus all honor and praise. But how can this forgiveness of sin be linked to a transformation of our character? If grace is an external gift, how can it ever become an internal possession or achievement? We can receive the gift—but can we participate in it as an accomplishment? Our actions seem to contribute only to the need for grace, not its fulfillment or its furtherance. The same set of problems emerges from an emphasis on predestination. The power of divine election is unquestioned, and it tends to overwhelm the human frame of reference. We might struggle and seek holiness, but the drama of our lives is always already established by the eternal decision of God. Predestination may secure all glory for God, but it can all too easily turn Christian faith into a fate given but not chosen, decreed but not inhabited. We seem near the realm of Vergil, for whom the individual man Aeneas draws significance from the greatness of the city he is destined to found, and whose participation in that greatness is seemingly tenuous.

The Protestant Reformation never doubted that grace could be inhabited nor that predestined salvation could be a drama of personal significance. Luther insisted that, through grace, Christ dwells within the faithful as an active and personal potency. Calvin's theology of predestination included a strong emphasis on the sanctifying power of Christ in word and sacrament. However, we do not wish to pursue the question of human participation in grace by way of systematic theology. Instead, we propose to examine the literary arguments of two great Protestant poets, Edmund Spenser and John Milton. Living in the century and a half after the first seeds of the English Reformation, their works are seminal poetic examinations of the human life charged with divine power. Both undertake to portray a Christian hero, one who participates in grace, and in so doing, takes on a personal excellence. The gift of grace has sins to overcome and triumphs to achieve, and this give epic drama to the life of discipleship. As a result there must be room and scope for *our* achievements. Yet the Christian hero does not rival or supersede God, the sole source of grace. Heroic achievement is ours but in a carefully circumscribed sense. For both Spenser and Milton, Christian heroism is Pauline, for the achievement is always *Christ's,* working *in* the hero.

Although Spenser and Milton never doubt the reach and reality of Christian heroism, they must labor poetically. They must describe this heroism—real and human—without tempting the reader to think in human scale rather than divine. They must depict heroes who are the consequence and not the alternatives to God's heroism. Spenser approaches this difficult task through symbol and allegory. His epic poem, *The Faerie Queene,* follows Ariosto's epic of romance, *Orlando Furioso,* which traces several heroes through different episodes. This allows Spenser to presuppose the singular role of God as the unspoken horizon of the action, while depicting the many roles of his followers. The several books of *The Faerie Queene,* then, follow the adventures of a series of symbolic knights. At the didactic level, these figures quest for the achievement of particular Christian virtues. However, Spenser's allegory is not only didactic, but also theoretical and theological. In the plastic world of allegory, he coordinates divine grace with human achievement. With plume and shield, the Pauline hero emerges.

Like Spenser, Milton adopts the heroic genre of epic. Milton, however, proceeds not through a sequence of allegorical romances, but focuses his efforts on producing a Vergilian, narrative epic with a single hero. Without an allegorical scrim, he confronts the problem head-on. *Paradise Lost* tells the story of God's creation and the fall of Satan and Adam, and *Paradise Regained* tells the story of the human and divine Jesus, and his restoration of man. Taken together, the two epics draw their characters and action from the biblical narratives, the only ones Milton thought authoritative, and narratives in which God is the singular hero. Of course, he does not simply retell the biblical story. His imaginative embellishments have so captured the Christian imagination that his account of the Fall nearly supersedes the story in Genesis. But embellishment is not his chief goal. Milton's main purpose is to identify and parse roles of divine and human power and agency in order to clarify the limits and possibilities of human heroism in an epic in which God is the surpassing hero.

Spenser and Milton are the first theoreticians of Christian heroism whom we consider. They self-consciously seek to appropriate not only the poetic imagery but also the heroic sensibilities of Homer and Vergil in order to explain and underline the Pauline vision of Christian heroism. Faithful to the Christian faith and hope, they present poetic accounts of the human person enlarged and perfected by grace. For both, the way of discipleship is the singular path toward an everlasting glory, and as such, they are confident that such a life is epic in scope and accomplishment. Whatever achievement the ancient poets thought worthy of poetic admiration and memorial, both Spenser and Milton thought that such heroism was surpassed by the glory made possible in Christ. For both, then, the heroic tropes of epic—its emphasis on testing conflict, its symbols of victory and badges of honor—are fitting raw material for the Christian poet. We may laud and magnify the hero of faith, just as Homer does for Achilles. The heroic disciple may serve as a model for our own lives, as Socrates was for Plato. Like Aeneas, the Christian hero participates in an eternal glory. Yet, in each instance, this use of heroic tropes does not stem from any innate or earned qualities possessed by the disciple. Here, Spenser and Milton break completely with the classical view of the hero. An epic of discipleship is possible solely because of the triumphant heroism of God. By grace alone does the hero of faith find a role in the Christian epic.

These appropriations by Spenser and Milton of classical devices for depicting the hero result in vast, magnificent poetic performances. It is beyond our scope to offer comprehensive explication and analysis of either author. Rather, we want to highlight specific poetic scenes that exemplify their visions of the hero as both grace dependent and genuinely worthy of recognition. To this end, we will treat books 1 and 2 of *The Faerie Queene*. Book 1 outlines the quest for holiness, the basis for Christian heroism, and book 2 treats its executive virtue, temperance. In both cases, Spenser artfully coordinates human agency and divine grace in order to fashion a distinctively Christian hero. Because Milton's epics are driven by narrative rather than allegory, which lends itself to self-contained units of episode and symbol, we cannot isolate illustrative passages. Instead, we will use his attack on censorship, the prose work *Areopagitica,* to bring our reading of *Paradise Regained* into focus. In the

Areopagitica, Milton argues that the disciple needs the test of temptation in order to fully realize the inner potency of faith. In *Paradise Regained,* the test of temptation is the focus. Jesus triumphs by resisting Satan's sustained effort to tempt him toward an active heroism that stands independent from God's sustaining grace.

SPENSER: THE QUEST FOR HOLINESS

The first book of *The Faerie Queene,* "The Legende of the Knight of the Red Crosse, or of Holinesse," describes the material basis for Christian heroism. The order of the books, and of the virtues they examine, is not random but cumulative; each virtue is built upon the one preceding. By placing holiness first, Spenser signals that all the virtues have their foundation in holiness. Without holiness, there is no virtue pleasing to God. But holiness is not simply a gift of grace; it is the object of quest, and thus a genuinely human project. Spenser presents this quest for holiness in the figure of a newly baptized knight, Redcrosse, who is marked for Christ with the sign of the cross on his shield. Narratively, Redcrosse quests on behalf of Una, whose land, Eden, and whose parents, the king and queen, are oppressed by a dragon from hell. But his quest is not simply a chivalric romance. The quest has an outward object—freeing Una's parents from their thrall to the dragon—but in keeping with the transferring power of allegory, it has an inner motivation and purpose as well. Una and the Edenic land of her parents signal that sinless perfection toward which Redcrosse quests.

Redcrosse, "full of fire and greedy hardiment" (1.i.14) begins his quest eager to prove his piety.[3] Yet through misadventure after misadventure, he proves rather the inadequacy of the outward signs of faith. To wear "on his brest a bloudie Crosse," even with heartfelt and undying faith, is insufficient. One must dwell in one's faith; it must become the animating principle of an active life that seeks a personal holiness. As Una says to Redcrosse at the outset, articulating the singular didactic imperative of book 1, "Add faith vnto your force" (1.i.19). The point is not that Redcrosse's faith is questionable. Spenser does not use misadventure in order to undermine the efficacy of baptism, or to suggest that Redcrosse teeters on the edge of faithlessness. Redcrosse falls into ignorance and sin, not unbelief. Nor is the cross-marked knight portrayed as innately weak; he consistently slays enemies and displays his "puissance." Rather, the complex drama of misadventure in book 1 concerns the difficulty of wedding faith with force, the difficulty of joining the human potency for action and achievement with the divine vocation of faith. The internal power of human character must merge with the outward sign of the cross in order for Redcrosse to fulfill his quest and achieve the Pauline vision of Christian heroism: transparency to Christ.

The first and dominant misadventure of Redcrosse is his separation from Una, his Lady fair. She represents purity and spiritual discernment, and through the deceptions of Archimago, Redcrosse ceases to recognize her for what and who she is. He abandons Una and soon after meets with the image of false purity and false spiritual judgment, appropriately named Duessa. She introduces herself to him as Fidessa, and in the context of the allegory, she represents the false papist faith, urging him to impious acts of piety. This false companion's consummating deception occurs when she guides him to compete in jousts in the House of Pride, symbolizing the traditional Christian insight into false piety: that one might use acts of outward faith for the purposes of self-aggrandizement. The didactic level of allegory is clear. If the image of Christ is made opaque by our vainglory, if we are the focal point of recognition, then faith has not been added to force. Outward signs of piety themselves become a deception, one of many ways to elevate oneself in the eyes of the world. Pious acts, in this sense, cannot be our own acts, and the glory of faith can not be our glory. Holiness cannot be won by human merit. Redcrosse's jousting victories must be transparent to the symbol on his shield, not to his own force, and his further misadventures spring from this need to subordinate his force to faith, for Redcrosse cannot achieve his quest apart from this unity.

Spenser not only shows this need for unity at the level of didactic allegory but also illustrates the difficulty and necessity of unifying faith and force at a theoretical level. Given the narrative device of the quest, Spenser must work against the presumption that faith is a heroic achievement. As Redcrosse's time in the House of Pride reveals, we are profoundly mistaken if we imagine that we derive any merit from our faith, as if it manifests a certain strength of character: a powerful will-to-believe, a victory of personal meaning against the abyss of Nothingness, a flash of transcendent insight. Faith is a gift of grace; it comes from without. Nonetheless our faith must become effective and active; it must be personal even as it finds its source in the external power of God. For Spenser, Redcrosse's martial force represents innate personal potency and power. Such inner resources propel Redcrosse forward on his quest. The theoretical level of allegory is devoted to showing how a faith that is wedded to this personal force becomes effective and active but utterly remote from the House of Pride. As Paul says enigmatically, but clearly, in his correspondence to the Corinthians, "I labored even more than all of them, yet not I, but the grace of God with me" (1 Cor. 15:10). Spenser's goal in book 1 of *The Faerie Queene* is to give the transparent flesh of allegorical action to this Pauline affirmation of heroic labor that is both his own and yet God's alone.

Three scenes illuminate Spenser's subtle vision of the quest toward the Pauline goal. The first finds Redcrosse in Orgoglio's prison. Orgoglio's name means "pride," and the particular way in which Redcrosse escapes testifies to the pure externality and unmerited quality of grace. Force of character cannot carry the knight forward. The second scene takes place after Redcrosse enters the House of Holiness in order to recover from his imprisonment to pride. From the culminating vision on the Mount of Contemplation, Redcrosse must return to the arena of trial and action. An inactive faith cannot achieve the quest; in order for grace to come into action, force must be added to faith. The third scene provides an extended allegory of the unity of faith and force. Fighting the dragon that has enslaved Eden, Redcrosse toggles back and forth between symbols of Christian dependence on grace and vigorous independent and worldly actions, just as Paul toggles back and forth, commending to the Corinthians his "labors"—"even more than all of them"—and God's grace. From a force without its source in faith, to a faith that lacks force, in these three episodes, Spenser builds toward a unity of faith and force in Redcrosse, the knight of holiness.

As a preamble to the scene in Orgoglio's prison, Spenser pulls aside the veil of allegory in the first stanza, as he often does, to articulate the didactic point of the coming action:

> Ay me, how many perils doe enfold
>   The righteous man, to make him daily fall?
>   Were not, that heauenly grace doth him vphold,
>   And stedfast truth acquite him out of all.
>   Her loue is firme, her care continuall,
>   So oft as he through his owne foolish pride,
>   Or weaknesse is to sinfull bands made thrall:
>   Else should this *Redcrosse* knight in bands haue dyde,
> For whose deliuerance she this Prince doth thither guide.
>   (1.viii.1)

Redcrosse "doth lucklesse lie" in the prison of Orgoglio, "Thrall to that Gyants hatefull tyrannie" (1.viii.2). Allegorically dispersed among the characters of the story, God's benevolent love and effective grace offers rescue. Una has learned of Redcrosse's predicament and has enjoined Arthur to rescue Redcrosse. Una needs Arthur's help, since she, as spiritual innocence, has no experience with pride. Redcrosse, too, needs Arthur's help, since his own power alone, however spiritual and animated by right desire, cannot break the bonds of pride—indeed, his faith in spiritual achievement has landed him in pride's prison. Thus, Arthur's rescue of Redcrosse offers Spenser an opportunity to elaborate on the necessity and effectiveness of external grace.

Arthur's squire Timias approaches Orgoglio's castle and sounds his trumpet to signal Arthur's advance. Before Timias's (honor's) trumpet blast, "Euery dore of freewill open flew" (1.viii.5), suggesting that pride's fantasies of false honor cannot stand before the force of true honor. The castle is not the only symbol of empty pride. When Arthur kills the giant Orgoglio, "That huge great body, which the Gyaunt bore, / Was vanisht quite, and of that monstrous mas / Was nothing left, but like an emptie bladder was" (1.viii.24). Spenser, by making Orgoglio's prison and its master ominous and powerful, but porous and hollow, hints that the prisoners of pride cooperate in their own imprisonment. Sin has no power but that which the sinner gives. One must believe in the efficacy of one's own personal force in order to fall victim to pride. After Arthur enters the prison, he takes the iron keys from the "auncient keeper of that place," senile Ignaro, whose keys of knowledge have grown rusty from disuse (1.viii.30). With those keys, "Each dore he opened without any breach; / There was no barre to stop, nor foe him to empeach" (1.viii.34). Like honor, knowledge punctures the pretensions of pride. But there is no key of knowledge for the iron door that imprisons Redcrosse, so Arthur "rent that yron door"[4] and hauls the "pined corse" of Redcrosse into the light. The prison of pride requires more than a key of knowledge. The prisoner of pride cannot free himself, not even with knowledge of pride's false and empty honor. Arthur, an external power, must break down the door and pull Redcrosse from pride.

Arthur is the knight perfected through God's grace and the symbol of Christ himself. He is both the bearer of grace, and grace itself. The reader's uncertainty about his identity reflects Arthur's already-achieved Pauline heroism. Spenser's allegorical conflation of Arthur, the perfect disciple, with Christ, his master, reiterates Paul's self-description: "Not I, but Christ in me." Arthur labors "even more than all of them," and yet not on his own, but with the grace of God in him. In this way, Arthur represents the external grace that Redcrosse must add to his force—Arthur saves Redcrosse—as well as the unification of faith and force which Redcrosse must become—Arthur is the exemplary hero. To guide the fallen knight toward the achievement of his quest, Arthur gives advice to Redcrosse: "Maister these mishaps with patient might" (1.viii.45).

This mastery cannot come from within; it must be "patient" and not "agent." Released from the prison of pride, Redcrosse has learned of the inadequacy of his own martial force. He cannot achieve the quest by his own power and strength, and this knowledge drives him to Despair, the personification of self-accusation. Redcrosse's self-dependent efforts have led to misadventure and not progress toward the achievement of his quest, and this casts a dark shadow of futility over the entire project of human life. When Redcrosse is brought to the brink of suicide by the accusations of Despair, however, Una intercedes and reminds him of the foundation of "patient might." Redcrosse should not despair of his own power, for God has not sent his follower to quest without his aide. Interposing the word of grace, Una asks, "In heauenly mercies hast thou not a part? / Why shouldst thou then despeire, that chosen art?" (1.ix.53). No amount of dialectical cleverness can defeat the arguments of Despair. As long as Redcrosse depends on his own strength rather than on grace, he is subject to the prison of pride and the recriminations of despair. But if he depends on grace, then his sinful inadequacy is covered by the surpassing power and purity of grace.

To facilitate his dependence on grace, Una brings Redcrosse to the House of Holiness. His limitations have been made all too apparent, and Spenser again steps back from allegory to make his general point clear:

> What man is he, that boasts of fleshly might,
>   And vaine assurance of mortality,
>   Which all so soone, as it doth come to fight,
>   Against spirituall foes, yeelds by and by,
>   Or from the field most cowardly doth fly?
>   Ne let that man ascribe it to his skill,
>   That thorough grace hath gained victory.
>   If any strength we haue, it is to ill,
> But all the good is Gods, both power and eke will.[5]
>   (1.x.1)

Redcrosse is so enfeebled from his previous travails and imprisonments that he is "vnfit for bloudie fight" (1.x.2). Redcrosse is debilitated, not because *his* strength is inadequate; his natural potency of character makes him a great warrior. Rather, he is "feeble and too faint" because the object of the quest transcends human power. His fitness does not depend on his natural powers but must be a matter of God's grace. This is the painful lesson he learns in the House of Holiness, painful because it requires an internal change, a drastic reorientation of the basis for his quest. Redcrosse learns the "wretched world . . . to abhore" (1.x.21); he is purged of "Inward corruption and infected sin" (1.x.25); he feels the lash and sting of bitter Penance, sharp Remorse, sad Repentance (1.x.27); and his conscience is cured (1.x.29). Redcrosse can only be fit for the "bloudie fight" necessary to achieve his quest insofar as he is dependent on grace.

In an arresting moment of insight, however, Spenser acknowledges that profound dependence on grace is itself incomplete in the attainment of the quest. After his rigorous disciplines, Redcrosse ascends the mount of the old hermit Contemplation, who gives him a vision of the new Hierusalem, the eternal city of heaven, which surpasses even Cleopolis, the earthly city of fame. This is an explicit echo of Aeneas's descent into the Underworld and his encounter with Anchises. Of course, as a Christian poet, Spenser offers a corrective to Vergil's reincarnative view of Rome and the true nature of blessedness. But just as Vergil has Aeneas bewildered at the souls' desire to return to life after he has seen the satisfactions of Elysium, Spenser has Redcrosse express a desire to abandon his earthly quest and enter into the heavenly kingdom: "O let me not (quoth he) then turne againe / Back to the world, whose ioyes so fruitlesse are" (1.x.63). Given the lessons learned in the House of Holiness, such a desire is understandable, but it is antiheroic. Both Spenser and Vergil agree on the necessity of enactment.[6] Redcrosse may no more forsake earthly life by way of mystical retreat than by way of suicide. He must fulfill his quest: to battle the dragon that oppresses Una's land and to restore the rule of her parents. His descent from the mount of Contemplation marks the need for enactment; faith must find force in the world. Within the conceit of chivalric romance, Spenser demonstrates the necessity of both sides—of faith and of force—for the attainment of Redcrosse's quest, and by extension, for true Christian heroism.

Redcrosse arrives in the land of Una's parents, called Eden, which is beseiged by a dragon bred in hell. Spenser lavishes detail on the dragon—his bulk, brazen scales, deadly tail, iron teeth, and fiery eyes and breath—to emphasize the Achillean nature of this public conflict. Heroic enactment of the God-given potency of faith admits of a grand scale. At first, Redcrosse appears to be no match for the dragon "that made the Redcrosse knight nigh quake for feare" (1.xi.15). He is tested by the very sight of the dragon, reminding the reader that human potency alone is insufficient. Fearful or not, he does fight, and there are three encounters, on successive days. In their first battle, the dragon burns him with fire. Redcrosse's armor heats up and causes searing pain. Like the "poysoned garment" of Heracles, Redcrosse's armor "that erst him goodly arm'd, now most of all him harm'd" (1.xi.27). In his battle with sin, his faith, symbolized by his armor, becomes painful to bear, and Redcrosse's allegorical figure now recalls the martyr burned by flames of persecution. His figure begins to become transparent to Christ. As Redcrosse falls toward death, he lands in a "springing well" of baptismal waters. This "well of life" restores Redcrosse, and with intensive emphasis on the renewing power of grace, Spenser writes, "So new this new-borne knight to battell new did rise" (1.xi.34).

On their second day of battle, Redcrosse is able to inflict more damage on the dragon, but he cannot yet defeat him. He is felled by the dragon's sting of death, and this time he falls at the foot of the tree of life. From the tree of life flows a "trickling streame of Balme" which could "reare again the senseless corse." It does so for Redcrosse, and once again, grace "did from death him saue" (1.xi.48). Thus restored to life, on the third day Redcrosse finally kills the dragon by driving his sword through its mouth. By his dependence on the healing balm of grace, Redcrosse is victorious. The victory completes Redcrosse's quest, and the final battle takes on a cosmic, salvific scope as a triumph over sin and death and the restoration of spiritual purity. The dragon of death is dead, and Eden is returned to its original harmony. Thus, the reader sees Redcrosse not only as completing his quest with the romance of the literal sense of the narrative, but also as an allegory of the exemplary Christian disciple. The young warrior has been transformed from the naturally strong but benighted man of faith into the Christ-like man of God.

Una meets Redcrosse on the battlefield after his victory. When she sees the "ioyous end" of his quest, "Then God she praysd, and thankt her faithfull knight, / That had atchieu'd so great a conquest by his might" (1.xi.55). Her words capture the conflation of the divine and the human in Spenser's unification of faith and force in Redcrosse. By this point of the allegory, Spenser hopes to have educated his reader in the proper understanding of the nature of Redcrosse's might and Una's recognition of his heroism. Like Aeneas, Redcrosse participates in a glory greater than the sum of his actions. Unlike Vergil, however, Spenser does not traffic in ambiguity or subtle suggestiveness about the nature of Redcrosse's participation in this greater glory. There is no question about the source and character of Redcrosse's successful quest. No thin thread of passion connects the hero to his destined achievement. Instead, it is grace-dependent, and subject to neither pride nor despair. Spenser is following Paul. Redcrosse never ceases to be a human, but in his human form he reenacts Christ's actions in conquering sin and death and redeeming Eden. As Redcrosse's victory allegorically recapitulates the victory of Jesus, whom God raised from death to glory, the knight of faith becomes transparent to Jesus in his sufferings and in his victory.

GUYON: ACHIEVING RESTRAINT

Holiness is the basis for Christian heroism, and book 1 has a strong theological interest in explaining how holiness is necessary for an active Christian life. However, we have to be convinced of more than its possibility; Spenser has to guide us also to the specific virtues that constitute such a life. Book 2 embarks on this task and the specific virtue illustrated in this book is temperance. Spenser's choice of virtue is not random: temperance serves as the executive virtue of the Christian life.

> Of all Gods workes, which do this world adorne,
>   There is no one more faire and excellent,
>   Then is mans body both for powre and forme,
>   Whiles it is kept in sober gouernment;
>   But none then it, more fowle and indecent,
>   Distempred through misrule and passions bace:
>   It growes a Monster, and incontinent
>   Doth loose his dignitie and native grace.
>   (2.ix.1)

Stability of character and self-restraint allow God to use the knight for his own purposes. Force, disciplined by temperance, is put at the disposal of faith. Thus, the quest for temperance fits the allegorical meaning of the quest of holiness, for temperance offers no rivalry with God. Quite the contrary, temperance is an achievement that prepares the way for God's heroic actions in and through the believer.

The aged Palmer, Guyon's guide and advisor throughout the book, has suffered at the hands of Acrasia (how, we are not told). He brings his complaint before Gloriana, and she commissions Guyon to seek redress for the Palmer (2.ii.43). With this, the structure of the quest is fairly straightforward. Acrasia, whose name means "weakness of will," and who dwells in the Bower of Bliss, must be conquered. Along the way to the

Bower, Guyon does battle with two brothers, Pyrochles and Cymochles. Pyrochles represents the fire of impetuosity. Cymochles, as his name implies, fluctuates between extremes, sometimes fiery like his brother, other times under the indolent sway of Acrasia.[7] Guyon meets with worldly temptations in his journey: he encounters the vile hag Occasion, loses his horse to the coward Braggadocchio, is spirited off by the frivolous maiden Phaedria. At each juncture he is tempted by the patently sinful extremes of uncontrolled passion or satisfied indolence. We intend to concentrate on two extended scenes of Guyon's temptation, in the cave of Mammon and in the Bower of Bliss. In both cases he is successful, but in the cave of Mammon his success is blank and lacks result, while his temperate journey into the Bower of Bliss culminates in its destruction. We will argue that the difference between these two outcomes constitutes Spenser's most important didactic point about the virtue of temperance, and by extension, Christian heroism in general: it must be active.

The cave of Mammon presents Guyon with the temptation of base worldly wealth and acclaim. Within the cave he is subjected to three temptations. Mammon offers riches as the key to "the worldes blis" and the goal "to which all men do ayme" (2.vii.32). Guyon rejects this false fulfillment of his quest. The happiness that he seeks is "in armes, and in atchieuements brave," not in possessions (2.vii.33). Mammon carefully forms his second temptation. He presents the busy world of commerce as a heroic enterprise, full of accomplishment. But Guyon sees the scramble for wealth as a "vaine shew" and states, "All that I need I haue" (2.vii.39). For his third temptation, Mammon offers marriage to his daughter Philotime, "Love of Honor." She represents worldly recognition and all its trappings of wealth and privilege. Guyon does desire honor, and his response to Mammon lacks the dismissiveness of his first two temptations. However, Spenser is working from the foundation of holiness, and honor, however visible and public, is otherworldly in both source and aspiration. Therefore, Guyon protests that he is betrothed to another lady. (Perhaps, in the nimbus clouds of allegory, his lady is the church, or Glorianna, the queen of Fairieland; Spenser gives no clue). Her honor, not Philotime's, must be his goal.

The cave of Mammon has been a fruitless exercise in restraint; Guyon's is a passive rather than active temperance. Of course, the dangers are quite real. Guyon is followed through the cave by a hell-fiend "Threatening with greedy gripe to do him dye / And rend in peeces with his ravenous pawes" (2.vii.27). But Guyon is unmoved because he desires none of it. Nothing that he faces in the cave of Mammon appears to

Guyon as anything but perversion, as "ensample of mind intemperate" (2.vii.40). Because of his temperate character, he avoids disaster, but just this passive or negative accomplishment marks his tour. Guyon emerges from the "hardie enterprize" of the cave of Mammon after three days of testing, and overcome by the "vitall aire" and "liuing light," he swoons rather than manifests triumphant vigor (2.vii.66).

Is the cave of Mammon, then, a sinful venture for Guyon? Is Spenser warning his readers that the temperate man should not advance into unnecessary tests and trials? Is Spenser being more literal, saying only that his human figure is hungry and sleep-deprived, reminding us of the malnourishing emptiness and poverty of worldly riches? For our purposes, Spenser's didactic message is more subtle, and more central to the nature of the temperance he is commending. Inner stength alone is insufficient for the heroic life. The cave of Mammon has been entered and exited without any consequence other than survival, and this signals Guyon's failure, not of constancy and resistance to temptation—after all, he does succeed in this sense—but in active, forceful achievement. Like Redcrosse, who must leave the mount of Contemplation and exercise his faith, so must Guyon do more than observe vice and abstain. He must act in order to achieve his quest.

The Bower of Bliss is one of Spenser's most masterful creations, theologically as well as poetically. Unlike the cave of Mammon, the Bower of Bliss touches Guyon, and Spenser intends it to touch his readers. Acrasia is mistress of the Bower of Bliss, and she is the "witch" whose demise is Guyon's quest. With Pyrochles, Acrasia serves as one of the two extremes that Guyon must mediate between: the lack of all power of will (Acrasia) and the fiery impetuosity of impulse (Pyrochles). But for the soul of temperance, Acrasia provides the more resonant temptation, because Guyon's own virtue, temperance, resembles indolence more than it resembles impetuosity. If he is to avoid this indolent, inactive side of temptation, then Guyon cannot tour the Bower as he did the cave of Mammon, with serene detachment.

Spenser signals the dangers of resemblance in his description of the Bower of Bliss. The Bower itself is filled with things lovely: the singing of birds, the growth of foliage, the splashing of waters. All is in perfect harmony, but at every turn, Spenser observes that such beauty is grounded in artifice and "semblance." Yet Guyon does not enter as an observer, as he did the cave of Mammon. His figure is active, and he does not wait for a guide or companion. When the gateskeeper Genius offers him his bowl of wine, Guyon "ouerthrew his bowle disdainfully; / And broke his staffe." When Excesse offers him her liquor, he "The cup to ground did violently

cast, / That all in peeces it was broken fond" (2.xii.49, 57). The beauty of
the place is supranatural, and therefore unnatural, and Guyon's ever-
temperate soul is unmoved:

> Much wondred Guyon at the faire aspect
>   Of that sweet place, yet suffred no delight
>   To sincke into his sence, nor mind affect,
>   But passed forth, and lookt still forward right,
>   Bridling his will, and maistering his might.
>   (2.xii.53)

His wonder without delight, his detached urgency, is challenged only by
"two naked Damzelles" cavorting in the lake. The "lilly paps aloft dis-
playd" arrest his step and attract his "melting hart" (2.xii.66). Spenser
does not dwell long on the internal processes of Guyon, however,
because they pass in an instant. The Palmer "much rebukt those wan-
dring eyes of his," and they wander no more (2.xii.69). Immediately
Guyon exercises his temperance internally. He is called back to his quest,
his active task: the destruction of the Bower of Bliss.

The conclusion of the quest comes quickly. They find Acrasia herself
in a bed of roses with a lover, bedewed with the pearls of postcoital sweat.
She lies slack, dreamy and preoccupied, fawning on her captive lover, her
loveliness covered only with a gauzy, translucent veil. Her lover, "some
goodly swayne of honorable place," sleeps (2.xii.79). His weapons hang
in a nearby tree, unused, and "his braue shield, full of old moniments, /
Was fowly ra'st, that none the signes might see" (2.xii.80). He is careless
of his honor and his quest "that did to his aduauncement tend." The
Palmer and Guyon approach unnoticed and rush upon them with "a sub-
tile net" from which they cannot escape. Acrasia they bind in "chaines of
adamant" (2.xii.82). The goodly swain, named Verdant, they release and
counsel.[8] And then Guyon destroys the Bower:

> But all those pleasant bowres and Pallace braue,
>   Guyon broke downe, with rigour pittilesse;
>   Ne ought their goodly workmanship might saue
>   Them from the tempest of his wrathfulnesse,
>   But that their blisse he turn'd to balefulnesse:
>   Their groues he feld, their gardins did deface,
>   Their arbors spoyle, their Cabinets suppresse,
>   Their banket houses burne, their buildings race,
> And of the fairest late, now made the fowlest place.
>   (2.xii.83)

Nothing is allowed to remain of the artificial fantasies. Echoing Aeneas's final blaze of anger, Guyon's temperance becomes passionate, even wrathful, as he puts it into action and attains his quest. His action in destruction clearly separates him from the serene indifference of a false and artificial temperance that would become as tolerant and indolent as Acrasia herself.

In the destruction of the Bower of Bliss, Spenser signals two allegorical themes. The first is didactic. In the figure of Guyon, Spenser steers us away from a weak, passive view of temperance. We too easily imagine that temperance has a private, internal goal. We can think it a self-serving virtue, where the temperate soul stands aside from the swift and violent currents of life. The race for wealth, the fight for honor, the endless search for sexual satisfaction: temperance seems appealing because it rescues us from these fruitless expenditures of time, energy, and passion. Temperance is, of course, internal. The constancy of character and purpose that marks the temperate soul is won with self-discipline. But Guyon's quest extends beyond the internal control of passion; if it had not, then the cave of Mammon would have marked the end of his quest. With the final scene, Spenser's argument, in book 2, is that the internal achievement of temperance is only heroic if it serves a visible, public, and active life. Christian temperance cannot be centripetal, a retreat from the world in order to attain serene imperturbability. Temperance is empty if merely a matter of detachment, for then it is unable to serve the active purposes of the Christian life. The force of passion must be restrained and shaped by temperance, not so as to produce apathy and inaction, but in order for faith to take command of the natural potency of passion. In the Christian life, as Guyon's final act demonstrates, temperance controls the natural passions of the believer toward the end of active discipleship.

The second allegorical meaning is theological, and it recapitulates Spenser's commitment to a Pauline vision of heroic faith. Guyon's quest and his attainment of it have a salvific and transformative effect. Verdant and the other captives of Acrasia (except the hoggish Grill) are released from their bondage to animality and sensual desire. Guyon's quest, then, is a reprise of Redcrosse's consummating victory. The dragon of sin is defeated and Eden restored to its natural state. In this way, the active agency of Guyon's fulfillment of his quest merges with Christ in his active destruction of sin's power and his reversal of sin's effects. Both Guyon and Redcrosse recapitulate the Pauline vision of transparency. Both disciple-knights merge with Christ and reenact his triumph over sin. The allegorical meaning is clear: the Christian is heroic only insofar as his life takes on the form of Christ. The goal of every Christian quest, however filled out materially by the particular contingencies of station, aptitude, and chance, is to vindicate Paul's words as he exercises authority: "Not I, but Christ in me."

MILTON: PRESERVING THE BOWER

Edmund Spenser is much approved by John Milton, not the least because of his success in personalizing the Pauline ideal of Christian heroism. In the *Areopagitica,* Milton cites Spenser favorably as a "sage and serious poet" and a "better teacher than Scotus or Aquinas."[9] But in the example that he gives of Spenser's sagacity, Milton subtly misrepresents the action of *The Faerie Queene.* Milton agrees with the intent of Spenser's allegory—to show how Christian heroism is real and visible—but he modifies the particular pattern for heroic enactment. Speaking of Guyon, the knight of Temperance, Milton says that Spenser "brings him in with his palmer through the cave of Mammon and the bower of earthly bliss, that he might see and know and yet abstain" (729). While this description works for the cave of Mammon, Guyon does more than see and know and abstain from the Bower of Bliss: rather than know it intimately, he razes it to the ground. Guyon adds force to temperance, just as Redcrosse adds force to his faith when triumphing over the dragon. Milton takes a more radical approach. Faith has its own force, and the trajectory of Christian heroism requires no independent action. Against the presumptive need for outward and active achievement, Milton argues that to endure, to "see and know and yet abstain," manifests the inner strength and glory of Christian heroism.

The tract in which Milton so approvingly refers to Spenser distills his vision of Christian heroism, and this vision explains his distortion of Spenser's use of Guyon. Parliment had passed an ordinance requiring licensing for the press, vesting the authority to censor in the ecclesiastical authorities of the Church of England. In the *Areopagitica,* Milton argues against this restriction of printed materials. His arguments are many. He warns against the dangers of clerical control, darkly hinting that such measures will draw England into papalist oppression. He illustrates the ineffectiveness of censorship by drawing on historical examples. He famously argues that intellectual restrictions hinder the progress of truth in its battle against falsehood. He advances an overheated picture of books as persons, and their destruction as very near to murder. However, his most passionate argument is neither political nor philosophical. Milton has intensely theological reasons for rejecting censorship, for it would undermine the possibilities for Christian heroism.

For Milton, like Spenser, Christian virtue must be exercised in order to be fulfilled. The danger of censorship rests in the diminishment of scope for this exercise. To emphasize his point, Milton draws on images of infancy and adulthood. "God," he writes, "uses not to captivate under a perpetual childhood of prescription" (727). Instead, in matters of sin and righteousness, "God commits the managing of so great a trust, without particular law or prescription, wholly to the demeanor of every grown man" (727). This image of the protected child over and against the free adult reflects Milton's view of world history. God created Adam free to sin so that he might win the merit of abstaining (733). Thus, Milton's England should not presume upon God's providence by restricting the scope of temptation through censorship.

Not only does censorship contravene Milton's view of divine providence, it also contradicts his understanding of true virtue and its enactment.

> I cannot praise a fugitive and cloistered virtue, unexercised and unbreathed, that never sallies out and sees her adversary, but slinks out of the race where that immortal garland is to be run for, not without dust and heat. That virtue therefore which is but a youngling in the contemplation of evil, and knows not the utmost that vice promises to her followers, and rejects it, is but a blank virtue, not a pure; her whiteness is but an excremental whiteness (728).

Untested virtue, which Milton deigns "fugitive and cloistered," is for him "blank"; enacted virtue, on the other hand, is "pure." Like Spenser, Milton reasons that the path from "blank" to "pure" requires exercise. Like film exposed but still undeveloped, virtue unexercised is less strong, less substantial, less *itself*, than realized, enacted virtue. Further, like Spenser, for Milton, enacted virtue is combatant, and he too uses martial language in describing victory over foes through conquest and warfare. However, unlike Spenser, Milton applies this language to the single temperate moment of obedience.[10] "He that can apprehend and consider vice with all her baits and seeming pleasures," writes Milton, "and yet abstain, and yet distinguish, and yet prefer that which is truly better, he is the true warfaring Christian" (728). Milton's virtue conquers in an enduring, not a destructive way. The temperate Christian hero participates in a footrace with evil, but he does not fight it to the death or raze it to the ground. The Christian, then, who wishes to run the race of faith, *positively needs* bad books to "apprehend and consider."

The striking conclusion that a reader, fresh from Spenser's allegorical pedagogy, must draw is that Milton does not oppose censorship out of an abstract commitment to tolerance or an imagined rational progress made possible by the free exchange of ideas. He wants to be free to take regular tours of the cave of Mammon and the Bower of Bliss. But Milton is no sensualist, and his desires are far from fleshly; they are motivated entirely by his goal of spiritual perfection. Under no circumstances does Milton want anyone, even a godly knight, to destroy the bower of temptation that provides opportunities to exercise a temperate faith. In short, his apparent hatred of authority, a hatred that manifested itself politically in his support of the beheading of Charles I, is integral to his belief that only in freedom of choice can true heroic virtue exist. Without such scope for the exercise of virtue, without the full range of apprehending, discerning, and abstaining, virtue is blank and not pure, circumstantially imputed, not personally possessed.

Milton does not eschew *all* authority, of course. He is not an individualist with a sunny optimism about the goodness within the heart of every person. His fierce Protestantism encourages his disavowal of all forms of spiritual authority other than God, but God's authority he never questions, and he is absolute in his adherence to the authority of the Bible as God's word. Indeed, Milton's defense of freedom is not motivated by an abstract or general commitment to freedom at all. In this sense, he is far from a modern man. Instead, Milton's defense of free choice grows out of his vision of Christian heroism under the supervening and cosmic achievement of God's omnipotent power. Precisely because God has such real and effective power, the faithful disciple has no great deed to accomplish, no mark to make. Thus, the passive act of temptation endured becomes, for him, the only possible human achievement. Such a temperate hero can give all active glory to God—he alone achieves the greatest of deeds, the defeat of the devil—while still possessing a personal, albeit passive, glory. Take away temptation, as the censorship established by Parliament threatened to do, and the opportunity for Christian heroism is diminished. A lesser test reveals a lesser hero.

In the *Areopagitica,* Milton, more than any other author whom we interpret, shows himself exquisitely aware of one of the questions that guides our study: the difficulty of human heroism under the supervening heroism of God. However, his tracts merely state his conviction. Only in his poetry does Milton set out to convince us of the truth of his vision by describing the Christian hero. Here, he is more ambitious than Spenser. His epic frame is Vergilian, and the hero is necessarily God. Moreover, unlike Spenser, Milton does not use the devices of allegory to parse the elements of heroic action, or to signal theoretical solutions to existential problems. Instead, Milton's epic is a narrative, and the heroic action, however deeply illuminated by his genius for image and argument, takes place within a human, realistic frame of reference. In short, Milton sets out to describe exactly how Christianity can be heroic.

FROM BLANK TO PURE

Milton was a ruthlessly consistent thinker, and his poetry expresses and perfects his insights. The repudiation of Spenser's active, destructive heroism shapes Milton's epic of Jesus' triumph, *Paradise Regained.* Already, in *Paradise Lost,* he foreshadows the heroism that will triumph over the powers of evil. When the fallen Adam asks the archangel Michael for details about the promise of the "capital bruise" that the Serpent will receive, ("say when and where / Their fight" 12.384–85), Michael responds clearly that violence is not the method of this victory, that it will not be "a Duel, or . . . local wounds":

> Not by destroying Satan, but his works
> In thee and in thy Seed: nor can this be,
> But by fulfilling that which thou didst want,
> Obedience to the Law of God.
>
> (12.394–97)

Milton does not disagree with Spenser about the importance of the contest. The excellences of faith must be made manifest in an agonistic context, otherwise, those excellences cannot be recognized and imitated. However, in the *Areopagitica,* Milton signals a change in the terms of victory, and therefore of obedience, shifting from active resistance to enduring and standing. As a result, Milton sets aside a straightforward use of the heroic tropes that Spenser employs to fill out allegorical quests.[11] Milton does more than ignore Guyon's destruction of the Bower of Bliss. He draws the ideal of passive endurance into the center of his Christian epic by rejecting the image of Jesus as triumphant warrior. His heroism does not entail destroying Satan, as Redcrosse kills the dragon and Guyon destroys the Bower of Bliss. He endures Satan, and this constitutes his heroic achievement and epitomizes the goal of Christian discipleship.

In order to effect this change in the content of Christian heroism, Milton shifts the dramatic hinge of Jesus' heroism away from the active potency of Golgotha. For Milton, the epic action in *Paradise Regained* focuses on Satan's test of Jesus in the wilderness. There, Jesus confronts Satan's power privately and secretly, just as Guyon is tempted in the cave of Mammon. Moreover, like Guyon's test, the temptations follow a three-fold pattern. However, Milton clings more closely to the biblical account than does Spenser, and his epic is an exegesis of Luke 4:1–13. Satan first suggests turning stones to bread: "So shalt thou save thyself, and us relieve / With Food" (1.344–45). In this way, he tests Jesus not just with appetite, but with "false pity"[12] and good deeds. The second temptation has Satan offering Jesus all the kingdoms of the world, if only Jesus will fall down and worship him. The final temptation takes Jesus to the pinnacle of the Temple in Jerusalem, where Satan urges Jesus to test the faithfulness of God. All three receive extended treatment, but the second temptation—the offer of worldly dominion and glory—takes up more than half of the poem, and not surprisingly, for it speaks directly to the question that so preoccupies Milton: the nature of Christian heroism.

Satan is defeated on the first day of temptation, and he returns to the infernal realm in order to regroup. Jesus will be difficult to deceive, and Satan is very aware that his task is difficult. "I summon all," says Satan, "Rather to be in readiness with hand / Or counsel to assist; lest I who erst / Thought none my equal, now be overmatch'd" (2.143–45). Satan knows that *he* is being tested. At this counsel another demon, Belial, suggests the pleasure of sex, but Satan rejects the suggestion. Jesus will require "manlier objects . . . such as have more show / Of worth, of honor, glory, and popular praise" (2.225–27). To the second day of temptation, then, Satan brings this important insight. Since he knows that Jesus bears the favor of the supervening hero of cosmic history—God himself—he will tempt Jesus with the "manlier objects" of heroism: the patterns and achievements that we ordinarily assume necessary for genuine heroism.

The second temptation undergoes many layers of development in the give-and-take of the colloquy between Jesus and Satan. Satan begins with an appeal to spiritual heroism. He recounts a list of biblical heroes who were driven into the wilderness, yet for whom God provided sustenance. Surely Jesus, a greater hero, deserves such treatment; anything less would be an insult to his honor (2.260–317). As Jesus rejects this temptation, Satan shifts. Echoing Paul's claim that all things are clean for the strong in faith, Satan observes that Jesus is surely permitted to eat as he pleases. Should he not show his spiritual strength by taking responsibility for his spiritual disciplines, choosing when to begin a fast, and when to end, choosing the adulthood of a self-directed fasting rather than the childhood of a fasting imposed from without? Again, Jesus resists, "Thy pompous Delicacies I contemn, / And count thy specious gifts no gifts but guiles" (2.390–91). Satan cannot tempt Jesus with spiritual prerogative, and he must shift his strategy.

"Great acts require great means of enterprise" (2.412), observes Satan. With this, he embarks on an extensive enumeration of many means of heroic achievement that he is willing to put at Jesus' disposal. Surely, thinks Satan, Jesus would like riches, for money is necessary if one wishes to field armies, motivate masses, and pay administrators. No great kingdom can be conquered or ruled without the lubricant of wealth and treasure. Jesus is not deceived. His kingdom is of a different sort and will require a "wreath of thorns" rather than "a Crown Golden in show" (2.458–59). Again defeated, Satan must ratchet up the heroic temptation one more notch. "These Godlike Virtues wherefore dost thou hide? / Affecting private life, or more obscure / In savage Wilderness," he asks (3.21). Now Satan is closing in on Milton's own insight into Christian heroism. A virtue unused is "blank," its excellence "excremental"; it becomes pure and internal only through use. In response, Jesus says that he needs to be visible only to God: "This is true glory and renown, when God / Looking on th'Earth, with approbation marks the just man" (3.60–62). Yet, if he looks down on Jesus, what does God see? What is Jesus doing that would merit God's approbation? "If Kingdom move thee not, let move thee Zeal," urges Satan (3.171), implying that if Jesus does not undertake a great work, then he shows himself lacking in zeal.

Jesus' response to this heightened temptation is crucial, for it articulates the basic logic of Christian heroism. "But why should man seek glory? who of his own / Hath nothing, and to whom nothing belongs / But condemnation, ignomy, and shame?" (3.134–36). As Redcrosse finally learned in the House of Holiness, the heroic project is undermined, from the outset, by human sin. No moral action, no righteous intention, no zealous project is free from the stain of sin, and therefore no action merits recognition and glory. Yet, Jesus does not rest with despair. God's grace, though not our own, brings glory. "Yet so much bounty is in God, such grace, / That who advance his glory, not their own, / Them he himself to glory will advance" (3.142–44). Thus does Jesus articulate the Christian vision of salvation by grace alone: If we set aside our own desire for glory and seek God's alone, then by his grace we shall share in that glory.

Faced with Jesus' utterly clear statement of Paul's vision of a self-emptying that is filled up by grace, Satan tacks into the headwind. He juxtaposes *his* quest and achievement with this view of Christian heroism. In a crucial passage, Satan explains why he has no fear of Jesus, why he, unlike Jesus or any Christian following in the path of discipleship, is in control of his own destiny.

> I would be at worst; worst is my Port,
> My harbor and my ultimate repose,
> The end I would attain, my final good.
> My error was my error, and my crime
> My crime; whatever, for itself condemn'd,
> And will alike be punish'd; whether thou
> Reign or reign not. . . .
>
> (3.209–15)

Whatever his fate, at least it is his own, self-wrought—"my error," "my crime." He has taken action, his own action, independent of God, and though the results may be impoverished, at least Satan can claim them as his own. In this self-description, Satan is challenging Jesus with a paradigmatically modern temptation: Be yourself!

Milton does not allow Jesus to respond, and instead, the scene shifts to "a Mountain high" (3.252) from which the two overlook three kingdoms: Israel, Parthia, and Rome. On the mountaintop, Satan continues to tempt Jesus with heroic achievement. The scriptures foretell Jesus' fulfillment of the Davidic kingship, and Satan urges Jesus to take possession of the earthly kingdom of Israel. Again, the scriptures anticipate the triumph of Jesus over all worldly powers, and Rome symbolizes that triumph realized. If only Jesus would assume his role as world emperor! Finally, after Jesus has refused all imperial powers, Satan turns him westward toward Athens and suggests a kingdom of wisdom (4.196–284). The scriptures teach that all truth is found in Christ, and Greece represents the empire of reason. If Jesus is to take possession of that truth, then he should assume a public, active role in the kingdom of the intellect. In all cases, Jesus refuses. The Christian hero does not act in order to attain glory; he endures and awaits the commands of God.

Milton's theoretical interests are clear. In the second temptation of Jesus in the wilderness, Satan argues that visible Christian virtue comes through action, and as such, it is an argument with which Spenser (as well as Athanasius) might not disagree. After all, how can recognition follow from invisibility? In Athanasius's account we *see* Anthony's discipline; we see him move from triumph to triumph. Temperance prepares Anthony for his works of sanctity—founding a community of monks in the desert, defending the faith in the city. In contrast, what do we see of Jesus in Milton's account? Satan's voice urges us to conclude that we see nothing. When Jesus will not act, but only refuses, Satan even questions the reality of his power: "A Kingdom they portend thee, but what Kingdom / Real or Allegoric I discern not" (4.389–90). Satan wants Jesus to *use* God's power to reveal himself; otherwise, Satan implies, he is invisible, and by failing to act, the heroism of Jesus is blank rather than pure. But unlike Spenser's knights, Milton's Jesus embarks on no quest, defeats no enemies, and certainly destroys no dragons or bowers. The epic ends with Satan departing unhindered, and Jesus, "hee unobserv'd / Home to his Mother's house private return'd" (4.639). Just as Satan predicted, the hero without action is unrecognized.

In *Paradise Regained,* the test does not constitute a preparatory element of a larger, active heroism. The test is entirely static, and it completes Jesus' heroic achievement. But this does not mean that Milton thinks the achievement less. According to Milton, he emerges from this test "By proof th' undoubted Son of God" (1.11). The testing is not a battle of deeds but of words and understanding, as the many layers of temptations offered and resisted peel away layers of readerly misunderstanding. Against our assumption that heroic achievement is active, and that personal glory must, somehow, stem from intentions and actions that originate within each person, Jesus is a passive hero who waits upon the will of God. In this temperate constancy of character devoted to obedient waiting, Jesus shows himself impervious to the active, conquering power of Satan. For Milton, this passive achievement is sufficient to secure victory for God on our behalf.

The arguments in the *Areopagitica* help us to understand the flaw in Satan's assumptions about Christian heroism. This, in essence, is Satan's one and only temptation of Jesus: Act like the Son of God. Do something. Reveal yourself in true glory. Let the world see. For Satan, he must act; otherwise, Jesus' virtue is invisible, untried and untested. However, if, as Milton argues, the singular Christian virtue is temperance, then standing firm and not acting under the duress of false desires for glory, false dilemmas of "Kingdom and Zeal," constitutes the full achievement of faith. The hero of temperance is, indeed, tested by temptation, and the virtue is revealed as pure and potent through exercise and triumph in endurance. Whether or not it becomes visible and effective in the affairs of men is a matter for God to decide. Jesus' public visibility must wait until the appointed hour. However, Milton's argument is that the more "heroic" fortitude that he will display in "due time" through his public trial and crucifixion is no different from his fortitude in standing and waiting "without distrust and doubt" during the private temptations in the wilderness (3.182). The patient obedience in the desert shows Jesus capable of the patient endurance of the cross.[13]

Milton is aware that he is stretching the limits of what might be identified as heroic. But rather than try to Christianize standard heroic tropes, as does Spenser, he mounts a direct assault on our imaginations. He declares in the prologue that the events of the temptation and the character of Jesus are "Above Heroic" (1.15). With such a description, he is not qualifying the results of Jesus' resistance to temptations. He is clear that the results are real and significant—no less than "Paradise Recover'd." This is a heroic achievement; indeed, it is the greatest possible achievement within the context of the biblical narrative. The "Above Heroic" comes from the means by which that great deed is done: "By one man's firm obedience fully tried / Through all Temptation, and the Tempter foil'd" (1.4–5). The "firm obedience" is not, itself, the source of potency and power. God is the hero of any truly Christian epic, and his will stands behind all the action in *Paradise Regained,* as Milton makes clear at the outset. But God is God, and his glory transcends that of mortal men, and is, therefore, "Above Heroic." Jesus' constancy proves him a willing servant of the Almighty God, and so proved, the way is open for God to act in and through his obedient servant. In this way, Jesus achieves what he predicts: "That who advance his glory, not their own / Them he himself to glory will advance" (3.143–44). Jesus' entire exercise is nothing more and nothing less than to obey, and this emptying of all personal and independent bases for achievement and glory prepares him for divine triumph and glory:

> What if he [sc. God] hath decreed that I shall first
> Be tried in humble state, and things adverse,
> By tribulations, injuries, insults,
> Contempts, and scorns, and snares, and violence,
> Suffering, abstaining, quietly expecting,
> Without distrust and doubt, that he may know
> What I can suffer, how obey? who best
> Can suffer, best can do; best reign, who first
> Hath well obeyed.
>
> (3.187–96)

To suffer entails not only enduring pain; in its wider sense, "to suffer" involves renouncing control and prerogative. We might suffer fools graciously, or suffer disdain without objection. The radical claim in Paul's

view of discipleship, reiterated by Milton with stunning consistency, is
that such suffering, such renunciation of self, prepares the soul for the
best action, the best heroic achievement: a faith that denies self in order
to affirm Christ within. By renouncing and abstaining, a vessel is formed
into which God pours his glory.

Milton's poetic argument is consistent. Obedient suffering—especially amidst the temptations of an independent and purely personal
glory—is the only heroic achievement that allows us to participate in the
greatness and glory of God. In this sense, Milton's Jesus does no more
than articulate the logic of Abraham's mute obedience, his ready willingness to do God's will. Milton's poetic genius lies in his ability to convince us that this obedient endurance is true heroic action and
accomplishment. Against the patient and suffering constancy of Christian heroism, Milton is able to portray all the active, independent, creative figures of hell as, in the end, empty and futile. As for our personal
significance, Milton declares not only that our enduring and obedient
standing is a real achievement, in fact, the only real achievement, but also
that it is ours. For Milton, obedient enduring is the one distinctive human
achievement that can be filled with, but not absorbed into, God's glory.
For God is above temptation, and our temperance cannot be his. Thus,
our constancy in his service, however much temperance might depend
on "Above Heroic" power of divine grace, remains a purely human
achievement even as its passivity is filled with the active glory of God's
triumphant redemption.

To a great extent, modern heroes of conscience follow the pattern of
Milton's Christ-hero. Their importance is not in their achievements or
creations, but their constancy of purpose. They claim our admiration
because they have stood strong against a storm of temptation. Outwardly,
Thoreau accomplished nothing by going to jail. But his fortitude against
the compelling powers of the state and the pressure of social disappro-
bation makes him a witness to the inviolability of conscience. Conscience, we imagine, is divine, and to endure in obedience to conscience
consecrates modern life with dignity. Even as the religious and moral
certainties of premodern life crumble, the image of steadfast faithfulness
to our inner sense of rectitude endures as an ideal. Obedience to conscience is easily transformed into obedience to self, and the narrow path
of rectitude quickly becomes a compulsive and scattered impulse to say
and do whatever constitutes the "real me." The dignity of conscience
descends into the banality of self-expression, alighting finally on that
most unhelpful of maxims, one frighteningly familiar to Milton as Satanic

advice: "Be yourself." As Milton recognizes, this is a counsel of despair, and the form of enduring obedience crashes to the earth, as ordinary veniality is sanctified as "genuine" or "authentic." If we choose to construct our dignity upon self-expression rather than inhabit it through obedience to conscience, then we are left with the very thin heroism of individuality for its own sake. Far from heroically "thick" human beings, the achievements of modern individuality disappear into the thinnest vapors of feeling, the spectral and labyrinthine delusions of the "real me."

Chapter Eight

Twentieth-Century Antiheroism: Camus and Bonhoeffer

To leave the mean is to abandon humanity.
—Pascal, *Pensées,* number 378

Our century has known many cruelties, and in this, it differs little from the past. History is a lifeline cut into the flesh of generations. Yet modern cruelties assume new and mechanized forms. Mustard gas and machine guns, sealed transport trains, crematoria, and atomic bombs—our time knows not only death, hardly a novelty, but manufactured and mass-produced death. The upshot has not been greater horror. We deceive ourselves about the past if we imagine that the career of a centurion was somehow more humane and less bloody than that of a GI. No, our century has no monopoly on blood and suffering and horror. But this mechanization of death has transformed the possibilities of heroism in the twentieth century. The vast scale and impersonal face of military conflict has effectively eliminated the battlefield as a public scene of heroic enactment. Except in cinema, warriors cannot see the greatest among them rise and turn the tide of battle; the smoke never clears to reveal a man of fury and power who transfixes the imaginations of lesser men. Anonymous bullets cut the air of modern battlefields; the thuds of artillery mark time; the clatter of tank treads replaces the taunts and yells of the adversary. War may remain necessary, even inevitable, but it no longer seems heroic.

To be sure, the twentieth century has seen any number of heroic soldiers. The masterful general orchestrates victory. The selfless private throws himself on a grenade to save his fellows from certain death. A small battalion holds a key town with grim determination during an enemy counteroffensive. Fair enough, but on the whole, the pageantry, the individuality, the sheer glory of war has been eclipsed by technology and the gray impersonal machinery of destruction. Millions of men went to war in 1914 with fears, dreams, and expectations far closer to those of Homeric warriors than most of us could now imagine. They went to war for the sake of glory! But the trenches, the endless barrage of shells lobbed from they knew not where toward a purpose inscrutable, the hail of bullets, the mud, the rain, the fever, the endless tedium of waiting—this and much more drained the glory out of warfare. Courage was still possible, indeed necessary then more than ever, as casualty rates soared and battle offered no compensations. Endurance was required; self-sacrifice redoubled. War has, in our century, been hard business indeed. Yet what could this soldier, that officer actually achieve, personally and publicly? What would compel recognition and motivate imitation? Where was the hill on which to plant the flag and rally the troops? How, in the mute contest of men and material, could one do something that would bring others to bow in awe and admiration?

Eisenhower was no fierce warrior or brilliant strategist. His greatest achievement seems to have involved managing the egos and petty rivalries of other soldiers so that the full might of a vast army could be brought to bear on a weakened foe. Even more telling, consider those who flew the plane that dropped the atomic bomb on Hiroshima. To pilot the Enola Gay was to shepherd an awesome power that overshadows anything the ancient Greeks possessed or even imagined. The pilot brought the bomb to its appointed destination, but when the button was pushed and the bomb fell, and the sky filled with the deadly fireball, where was the heroism? We need to see that the issue is not the rightness or wrongness of nuclear weapons. Thucydides describes the Athenians achieving deeds as horrifying and thorough in destructiveness. The issue is the possibility of human greatness associated with this overwhelming power. One can be repelled by Achilles' rage and Aeneas's blaze of anger. Perhaps men should repent of the weapons of death, both sword and bomb. But all the same, readers of the *Iliad* and the *Aeneid* cannot help but see Achilles and Aeneas as intimately connected to the violence and power of their deeds. Even if we turn from them in horror, we turn from *them*, because they dwell in their deeds. They are welded to what they have wrought, and we cannot separate them from their achievement. Notice the contrast to our time. The name of the airplane, the Enola Gay, is remembered; the pilot forgotten.

Warfare has become dissociated from individuality, and as a consequence, a dominant form of public contest and trial has been drained of its potency as a poetic resource for heroic description and demonstration. The battlefield now supplies poets with images of suffering and futility, or at best, with an occasion to portray the endurance of humanity under the burdens of senseless slaughter. Comrades huddled in the trenches, sharing a precious cigarette; or a shell-shocked soldier transfixed by the beauty of a surviving butterfly—these are twentieth-century images of warriors. They survive, or they die, but they do not triumph, or they triumph only in surviving. Nations and ideologies clash, suffer defeat and claim victory. Men are merely raw material fed into the assembly line that eventually produces a winner and a loser.

If heroic achievement is no longer possible in the many and real battles of our time, then some breathe a sigh of relief. The world does not exist for the purpose of supplying poets with potent images of greatness, or men with the opportunities for glory. We must live in this world of violence and conflict, and most of us never enjoy overwhelming strength, great intelligence, or the blessings of the gods. Victory would be impossible no matter how the battles were conducted. Most of us are among the nameless multitudes that have populated battlefields since the beginning of time, those who would run from danger, or be cut down by men with larger shoulders and a more martial spirit. The loss of battle glory for the few Achillean souls may, indeed, be a gain for the rest of us. We are less likely to go to our deaths with illusions of a glory we can never possess.

This is Albert Camus's conclusion. The cosmos is inhospitable and unforgiving, and for Camus, our vocation as human beings is not greatness but solidarity. The eclipse of the heroic warrior is a blessing, for it crops our ambitions and drives us back into the common and ordinary run of men. This antiheroic vision is most evident in Camus's allegory of Nazism and the French resistance, *The Plague*. In this story of pestilence, the adversary is an impersonal power of infection, sickness, and death. It does not advance against us singly, but as a collective. Like troops hunkered down while under bombardment, the evil that Camus depicts as aggressive and deadly assaults impersonally. Heroism of the Greek or Christian sort is, then, an illusion, and it reflects the desire to break ranks. Against a ubiquitous plague, such an illusion yields nothing real or enduring. Our task, as Camus develops his story of resistance, is to remain with each other, sharing a common fate. This task requires courage and endurance, to be sure, but Camus insists that our resistance to evil must not become elevated, unique, and distinctive. We should not regard our achievements as lofty, as worthy of exalted recognition, for to do so opens a gap between ourselves and others. We should resist evil, but also resist the temptation to aspire to the heroic. We should cherish our ordinary, and even venial, humanity. We should want to live simply as human beings, and not as supra-human heroes.

Camus was not the only author to endure mid-century bombardments. Dietrich Bonhoeffer, like Camus, faced the pressing question of how to endure against a mechanized and seemingly irresistible power of evil. A German theologian whose budding career corresponded to the rise of Nazism, his life was shaped by resistance. He recognized the cancer of Nazism early and was active in leading the Confessing Church, a small group of German Protestants who refused to accept the Nazification of church structures, leadership, and theology. Bonhoeffer was head of an illegal seminary in East Prussia in the late 1930s, and his opposition to Nazism hardened. Through family connections, at the outset of the war, he became a civilian agent of the *Abwehr,* the German military intelligence that was the equivalent of the CIA. This secretive organization was the source of a number of plots to topple the Nazi government, and apparently, Bonhoeffer cast his lot with such efforts from the outset. The webs of association and implication remain largely hidden—the leading participants were all killed before the war ended. Nonetheless, Bonhoeffer was suspected of participating in a very nearly successful plot to kill Hitler in 1943 and was imprisoned after that plot failed. The odd combination of legal punctiliousness and ever-heightening lawlessness that characterized Nazi Germany sealed Bonhoeffer's fate. The *Abwehr*'s impenetrable secrecy prevented prosecutors from making progress toward convictions. But the legal system did not, in the end, carry the day. Bonhoeffer remained in prison for two years. In the final months of the war he was moved from a military prison to a Gestapo prison. Now outside the reach of legal compunction, he was sent to the Buchenwald concentration camp. In the final days of the war in Europe, moved again by the Gestapo to keep him out of the hands of Allied armies, he was summarily tried by an SS court at the Flossenbuerg concentration camp and executed 9 April 1945. Four days later, Allied troops liberated Flossenbuerg, and less than a month later, Germany surrendered.

Because of his manifest courage, Bonhoeffer is often cast as a wartime hero and a modern-day saint.[1] We are not concerned, however, with the drama of his life. Instead, our interest falls on Bonhoeffer's considered assessment of the shape of Christian witness in those demanding times. In his most influential book, *The Cost of Discipleship,* published in the mid-1930s as the face of Nazism was increasingly clear, Bonhoeffer, like Camus, rejects heroism. We must give up the illusions of personal power sufficient to secure victory. However brilliant Spenser's achievement, however towering Milton's poetic genius, the desire to assimilate discipleship to visible forms of human achievement—the faithful knight, the desert solitary—creates illusions of human potency, a personal zone of power and achievement. These illusions may be innocent in easier times, but for Bohoeffer, when the Adversary bears down upon us in earnest, such a mixture of divine and human endeavor tempts us to a false confidence, or despair. The machinery of death, the efficiency of a faceless bureaucracy, the numbing cannonade of propaganda, all overwhelm individual powers. The Adversary even overwhelms the collective wisdom and achievement of a great learned, urbane, and humanistic culture. Christ alone has the power of resistance, and as Bonhoeffer insists with stringent clarity, the Christian can only drop his worldly projects and purposes and follow him. In dark times, there is no luxury of heroism, no splendid dais on which to celebrate human achievement. There is only the hard and anonymous labor of discipleship.

With Camus and Bonhoeffer, we turn away from the literary accomplishment of Spenser and Milton. Neither compares in depth and scope of poetic achievement. Camus remains an important period author. He has a genuine gift for lyrical prose, and one cannot help but be moved by his descriptions of the power of the sky, the ocean, and the common graces of human life. For this reason, Camus's novels are able to create a spiritual or existential atmosphere that exerts an effective influence on readers. Nonetheless, his novels do not seek to develop a sustained philosophical position. Camus is satisfied with displaying the profound personal and communal price of maintaining spiritual integrity, the difficulties of pursuing excellence while still living an altogether human life. This is especially true of his allegory of resistance to evil, *The Plague.* The novel manifests a modern sensibility—the antiheroic—and does so with remarkable nuance and insight.[2] The bulk of this chapter will be devoted to showing this antiheroism, and bringing to light Camus's vision of the "hero" who lives "as a man." We must remain connected to the passions of ordinary life, for only then can we resist evil on behalf of the concrete reality of human life rather than on behalf of spectral and vaporous ideals.

Bonhoeffer, unlike Camus, was interested in the theoretical structure of our relation to God's glory. His was a singular mind, and by all accounts, he was one of the most promising theologians of his generation. However, the urgencies of church life in the 1930s, imprisonment, and execution blocked full expression of Bonhoeffer's theological project. Moreover, amidst the urgent demands of the late 1930s and early '40s, Bonhoeffer had neither time nor inclination to fit literary form to theological substance. His prose is powerfully direct. It is saturated with biblical language and image, often, as we shall see, set against the ideological horizon imposed on his readers by Nazi illusions of heroic achievement. But Bonhoeffer's works are not literary in intention or effect. He does not conjure; he declares. He does not call upon the Muse; he turns to scripture for powerful words. As a consequence, once we have dwelt rather extensively in Camus's antiheroic vision, we can turn to Bonhoeffer, and rather quickly and efficiently chart his very different and exclusively Christian reasons for rejecting heroic ambition in the struggle against evil.

Two Saints

The setting for *The Plague* pushes the heroic to the periphery and signals Camus's vision of a "mild, benevolent diabolism" that preserves human life.[3] Oran is a town on the Algerian coast, a town that the narrator inhabits with an evident affection, but which he describes with ruthless objectivity. It is smugly prosperous, ugly, and "completely modern" (5). It is a town dedicated to commerce and little else, a city of unexceptional humanity. People work; they fritter away evenings in cafes talking of nothing in particular; they love; they marry and come to take each other for granted. Oran is, in short, no city of great beauty, vibrant culture, or surpassing glory. Rather, for the narrator, Oran is "treeless, glamourless, soulless" (6). But this is not, finally, a terrible defect. For in its simple ordinariness, "the town of Oran ends by seeming restful and, after awhile, you go complacently to sleep there" (6). It is no place for heroes—no great artists, statesmen, or captains of industry—Oran is just a city in which normal people can live without troubling themselves about "higher" things. One can be quite ordinary and fit into the everyday life of Oran. This may seem damning to the reader, but for the narrator of *The Plague*, the banality of the setting marks its true and enduring virtue. There, one can live a merely human life.[4]

Into the city of sleepy complacency comes a deadly pestilence. Rats emerge out of shadows and sewers, reeling with disease and dying in the streets. The people of Oran are mildly disturbed but continue in their normal ways. Then a few people contract a virulent disease and die cruel deaths. The main protagonist, and narrator of *The Plague*, is Dr. Bernard Rieux. He treats the early plague victims, and has suspicions that their peculiar symptoms are signs of coming disaster. He tries to mobilize the town officials, but ever concerned about public morale and the possible disruptions of commerce, Oran's leaders temporize and delay acknowledging the emergency. The plague gains a foothold and then explodes into the population as a whole. The authorities are forced to act. The city gates are closed and Oran is sealed off from the outside world. Plague victims are taken to special wards and family members are quarantined. Volunteer sanitary squads are organized to fight the spread of disease. The altogether ordinary daily life of Oran is transformed. A city whose singular virtue is its congeniality to mere life becomes a charnel house of death. Bodies pile up. Mass graves become necessary. Eventually, smoke begins to rise from the crematorium as the sheer volume of rotting flesh overwhelms compunctions about the dignity of the dead.

Camus intends this story of pestilence as an allegory of the Nazi domination of France in the early 1940s, and readers have needed little encouragement to understand it as such. The crematorium and its ominous black smoke is enough to evoke the horrors of Nazism. The volunteer sanitary squads mirror the resistance cells in occupied France. Ignoble and ineffective civil authorities parallel the disarray of French leadership on the eve of the war, and suggest the complicity of the Vichy government. Yet, we must beware of seeking a one-to-one correlation between narrative elements and historical events. For example, the rats may represent the first wave of refugees from the Third Reich in the late 1930s entering the everyday complacency of France with stories of careers ended, businesses confiscated, homes abandoned, relatives hounded by Brownshirts. They were harbingers of the coming storm of death and destruction throughout Europe, a storm that engulfed France in 1940. But like Oran, France ignored the warning signs, confident in its supposedly impregnable defenses. The threats of Nazism could be met without disrupting commerce, or so most thought in 1939. However, the correspondence is not exact. The rats of Oran are carriers of infection, not innocent victims. More significant still, the threat of Nazism was human, while the plague that overwhelms Oran is a force of nature. Ideology may be as cruelly indiscriminate as natural disaster, but human agency shapes it and puts it into action. The Resistance did not fight an infection; it fought against domination enforced by other human beings.[5]

These allegorical failures should not trouble us. Camus is not interested in an analysis of the causes and propagation of Nazism or even an
allegorical display of evil in general. In this sense, *The Plague* is not an
allegory of Nazism, but an allegory of resistance. The evil of the plague
is part of the setting of the novel, just as fixed and immobile as the city of
Oran. It is taken for granted, and the main focus of narrative inquiry rests
in the possibilities for resistance. Here, Camus does not proceed with a
historical allegory. There are no clear antitypes to the various figures of
resistance in *The Plague*. The main protagonists are characters with their
own motives, histories, and actions, and Camus makes no effort to shape
them to suggest actual French Resistance leaders or participants. They
are types, to be sure, but not types who mirror other, historically particular and distinct men. They are types of human beings in general, men
who find themselves drawn to resist suffering and death. In this sense,
their stories are allegories, not of the French Resistance, but of resistance *simpliciter*. They provide windows on the struggle against assaults
on our common humanity. And by inviting us to look through the windows of these characters, Camus wishes us to see how heroism fails as a
category for understanding any sustained human endeavor to stem the
floods of evil that periodically engulf human communities.

Camus tends to think that so-called "great men" are more often than
not papier-mâché. Commenting on the town leaders, the narrator
observes that such men may have "high qualifications and evident good
intentions . . . but as regards the plague their competence was practically
nil" (106). However, Camus does take one traditional type seriously, that
of the saint. He gives sympathetic attention to the possibilities of Christian martyrdom in one of the subordinate characters, Father Paneloux.
More importantly, Camus assigns the role of secular saint to one of the
main characters, Jean Tarrou, a personality with strong parallels to
Camus's own convictions about the immorality of the death penalty and
the moral failures of communist revolutionary programs. Both offer real
paths toward resistance. Neither seems compatible with the kind of life
that people in Oran—and everywhere—must actually live.

Father Paneloux is a Jesuit priest, a man of profound learning and conviction who joins the sanitary squads and struggles, with the others,
against the plague. The narrator has no faith in Christianity, but nonetheless, Paneloux evokes his admiration. Indeed, the overall sympathetic
treatment of this clerical character in *The Plague* tends to make Christian readers think Camus is an author friendly to faith. Perhaps, but
Camus's unwillingness to adopt the dismissive superiority of twentieth-

century atheism testifies more to his humane concern for the ways in which people actually live than an active sympathy for Christianity. Moreover, as the narrative develops, Paneloux's courageous faith escapes the usual criticisms of fanaticism and superstition, but the way of martyrdom that he represents is implicitly criticized as a renunciation of common humanity.

Father Paneloux gives two sermons, one in the first month of the plague, and the second near its end. They are very different in tone and sentiment. The first sermon warns "them" that the plague is a judgment on "their" unbelief. Under the burdens of pestilence, the sheep are to be separated from the goats. The second sermon speaks of "us," and quietly, but forcefully, argues that the plague is a profound test of "our" belief. Will we drink the bitter cup that has been given us? However much weight a reader may wish to place on this shift, an underlying continuity obtains. Whether as dividing judgment or as ultimate test, the evil of the plague, for Paneloux, serves as a winnowing force. It raises the stakes of common life, forcing the question of our ultimate loyalty and destiny to the forefront. Faithfulness, or unbelief, will become evident, and no matter how much Paneloux's tone might have changed by virtue of his chastening experiences fighting the plague, in both sermons he relishes this clarity. God has sent evil into the world in order to reveal the distinction between the holy and unholy (the first sermon), or to provide a heightened conflict that gives opportunity for a sanctity purified of everyday compromise (the second sermon). For Paneloux, then, the most important aspect of the plague is this: evil draws men to the heights of heroic faith—or shows their faith to be hollow and empty. Moreover, this evil is a blessing. To be given the clarity of a test, to be provided a stage on which to enact the fullness of one's faith, this is an opportunity to be cherished.

Paneloux's faith is traditional, if not Miltonic in its desire for the test. Camus may have rejected Christianity in his own life, but he had no interest in revising or softening it in his literature. Moreover, Camus demonstrates a profound grasp of just the sentiments that animated Ignatius of Antioch as he celebrated his coming execution. Heroic faith is martyrdom, and the bright light that such an achievement casts upon the life of the believer marks the believer as holy. Paneloux's first sermon is explicit. Against the wishy-washy humanism of ameliorative half-measures and Sunday morning conviction, Paneloux relishes the coming horrors of the plague. He evokes the heroic sacrifices of Christians in plagues past, and though he adds the traditional caution against a too hasty desire for martyrdom, he urges his listeners to "learn a salutary lesson from that zeal"

(98). In darkness, the light of faith is more visible, and all will see whose convictions extend beyond the conventional and habitual. The second sermon strikes the same note. "My brothers," says Paneloux with a solidarity born of several months of serving the dying as a member of the sanitary squads, "a time of testing has come for us all. We must believe everything or deny everything" (224). In a time of darkness, one either clings absolutely and without reservation to the light, or one is overwhelmed by the darkness. Only the supra-human zeal of faith willing to embrace "everything," even the cross of Christ in which suffering and death have the power of salvation, only this zeal, for Paneloux, can resist great evil.

Camus does not mock this Christian approach to resistance. He is clearly repulsed by the idea that suffering and death can be redemptive. He cannot believe in such a God. The voice of Dr. Rieux expresses a characteristic horror. After witnessing the death of a young child, Rieux says to Paneloux, "Until my dying day I shall refuse to love a scheme of things in which children are put to torture" (218). However, Camus is not, finally, interested in what he, or any of his characters, can and cannot believe. He wishes to count the human costs of resistance, and here, he charts the severity of Paneloux's approach with exact clarity. "The love of God," Paneloux preaches in his second sermon, "is a hard love. It demands total self-surrender, disdain of our human personality" (228). This love requires us to "aspire beyond ourselves" and to reach toward a "summit" of "high and fearful vision" in which the divine purpose will be revealed in seeming senseless suffering and injustice (228).

Paneloux does not fill out this mountain-top vision, but Camus carefully shapes Paneloux's death to ensure that the readers see him as scrupulously faithful to his own aspiration. Paneloux falls victim to the plague. He refuses the assistance of a doctor, much as Ignatius refused the interventions of his supporters. Suffering alone, Rieux discovers that he is ill and comes to his side. Near death, the priest rejects Rieux's offer to stay with him. "Thanks," he says with difficulty, "But priests can have no friends. They have given their all to God" (233). Paneloux soon dies alone, a martyr of resistance. The medical assessment is telling. Paneloux's symptoms were inconclusive, and Rieux labels his case "doubtful" (234). Doubtful indeed. Paneloux loved God, not humanity. He valued faith over friendship, the "high and fearful vision" of holiness over the altogether ordinary constraints of a merely human life. Perhaps we should be thankful that such men exist. Resistance may need their supernatural faith. But it is by no means clear that saints such as Paneloux are resisting evil for the sake of life. They seem to resist for the sake of the glory of faith. They resist in order to rise to that "lofty plain." To the extent that resistance, for Camus, must serve life, Paneloux was a doubtful case. His courage was real, his sacrifice ultimate, his labors cherished, but Paneloux was not, finally, a trustworthy ally. He lacked a final loyalty to the inevitable mediocrity of life, a mediocrity so intimate to a place like Oran.

Jean Tarrou is a very different kind of saint, one far closer to Camus's heart, but nonetheless troublesomely close to Paneloux in his moral ambition. As an agent of resistance, Tarrou is decisive. He organizes the voluntary sanitary squads to fight the plague and spearheads resistance efforts. Moreover, in his attitude toward life, Tarrou manifests existentialist virtues of solidarity with common life. He keeps a daily journal devoted to observations of seemingly trivial events and personalities. In all things, then, Tarrou manifests a love of humanity. All deserve careful and loving observation, even the strange man next door who spits on cats every afternoon at four. All deserve protection against suffering and death. Tarrou, then, is a resistance leader seemingly different from Paneloux. He loves humanity, not God. But to say it this way puts the difficulty front and center. Tarrou loves humanity, and the ambition of this universality of his love drives him toward a sainthood quite different from Paneloux's, but nonetheless extreme.

Tarrou's ambition becomes clear in a long monologue in which he explains his life and motivations to Rieux. They have retreated from the front line of resistance for an hour, an hour "off" for friendship (245). In this time of quiet conversation, Tarrou recalls his childhood and youthful convictions. His father was a government prosecutor, and once Tarrou had gone with him to court. The scene in the courtroom transformed his life. He could not bear the idea that the justice his father represented required the death of the criminal. The horror of execution drove him from his home and into an underground revolutionary cell. He committed himself to resisting "the plague" that infected inhumane systems of justice. Yet, after some years of activism, he was invited to the execution of a traitor to the revolution. Again, he was struck with horror. The plague that infected his father's courtroom also infected revolutionary opposition. This taught Tarrou a second and terrible lesson: the plague is a deadly terror that spreads its infection far more widely than we imagine. Anyone who thinks that others "deserve" to die has the plague. Indeed, observes Tarrou, "what's natural is the microbe. All the rest—health, integrity, purity (if you like)—is a product of the human will, of a vigilance that must never falter" (253). The upshot, for Tarrou, is a Herculean task. To avoid infection requires "tremendous will-power, a never end-ing tension of the mind" (253). One can hardly live without succumbing to the plague.

Seeing the true nature of the plague and the strenuous exercise of the will necessary to avoid complicity with its horrors, Tarrou feels a "des-perate weariness." The overriding imperative of a truly moral resistance to the plague requires fighting evil without causing others to suffer. Of course, because the plague is carried by human beings in its thrall, resist-ance inevitably requires fighting against the wrongful desires of others. Camus captures this reality by describing the desire of families to stay with infected victims, and the sanitary squads must often struggle against the very people they seek to save. In the real world of underground resist-ance against the Nazis the struggle was lethal. Cruel measures were often required, and very often, one took action that one knew would lead to Nazi reprisals against innocent victims. Tarrou's desire for resistance that does not harm seems impossible, and Camus signals this impossibility when he has Tarrou sum up his aspirations with an oxymoron. "I try," he says to Rieux, "to be an innocent murderer" (254). Yes, to be an innocent murderer. To resist evil effectively and actively, but to do so without anger, without hatred, without violence, such a hope would, indeed, induce a "desperate weariness." It is a hope that Paneloux never harbors. Faith sacrifices itself before the power of evil; it does not conquer. He makes no claims about the worldly effectiveness of Christian martyrdom. Such matters are in God's hands, not ours. Not surprisingly, then, Tar-rou reports that his ambition leads to a weariness "from which nothing remains to set us free except death" (253).

Tarrou does die. Within Camus's allegory of resistance, it seems inevitable that saints, whether religious or secular, must become sepa-rated by their ambition from life. And death, garlanded by self-sacrifice and sealed in fierce commitment, is the ultimate separation. Unlike Pan-eloux, Tarrou does not refuse the comforts of friends. He dies in Rieux's apartment, under his care and the benevolent gaze of Rieux's mother, a silent icon of eternal motherhood. But he does die, and rightly. It is the only possible peace for a man who seeks both to resist evil and do no harm. Tarrou, then, is an inspiring character in *The Plague*, but in the context of Camus's narrative, he has failed to live as one must in a city such as Oran—to live with compromises and mendacities, with failures and injustices. In fact, Camus places Tarrou in judgment of himself. In his journal, which constitutes crucial parts of the narrative, Tarrou offers a definition of the heroic or saintly form of life. "Perhaps," he wrote, "we can only reach approximations of sainthood. In which case we must make a shift with a mild, benevolent diabolism" (276). Such a "saint" would have the courage for cruelties, a necessity, perhaps, in times of plague, but always under the guidance of a mild, benevolent sensibility that wished nothing more than the return of ordinary life with all its limitations and failures. But Tarrou was not satisfied with approximations, and he could not make the shift. His ambition took him away from the land of the living, and like Paneloux, he ascended to a plain very different— no God, no redemption—but no less lofty.[6]

"What Interests Me Is Being a Man"

However important Father Paneloux and Jean Tarrou are as two different kinds of saints, the dominant figure in *The Plague* is Dr. Bernard Rieux. He is both the main protagonist and the narrator, who remains anonymous until the end of his tale. As a physician, Rieux is thrust forward in the task of resistance. He is a healer by profession, a man dedicated by training to alleviate suffering and fend off the powers of death. From beginning to end, Rieux is at the center of the struggle against the plague. His daily rounds make him aware of the disease at the outset, and as the situation worsens, Rieux takes charge of isolation wards and oversees the largely ineffective efforts to stem the tide of infection. Moving among the afflicted, his life is always in danger. Working from dawn to dusk, his labors stretch him to the point of exhaustion and collapse. Rieux seems, then, an obvious hero of resistance, a paragon of commitment and self-sacrifice. Yet, both in conversation and as narrator, Rieux expresses a profound rejection of the very idea of heroism.

The voluntary sanitary squads that so clearly parallel the resistance cells in occupied France offer the clearest object of Rieux's antiheroic sentiments. Speaking with the cold objectivity of the narrator, Rieux warns that we tend to favor deceptions and falsehoods, especially if they give us an uplifting sense that high ideals and great achievements lie at the heart of the human drama. We are, he warns, inclined to think of those who volunteered to risk death in the service of resistance "in over-glowing terms," to ascribe great "courage" and "devotion" (131). We want something spectacular to inspire us, "some heroic feat or memorable deed like those that thrill us in the chronicles of the past" (179). When we face evil, either in reality or in our imaginations, we wish to think of heroes who rise above fear and despair, complicity and half-measures. But reflecting back on the time of the plague, Rieux insists that those who resisted had "no such great merit in doing as they did" (132). To be sure, their witness inspired the whole town to come to terms with the disease, and to endure and perhaps fight in their own less direct ways. "But," Rieux continues, "we do not congratulate a schoolmaster on teaching that two and two make four" (132). That a man might say no to suffering and death is no different. "There is nothing admirable about this attitude," Rieux observes, "it was merely logical" (133), and we should not view logic—or common decency—as heroic. For Rieux, to make such a man a hero lowers the standards of humanity, and of heroism. We should not say that completing a syllogism, or resisting suffering and death, wins garlands. We should simply say that both constitute a natural, altogether human response. We should not look up to those who resisted, for to do so entails looking away from the ordinary run of men and women, as if they were, somehow, incapable of a normal human response to suffering and death.

The voice of the narrator differs not at all with the direct speech of Rieux. Two conversations come into focus over the question of heroism. First, Rambert, a visiting journalist unable to leave Oran because of the plague, befriends Rieux. Rambert wishes to escape and rejoin his wife. Rieux assures him that he bears no grudge; indeed, he insists that Rambert is taking the proper course of action. Rieux is adamant. "There's no question of heroism in all this," he says to Rambert, "It's a matter of common decency" (163). Behind Rieux's rejection of heroism is Camus's overriding justification for resistance. Our shared humanity is the only basis for resisting evil, and that humanity rightly claims its private loves and personal satisfactions. The purely personal need that each of us has for love should have as much of a claim on our souls as our communal obligations to others. Rieux does not want to override humanity in order to save humanity. Here, Camus depicts Rieux's character with the utmost consistency. Rieux does not want Rambert to renounce the very happiness and urgency of love that he, Rieux, hopes that his medical efforts will make possible for others. Rambert has a right to his love, a right to his hopes for ordinary life far from the demands of a plague-ridden town. The conversation ends inconclusively. Rambert wishes to know what, exactly, is entailed in "common decency." Rieux knows only that it consists in doing his job. Rieux is a doctor; Rambert is not. That marks the only relevant difference between them. Rieux is not a hero who somehow rises above Rambert.

The second conversation takes place at the height of the plague, when Rieux and his closest companion, Tarrou, are near collapse from stress and exhaustion. They take a moment of rest on a terrace overlooking Oran and fall into a conversation. Tarrou speaks of his motives for fighting the plague. As we have seen, Tarrou sums up his impulse by appealing to the ideals of sainthood. Rieux's response is decisive. Against Tarrou's explanation of resistance, Rieux expresses direct opposition, and in so doing, articulates the central commitment of Camus's antiheroism. "Heroism and sanctity," he says, "don't really appeal to me, I imagine. What interests me is being a man" (255). For Rieux, one resists simply because one is thrown into the world as a human being, inescapably connected to others by a shared need for love and a common vulnerability to death. All thoughts of holiness and heroism strike Rieux as attempts to lift oneself out of this common condition, and in so doing, to establish distance between oneself and others. "Ah yes, I am special," we too easily think, "Unlike most, I have made great sacrifices; I have done great deeds." This distance, however much it might motivate us in the moment, ultimately undermines the conditions for resistance. Only if one lives as man, as one committed to life, given by fate a certain job in a certain town under the contingencies of one's time, can one find the basis for the elusive "common decency" Rieux commended earlier to Rambert.

This very sentiment is expressed at the outset of the story; Camus does not want his readers to miss the point. Rieux's wife suffers from tuberculosis and must leave town. The first victims of the plague are dying with mysterious symptoms. Camus wishes to remind us that the plague, while a heightened threat, is not fundamentally different from the ongoing and all-too-common threats to life. Rieux is disoriented and world-weary even before the trials of the plague begin. Against a sense of futility and despair, Rieux clings to the world into which he has been thrown. He does not take refuge in an ideal. He does not construct a reassuring picture of himself as uniquely afflicted, or uniquely triumphant. "There lay certitude," he reports in the omniscient voice of the narrator, "there, in the daily round. And the rest hung on mere threads and trivial contingencies; you couldn't waste your time on it. The thing was to do your job as it should be done" (41). Rieux's job is to fight disease. That is the kind of man fate has made him. It is as simple as that. Were he a baker or policeman, his responses to suffering and his role in the resistance to the plague might well be far less central and seem much less "heroic." For Rieux, the daily round sustains us. He does not want to be a hero, and certainly not a saint, but he does want to be himself, a doctor whose duty is to alleviate suffering and fend off death. For this reason, he rises each day and throws himself into the task of resistance.

Should we not say, then, that Rieux succeeds? He does his job until the plague abates. He lives as he has been thrown into the world. So is he not an existentialist hero of sorts? However, the man who repudiates heroism is no hero himself, not even an existentialist hero. In his conversation with Tarrou, after Rieux says that he wishes to do no more than live as a man, Tarrou asserts that they really agree. "We're both after the same thing," he says, but enigmatically Tarrou concludes, "but I'm less ambitious" (255). To live as a man in inhuman times is no mean trick. And Camus hints that Rieux must sacrifice too much of his humanity to his profession to make any claim to live as a man. He must abstract himself from his personal needs, from his love and anxiety about his wife, even from his friendship with Tarrou. So abstracted has he become that the news of his wife's death is but one suffering more piled upon the many months of suffering he has both witnessed and endured. The final scene of the novel is telling. As Oran celebrates and lovers are reunited, Rieux walks the city alone. He returns to the high terrace where he and Tarrou had shared their friendship in a rare moment of unguarded conversation. Rieux overlooks the city, but he cannot abandon himself to its bacchanalian celebrations of the return of ordinary life and its venial pleasures. He visits a patient, an old, solitary asthmatic whose days are taken up with the solidity of a never-ending task—counting peas from one pan to another—and Rieux is quietly assimilated to his isolated chamber. He has done his job, he has clung to the daily round as the sure anchor of common decency, but has he lived as a man? An abstraction and isolation seems to have been the price he had to pay in order to resist effectively, and that price blocks him from the immediacy of passion that is so essential to ordinary life.[7]

Rieux's failure makes him the pivotal figure in *The Plague*, for he wishes to avoid heroism and its transcendence of ordinary life, but he cannot connect himself to the common run of human emotion. He respects Father Paneloux's commitment and does not reject otherworldly faith as superstitious and foolish. Camus has no time for easy and superior atheism, either in his literary characters or in his own life. Even more does Rieux empathize with Tarrou, the humanist saint. He never tries to talk Tarrou out of his moral severity, and Tarrou's death deprives Rieux of his closest friend in resistance. Yet, as narrator and protagonist, Rieux articulates the strongest objection to both Christian and secular sainthood. Both Paneloux and Tarrou abstract themselves from the everyday life, its banalities and compromises, its failures and inevitably self-centered emotions. Both leave behind the constraints of the daily round. Indeed, it is telling that neither suffers the constraining attachment of love, the priest by formal vow and Tarrou seemingly by virtue of the kind of man he wishes to be. Both seek to live on the "lofty plain," the summit that overlooks humanity, even as it serves human needs so selflessly. Here, Rieux' sympathy for both men seems to stem as much from the sense that he shares their fate as it does from the camaraderie of resistance. Rieux too has become "abstracted" from life. It was the only way to carry on the resistance. He manifests the cold objectivity of a medical doctor, treating symptoms and disease with an urgency that necessarily overrides the emotional needs and attachments of patients and their families. Further, as a man, Rieux has a skeptical temper, and with almost superhuman detachment, he records events without passing judgment. In the end, though he lacks the singularity of Paneloux and Tarrou's ambition, Rieux shares their ascent to a "lofty plain," even as he rejects such an ascent as an achievement to be lauded or sought. Rieux, like Paneloux and Tarrou, has something of the holiness that Spenser thinks necessary for heroism, but he cannot join it to the force of passion that Spenser also thinks necessary.

THE HEROISM OF INNOCENT CONSCIENCE

Are there any true antiheroes in *The Plague*? Are there men who resist and succeed in simply being men? As narrator, Rieux commends one man, Joseph Grand, a minor municipal clerk, failed novelist, and statistician of the resistance to the plague, as the "hero" of the story. He is an "insignificant and obscure hero who had to his credit only a little goodness of heart and a seemingly absurd ideal" (37). Grand is a hero, then, who is unable to pretend toward the "lofty plain" and who will not tempt others toward imitation. He is a hero who is quintessentially a man, and nothing more. To this hero, designated by the narrator, we also add Raymond Rambert, a foreign journalist trapped in Oran by the plague. Both men offer resistance, but neither abstracts himself from his humanity. The key, for both, is a courage for selfishness combined with a goodhearted concern for others. Grand and Rambert have innocent consciences, Grand by nature and Rambert by the contingent influence of event. That is to say, they can resist the plague wholeheartedly while they give free play to their personal passions and needs. This, for Camus, is the true mark of the antiheroic hero.

Joseph Grand works as a permanent temporary employee of the city government of Oran, doing his job day in and day out, hoping for advancement, but never asking for a promotion. His reluctance does not stem from a lack of courage. Rather, he never advances because he lacks the proper words to request a promotion. The vocabulary of self-advancement seems beyond his grasp. This same lack of words characterizes Grand's novelistic efforts. For years he has sought to write a novel but never progresses beyond the first line. With innumerable revisions he tries to capture, with words, the picture in his mind's eye. But just as self-advancement eludes him, self-expression never seems possible. The sentence must be forever rewritten. Grand is not, then, the sort of man who makes a name for himself, either in his profession or in literature. He is what we would commonly regard as a failure, unable, like most of us, to set himself apart from the common run of men.

Camus pairs this mediocrity with an immediate and overriding decency. A neighbor tries to commit suicide and Grand intervenes, and he does so immediately and without thinking of the costs or consequences for himself. The fellow was in need; common decency guided Grand to step in and save his life. The episode foreshadows Grand's involvement in the resistance. It is unpremeditated and almost unconscious. He is needed, the cause is clearly important, so Grand does what he can with no thought of heroism or saintliness or self-sacrifice. He resists as a matter of course. However, Camus does more than construct Grand as a character of ordinary decency. He also invests Grand with intense private passion.

Grand's literary ambitions are very real and central to his character. At no point in the grim progress of the plague does he stop working on his first sentence. No matter how pressing the communal obligations of resistance, Grand will not renounce his purely personal need to write the perfect first line. Even after Grand contracts the illness and the fever prohibits him from working on his novel, he continues to be preoccupied with this passion. Thinking himself close to death, he begs Rieux to burn the hundreds of pages of manuscript (all versions of the first line revised again and again). This absurd project—the quest for a perfect sentence that is unique to Grand's private vision—takes pride of place, even in the jaws of death. Grand survives, and as he recovers, he recommits himself to his novel. The victory, for Camus, is double. Grand has overcome the death-dealing power of the plague, but more importantly, he has persevered in his idiosyncratic passion. The power of the merely personal, something found in ordinary men and women, triumphs over the plague.

This combination of decency and loyalty to private passion makes Grand the "true hero" of resistance. "In a certain sense," writes Rieux as narrator, "it might well be said that his was an exemplary life" (46). Grand is capable of "acts of kindness" and has "a capacity of affection," not because he has disciplined himself to live up to a superhuman ideal, but because "he was one of those rare people, rare in our town as elsewhere, who had the courage of their good feelings" (46). Grand trusts his humanity, and this allows him to both respond to the needs of others and remain true to his loves and eccentricities. The "courage of good feelings" typifies Grand's innocent conscience, unburdened by aspirations of saintliness, free from lofty ideals. He could live as a man, open to the needs of others, and yet remain within a life defined by personal memories and idiosyncratic and private aspirations. Grand's success, his "exemplary life," makes Grand the greatest bulwark against the plague. The plague never broke Grand's will to resistance, but it also failed to abstract him from himself. Grand never separated himself from humanity, either with the high ideals of Paneloux and Tarrou or with the Stoic detachment of Rieux. His triumph was, quite simply, an endurance. Even in resistance, Grand remained who he was, laboring over the first sentence of his never to be completed novel, unchanged by the onslaught of suffering and death.

Grand is fated to be the exemplary antihero. His innocent conscience is innate; he is unreflectively decent and necessarily self-preoccupied at the same time. One may recognize such a man and give him the existentialist garland: "an insignificant and obscure hero." However, like Achilles, son of a goddess, one cannot imitate Grand. One is either born with an innocent conscience, or one is not. Camus does not wish to leave his readers in such a predicament. Ever the moralist, Camus intends to offer a pattern for imitation, an innocent conscience achieved rather than given, a way of resistance that does not depend on being born with an absurd character. Raymond Rambert, a foreign journalist trapped in Oran by the plague, provides an imitable pattern. His innocent conscience, his commitment to resistance and loyalty of private passion, is achieved rather than simply given. To him we must turn.[8]

Trapped in Oran, Rambert desperately wants to return to Paris to be reunited with his beloved. Throughout most of the narrative, as the other main characters throw themselves to the tasks of resistance, he is preoccupied with schemes of escape. Yet, rather than portraying Rambert as a man fleeing from duty, Camus takes a sympathetic stance. In a conversation with Rieux and Tarrou, the outlines of Rambert's character, and Camus's recommendation of him to the reader, emerge clearly. Rambert wishes to justify his efforts of escape to Rieux and Tarrou. He tells them that he does not fear the plague or shy from the sacrifices of resistance. He had served in the Spanish Civil War, and he knew himself capable of heroic deeds. Yet, that experience in Spain taught Rambert a lesson about humanity. "I know that man is capable of great deeds," he tells Rieux. "But if he isn't capable of great emotion, well, he leaves me cold" (162). Men can work themselves up into frenzies of conviction and idealistic aspiration, and in such a state, remarkable actions are possible. However, Rambert finds this greatness hollow. "Personally," he continues, "I've seen enough of people who die for an idea. I don't believe in heroism" (162). For Rambert, and for the novel as a whole, conventional ideals of heroic commitment and sacrifice abstract from common emotions, attachments, and feelings. This, Rambert suggests, corrupts the very humanity the idealistic hero seeks to defend and save. His decision to escape Oran, then, is part of his rejection of heroism. He intends to remain loyal to his feelings of love. He will not allow these private feelings to be eclipsed by abstractions of duty and obligations.

Whatever lessons Rambert may have learned, his conscience is not innocent. He lacks Grand's matter-of-fact combination of decency and self-absorption. As the conversation moves forward, he admits his doubts. "Maybe I'm all wrong," he says to Rieux, "in putting love first." Rieux's response is telling. In a singular moment of emphatic, even violent judgment, Rieux insists that Rambert is *not* wrong. The personal, however selfish, must have authority over our lives; otherwise, we become mere abstractions, shadows in the service of an ideal. Rambert does not escape. His efforts come to naught as the authorities tighten security. Soon, Rambert joins the resistance and fights courageously and effectively. Yet, precisely because he was willing to allow love to trump duty, Rambert retains a capacity to achieve Rieux's goal: "to live as a man." As the plague lifts, his beloved joins him in Oran, and like so many others on the train platform, Rambert is utterly absorbed into the overwhelming private passions of reunion, drifting with his wife into the anonymous humanity of the crowds celebrating the end of the plague. Rambert may lack the immediacy of Grand's innocent conscience, but he follows the same pattern. He serves others, but he retains a capacity for the profound selfishness of private love, a selfishness that merges him with the common run of men and prevents ascent to the lofty plains of an ideal.

For Camus, the imperative of antiheroism stems from a commitment to the unsurpassable value of our shared humanity. The contrast with classical views is patent. Achilles remains loyal to a passion uniquely his own, and he actively repudiates the shared world of ordinary heroic recognition, the common currency of golden tripods and swift horses. The same holds true for the Platonic and Vergilian hero. Socrates eludes our grasp, both paying homage to and mocking Athenian conventions. The larger poetic project of the *Aeneid* involves an extended effort to persuade us that Aeneas participates in his unique and divinely guaranteed destiny. In each case, the picture of excellence crowds out simple patterns of human solidarity. Achilles does not converse with the nameless soldiers who populate the fields of battle. Socrates does not live as an ordinary Athenian. Aeneas, in his final act of passion, transcends the mold of *pietas*. Camus resists just this transcending uniqueness, the surpassing excellence. For Camus, the baseline of common decency arises out of the ordinariness of human life, its mediocrity and veniality, as well as its quiet dignity and enduring emotional needs. To transcend this commonality entails cutting oneself off from the taproot of humane existence, and risks making the hero an enemy of humanity. The lofty heights of the hero and saint encourage arrogance and superiority, and even if such vices are resisted, the thin air and emotional aridity of "pure ideals" eventually weakens the hero and diminishes his or her power for existence. Thus, for Camus, we must dwell in the world as ordinary men and women. This is the highest possible vocation, and it marks out the only true heroism. There can be no quest for surpassing achievement. Only the broad and fertile plains of human mediocrity—its private passions and purely personal needs, as well as patterns of decency and fellow feeling—can sustain resistance to the brutal ideologies and mechanization of death that so dominated the decades of Camus's short literary career.

CHRISTIAN ANTIHEROISM

Written after Hitler's rise to power and during the decade of the Nazification of German society in the 1930s, *The Cost of Discipleship* serves as Dietrich Bonhoeffer's meditation on the conditions for Christian resistance. This meditation is easily misread. Books were censured by Nazi authorities, and Bonhoeffer could not speak directly. Nonetheless, in pointed antitheses, often using the dominant terms and rhetoric of Nazism, Bonhoeffer contrasts the heroic vision of Nazi propaganda with the Christian gospel. The Leader whose special destiny entailed founding a new Reich through conquest is the antithesis of the Christian Lord, who founded the kingdom of God through a willingness to die for others. Where Nazi propagandists planned great public rallies and built monuments to the glory of Germany, Bonhoeffer emphasized the hiddenness of Christian discipleship. Where Hitler insisted Germany needed *Lebensraum,* "space for living," darkly threatening military invasions, Bonhoeffer wrote that Christian discipleship needs *Lebensraum,* and in so doing, established the church as a public institution that contests the state's claim on the loyalty of citizens. But most importantly, where Nazism gloried in great achievement and feats of courage and eagerly showered athletes and daredevils with medals and accolades, Bonhoeffer describes Christian discipleship in profoundly antiheroic terms.

In these contrasts, his contemporary German readers who had eyes to see and ears to hear were entirely sensible of the profound contemporary relevance of Bonhoeffer's seemingly pious meditations on questions of grace and freedom, gospel and law, church and world. Yet, even if the contemporary American reader grasps the contrast, he or she is quite likely to be mystified. For our common assumption is that heroic evil must be met and defeated by heroic goodness. Across these contrasts, Bonhoeffer argues otherwise. The call of Jesus leads to single-minded, even childish obedience, and this leaves no room for human achievement. "Beside Jesus," he writes, "nothing has any significance. He alone matters."[9] There is only one power, one excellence to recognize and admire, and in keeping with the New Testament, Bonhoeffer identifies Jesus as the sole bearer of that singular and surpassing greatness. His alone is the power to resist evil, and our role is to follow and obey. The faithful are commissioned to do Christ's work, not their own, and thus, "their commission is not a heroic struggle" (211). No disciple stands as a hero; they stand only with and in the singular heroism of Christ.

This rejection of heroic resistance follows some of the same patterns as Camus's antiheroism. For Camus, we must not separate ourselves from the common run of humanity; we must not reach upward to the lofty plain of heroism in order to differentiate ourselves. Bonhoeffer also rejects the will to differentiation, but not in the interests of preserving human solidarity. Instead, the antiheroism stems from Bonhoeffer's affirmation of the self-negating aspect of the Pauline vision: "Not I, but Christ in me." Jesus Christ is a greatness singular and sufficient; he bears the glory of God in his person. Christ alone is the anchor and dynamic power of Christian discipleship. The disciple must resist all temptations to separate himself from Christ, all temptations to differentiate himself, his life and work, from Christ. Bonhoeffer rejects heroism, then, in order to preserve our solidarity with Jesus. We can only participate in him to the extent that we renounce all bases for life outside his authority.

For Bonhoeffer, the Christianity of twentieth-century Germany tends toward two errors, both of which undermine Christian resistance to evil. The first temptation affirms the sole sufficiency of grace as the foundation and basis of the Christian life, but transforms Jesus' call into spiritual platitudes that have no weight and consequence in ordinary life. This leads to the error of cheap grace. The second temptation seeks to make the call of Jesus effective by carefully coordinating human achievement with the power of God's grace. This yields the error of domesticated grace. For Bonhoeffer, both errors diminish the real potency of the gospel, and both undermine the basis for discipleship. We need to understand both errors if we wish to grasp Bonhoeffer's vision of the narrow path of Christian resistance, an antiheroism that can triumph over the redoubled pagan heroism advanced by Nazism.

The first error involves a tacit assumption that the gospel has no real power in human affairs. Bonhoeffer calls this error "cheap grace." The gospel becomes a purely "spiritual truth" that leaves the world unchanged. In a sustained polemic against Lutheran preaching of justification by faith alone, Bonhoeffer denounces the view of God's power as easy forgiveness of sins. The message of Christ is not a wink and a nod that somehow overlooks sin and accepts the sinner, unchanged. It is not forgiveness without repentance, baptism without church discipline, absolution without personal confession (44–45). It is not a grace that turns on us, our strengths and achievements. Rather, for Bonhoeffer, grace is the costly decision of the Father to give up the life of his Son, the decision of Jesus to take up the cross and die for the sin of the whole world. In Jerusalem, before the high priest and the Roman governor, and on Golgotha, Jesus did something in the world. Even in suffering and death, his life took up space and time. For just this reason, Christians must assume that God's grace is effective in the world, effective in space and time. Justification of the ungodly, then, is not "acceptance of the unacceptable." It is transformation of the sinner into a servant of righteousness. This grace is costly. It cost Jesus his life, and it may well cost the same for any who would follow him. Just because grace involves no human achievement, no human power or possession, does not mean that grace is spectral, spiritual, and ineffective among the worldly doings of man. Quite the contrary, precisely because grace is God's alone, it has the power of eternity.

As Christians try to combat the temptation to spiritualize the gospel, they too easily fall back into the second error, a tacit dependence on human and worldly patterns of power and effectiveness. To show the reality of grace, one carefully coordinates the divine power of Jesus with the subordinate, but real, powers of the faithful person. Christ is the way, the truth, and the life, to be sure, but the human powers of reason and judgment allow us to recognize and follow him. Jesus's commandments are righteous and true, but individual conscience is a necessary complement to the objective requirements of scripture. Christian faith is spiritually pure, but a general human tendency toward cosmic trust provides the proper basis for a distinctively Christian form of belief. The particular conjunctions of divine and human are many, but for Bonhoeffer, the details are irrelevant. All attempts to supplement, undergird, or prepare for the power of the call of Jesus add a "superstructure of human, institutional, and doctrinal elements" (36). Far from enhancing the power of the gospel, the "human ballast" domesticates God's power, diminishing its effectiveness and muting its distinctive demands (36). Instead of preaching God's word (no matter how subordinate the human element, no matter how carefully coordinated the junior partnership of the human person) one who carries this "ballast" preaches the limitations of human power and achievement rather than the unlimited scope of God's power.

Bonhoeffer combats the errors of cheap grace and domesticated grace at every turn. His constant engagement with the rhetoric of Nazi propaganda and his self-conscious articulation of the shape and purpose of Christian discipleship in terms of that rhetoric testify to his assault on cheap grace. The currents of Christian faithfulness run in direct opposition to the Nazi regime, and open conflict is inevitable and necessary. At the same time, Bonhoeffer's renunciations of Christian heroism serve to bar the way toward domesticated grace. The believer possesses nothing and has no basis on which to stand other than Jesus' call. The call of Christ comes into conflict with Nazism, not the strength, virtue, or piety of the Christian. The combination—effective opposition and the rejection of any human basis for opposition—is manifest in Bonhoeffer's careful coordination of the visible and hidden character of discipleship. Grace makes a difference in the world; we do not.

Lutheran theology has understood the relation between the gospel and worldly power with a doctrine of two kingdoms, a spiritual kingdom inaugurated by Christ, and a worldly kingdom in which civil authorities govern to restrain sin. A superficial use of this two-kingdoms doctrine can treat "spiritual" as private and subjective, a matter of personal convictions and religious ideals, and in this way, concede all public and social existence to civil authorities. Bonhoeffer opposes this spiritualization of faith. The initiation into faith, baptism, is "a public event," writes Bonhoeffer. Baptism marks citizenship in a new kingdom, governed by Christ. It signals a change of loyalty and requires us "to stand visibly in the fellowship of Jesus Christ" (234).

The visible mark of baptism is more than initiatory. One is called to stand visibly with a community of teaching and worship that is continuous through time, and which, moreover, is a public reality, a church with its own order and discipline. Here, Bonhoeffer uses Nazi rhetoric in a very pointed way. The aggressive policies of Hitler's regime were justified by the claim that the German people needed *Lebensraum*, living space. This *Lebensraum*, moreover, must be purified of contaminating races, especially Jews, in order to allow for the full flowering of Aryan greatness. Bonhoeffer does not offer liberal criticisms of this aggressive desire for a visible community of Aryan purity. He does not insist on a principle of tolerance. He does not preach the virtues of diversity. He does not defend the rights of the individual. Instead, he depicts the church as a public reality, a polis, that "takes up space in the world" (248). The church needs *Lebensraum*. In its worship and discipline, the church makes a claim over the entire life of the baptized, and with the claim, "the Church invades the life of the world and conquers territory for Christ" (258). Moreover, the church not only needs space for living but also must purge and purify. Here, Bonhoeffer meets the Nazi rhetoric at every point. The church must expel heresy; it must renounce compromises and complicity with worldly powers. There can be no question of Christian nations, Christian races, as some German theologians had speculated during the 1930s in hopes of baptizing Nazism. Territory must be taken, Bonhoeffer argues, and that territory must be sanctified through service and turned to the purposes of worship. By these means, he writes, the church "makes a deep invasion into the sphere of secular life" (267). And this invasion is as saturated with blood, sacrifice, and suffering as anything imagined by Nazi propagandists. For the church meets resistance, and her *Lebensraum* "has been torn from the clutches of the world."

Bonhoeffer's images of struggle, conflict, and invasion seem to suggest that the Christian life is, indeed, a heroic vocation. Against this illusion, and the consequent tendency to annex human virtues and achievements to the singular greatness of Jesus, Bonhoeffer emphasizes the hidden character of the Christian life. The Christian has nothing that can be recognized and honored, for Jesus does not give us a task that we can make our own, that we can possess and make the basis for our own glory. Reflecting on Matthew 6:1 and Jesus' exhortation that his followers keep their righteousness hidden, Bonhoeffer observes that discipleship entails nothing more than heeding Jesus' call. And in heeding his call, disciples should take no account of public consequences. Instead, Bonhoeffer writes, "Our task is simply to keep on following, looking only to our Leader who goes on before, taking no notice of ourselves or of what we are doing" (158). The Christian should not think of his or her impact on others and should not cultivate a persona, either pious or ironic, either vigorous or contemplative, either liberal or conservative, in order to enhance the power of the gospel, in order to make Christ's call more winsome, more effective, more attractive. Here, Bonhoeffer is insistent. Jesus gives his follower nothing to do other than to follow him, and he gives all that is necessary in order for us to follow. "Jesus asks nothing of us," Bonhoeffer writes, "without giving us the strength to perform it" (38). There is no room and scope for us—our needs, our intuitions about morality, politics, or religion—in the singular and sufficient power of God in Christ. There is room only for us to follow and obey.

This antiheroism can confuse readers. Students find Bonhoeffer's personal story inspiring. He courageously resisted, and he died a martyr. Yet they consistently find *The Cost of Discipleship* a baffling book. Surely, we think, Nazism must be resisted on a moral basis of some sort. Our humanistic age diagnoses Nazism as a mass phenomenon in which a vulnerable population, humiliated by military defeat and prostrate in economic depression, sought security and deliverance in obedience to an authoritarian demagogue. The antidote, then, is a heroism of critical thought, a courage of individual freedom. Resistance to Nazism, we assume, is best conducted as a defense of human rights, the recovery of moral ideals, a restoration of liberal democracy. Yet, however pointed Bonhoeffer's use of Nazi rhetoric, his references to Jesus as *Führer,* and his claim that the church needs *Lebensraum,* he never prescribes these antidotes. Indeed, Bonhoeffer entertains no theory of resistance other than the sheer power of God in Jesus Christ. His way is, like Milton's, "Above Heroic," and it requires obedience to "the absolute, direct and unaccountable authority of Jesus" (57). For Bonhoeffer, obedient discipleship shifts attention away from human achievement. Nothing arises from the faithful person. Everything flows from the power of divine purpose in Christ. On this point, Bonhoeffer insists, "External privation and personal renunciation both have the same ground—the call and promise of Jesus. Neither possesses any claim to recognition" (106). No Christian *possesses* the strength to resist the world and the evil that rises and falls like waves in the ocean. There are, of course, faithful individuals who have the courage to speak the truth, who take personal risks of resistance, and who endure suffering and even death for others. Yet, the fact that Christian discipleship takes such forms in no way permits us to speak of achievement or greatness. "There is nothing for us to glorify in the disciples who bear the cross," writes Bonhoeffer, echoing Paul, "only the Father which is in heaven can be praised for the 'good works'" (119). To him goes all glory, laud, and honor.

The immediate context for the antiheroism of Camus and Bonhoeffer is telling. For both, the moral aspirations and political idealism of modernity failed to provide a basis for resistance to Nazism. For Camus, the profound evil of Nazism was not so much its violence and aggression but the dehumanizing force of Nazi ambition. The goal was not just to conquer and rule—such ambitions are as old as human history, indeed, they are the very core of history. Rather, the Nazi project involved absorption and digestion, and the primary means for achieving that end was to drive men and women from the ordinary tissue of life with relentless assaults. Fear submerges life into a sub-human struggle for survival. For Camus, resistance to this evil should not turn on a courage that reproduces the alienation of fear. We should not forsake the passions that connect us to everyday life, however venial and egotistical, in order to combat a plague. To do so risks defeat in victory. One should resist the sub-human with the human; one should resist the temptation to combat the ideology of the Superman, and his extra-moral rights to conquer, subdue, and digest, with a supra-human courage, a supra-human ideal. For Camus, one should not seek to escape hell in order to live in heaven. One should seek always to defend the rightful prerogative of mediocre earthly places like Oran and mediocre lives such as Grand's.

Bonhoeffer's antiheroism was both more closely tied to the specific threats of Nazism to human life, and less so. For Bonhoeffer, a member of a very prominent German intellectual family, one of the most painful revelations of the 1930s was the inability of his cultivated, intelligent, and deeply moral culture to resist Nazism. In the end, the pagan heroic ambition of Nazism could not be resisted with parlor room meetings of concerned citizens or petitions signed by university professors. Bonhoeffer could not sustain confidence, then, in a moral or humanistic heroism. The thin reeds of "critical freedom" and "moral ideals" are easily broken. Life is terribly complex; our civic responsibilities are often opaque and our personal obligations often require protective retreat. For Bonhoeffer, the Christian must renounce all independent and merely human bases for resistance. The pathos of *The Cost of Discipleship* is patent.

Against the labyrinths of reflection and moral judgment, Bonhoeffer juxtaposes the singular call of Jesus: follow me. One can never be a hero in such a simple turn toward total obedience: we hardly preserve anything of ourselves that could be called yours or mine. Bonhoeffer's disciple can never accept the palm. "But I was only following Jesus. That is, after all, nothing more than what it means to be a Christian."

In the end, however, Bonhoeffer is not concerned with effective means of resistance, and in that sense, the proximate cause of his most influential writings recedes from view. Bonhoeffer worries, finally, about the same problems that animated Paul and the great Protestant poets, Spenser and Milton: Jesus Christ, his greatness, and our participation in his achievement. He is worried about the salvation of his soul, and in so doing, he turns away from Hitler and the urgencies of his time. For the Christian is not concerned with resistance. Christ has triumphed, and he shall be all in all. Discipleship entails entering into that triumph, and in so doing, the Christian resists nothing, but rather, accepts all. Of course, the world may throw up blockades and launch attacks on the disciples' acceptance of the call of Jesus, but then the resistance is the world's, not the Christian's. To the extent that Bonhoeffer, the man, lived as he preached—and we should have no illusions here—he did not die resisting Nazism. No heroism here. Rather, his death was one of the final acts of Nazism to resist those who had been called to follow Jesus. The Gestapo henchmen, the SS court, the executioner, and Hitler, who took a personal interest in the execution of Bonhoeffer and the rest of the conspirators—they were active, Bonhoeffer was passive. He was made a martyr; he did not choose or make himself a martyr. But of course, that is precisely the way in which the Christian tradition has understood that strange power that Paul thought to be the inheritance of the baptized. Not I, but Christ in me.

Chapter Nine

Reclaiming Excellence

No longer the Saint, but the instinctual Everyman, twisting his neck uncomfortably inside the starched collar of culture, is the communal ideal, to whom men offer tacit prayers for deliverance . . .

—Philip Rieff, *The Triumph of the Therapeutic*

Spenser's gallant knights may charm contemporary readers, but his underlying poetic argument—that Christian faith has arresting glamor and heroic achievement—fails to persuade us of the reality behind the allegory. Jesus can be terribly appealing: a countercultural activist who expresses solidarity with social outcasts, a wise and spiritual teacher, a committed and courageous prophet. Joan of Arc can attract admiration as a feminist before her time, and militant popes can win accolades from patrons of Realpolitik. The witness of modern Christians such as Dietrich Bonhoeffer can testify to the importance of strong convictions in troubled times of mass hysteria. But the kind of faith that Bonhoeffer describes, a faith that Paul and early Christians demanded of those who would follow Jesus, a faith that animated Joan of Arc and defined the office if not the conviction of the bishops of Rome, extends far beyond what most of us seem willing to entertain.

The reasons for this deep reluctance regarding the strenuous heroism of obedient discipleship are many. For the freethinker, the dogmatic form of Christian teaching is a diminishment of our intellects. "Life is all about asking your own questions, not accepting other people's answers." Authority suppresses our impulse to question, we are warned; thus, the traditional Christian claims on our souls are kept at arm's length, neutered by the "obligations of critical responsibility." The avant-garde artist may reject the analytic reserve of the freethinker and embrace any number of fevered passions as the basis for creativity. But there are limits even for those who would "explore the boundaries of human experience." We often imagine that subservience to the past undermines our creativity, and that obedience to an authority outside ourselves is an act of bad faith that destroys authenticity. The avant-garde, the "going before" that John the Baptist urges in the Gospel of Mark, and that the martyrs and saints of the church undertook with such evident extremity of both passion and action, is too far beyond the boundaries of those who proclaim to renounce all boundaries. For them, all forms of human experience must be affirmed and explored—except a human experience born of and directed toward dependence on the something other than ourselves.

Most of us are neither freethinkers nor avant-garde artists. We are not preoccupied with critical responsibility; we do not find ourselves rebelling against dependence. We are just ordinary folks who are trying to live decently and without unhappiness. Here, Christian heroism offers little aid, and too often its demands and aspirations seem only to add to the burdens of life. However righteous and saintly the Christian hero, the shape of his life is not decent, not appropriate to the vast array of daily interactions: career, family, friends. One has a distinct sense that Francis of Assisi would throw a terrible chill over a good party, and Dietrich Bonhoeffer, however admirable in his convictions, certainly brought deep grief to his parents and fiancée. The urgency of discipleship, then, does little to smooth out the rough spots of life. Further, the moral teachings of Christianity, however noble in some aspects, entail intensive repressions of our sexual desires, our lust for possession, even our desire for achievements we can call our own. In each instance, we worry that Christianity proposes a narrow and ultimately diminishing framework for the pursuit of human excellence. Often, the call of Jesus seems to come as a horrible "No!" With respect to both the strenuous "yes" and the repressive "no," most of us adopt a therapeutic strategy. Of course we need to have ideals, but not unrealistic ideals. We do not wish to become fanatics. Many of us feel the need to discipline ourselves, but not too much, for we all need a little space to "be ourselves." We do not want to take on the ashen complexion of the ascetic, hungry and alone, perched on a pillar in a desert.

Whether taking cues from the freethinker's concern for intellectual honesty or the avant-garde artist's desire for something purely new and undefiled by dependence, or just sensitive to the weakness and already heavily loaded consciences of ordinary folks, much of what passes for modern theology entails translating the extremities of Christian heroism into something more ordinary and reassuringly human. The freethinker need take no offense; truly modern Christians affirm the high labors and strenuous tasks of "critical responsibility." Faith willingly submits to rational criticism, we are told, and when "modern man" can no longer believe in the miracles and superstitions of the past, then so much the worse for traditional Christianity. The avant-garde artist need not worry. The conscience of the believer always trumps ecclesiastical authority, and the past doctrines and disciplines of the Christian tradition are nothing more than symbolic resources for our present spiritual quests. Why not employ the Blessed Virgin and the cross in ever new and transgressive ways to express the spiritual truths within? For the burdened consciences and busy lives of ordinary folks, modern theology wishes to fashion its own word of grace: moral teachings are part of the ever-changing contextualization of faith. We should not trouble ourselves overmuch with Jesus' strenuous call, for the simple agrarian setting of first-century Palestine is really so different from our own complex modern situation that no commandment can be taken literally. But above all, modern theology seeks to reassure. Be not anxious, the call of Jesus is not really a call to self-denial. Faith is an ornament for our already very wonderful lives, or it is part of a menu of therapies for sick souls who want to feel good about themselves. After all, Jesus came to bear witness to God's love, and surely a loving God would not want to place the burdens of excellence and spiritual achievement on us.

These responses to the freethinker, the avant-garde artist, and ordinary folks are widely disparate. Sometimes modern theology downplays miracles and the supernatural when trying to answer the criticisms of the freethinkers of our age. Moral seriousness replaces the resurrection of the dead as the focal point of Christian teaching. In the next breath, modern theology can turn to the poetic souls of avant-garde artists and claim that Christianity enhances our spiritual journeys and deepens our experience of the transcendent. The abyss of mystery speaks to us out of the symbols of faith. At other times, with constant adjustment and revision, modern theology tries to help ordinary folks by translating the vertiginous contours of discipleship into something less exposed and precipitous. Christianity provides a sense of community in our atomized society; it adds grace notes of beauty and spiritual experience to the gray tasks of daily survival; it helps make us better wives and husbands, mothers and fathers; it offers hope to the hopeless, love to the loveless.

Across all these different formulations, however, a single theme endures, one that has been central to the Christian writers we have engaged. The freethinker, the avant-guard artist, and ordinary folks rightly sense that the Christian ideal of heroic discipleship involves an extraordinarily ambitious renunciation of a merely human basis for greatness, and this renunciation engenders suspicion. The freethinker sees the prerogatives of reason usurped, and the avant-garde artist recognizes an assault upon the immortal "I." Both rush forward with critical weapons and the battle cries of "reason" and "freedom." Ordinary folks are less clear about the dangers of excellence. They are no heroes of the intellect or bold explorers of experience, but they do have an investment in normalcy, and the ambitions of heroic discipleship seem to promise only endless turmoil and imprudent risks.

A recent Roman Catholic encyclical on the controversies in moral theology that stem from modern efforts to allay the fears of Christian heroism, *Veritatis splendor,* reinforces rather than relaxes such worries. For John Paul II, Christian moral teaching is fundamentally simple, differing not one iota from Bonhoeffer's fundamental imperative: follow Jesus. This entails "abandoning oneself to him" and "letting oneself be transformed in his grace" (para. 119). The Virgin Mary, the encyclical continues, is the exemplar of this self-abandonment; she is the perfect form of Christian heroism. "By accepting and pondering in her heart events which she did not always understand (cf. Lk 2:19), she became the model of all those who hear the word of God and keep it (cf. Lk 11:28)" (para. 120). She accepts what she cannot understand, follows whither she knows not where. This Marian pattern expresses the dynamic of Christian heroism that has been constant, from Paul, through the early Christian writers, to Spenser, Milton, and Bonhoeffer. By emptying ourselves of self-will and abandoning ourselves to the will of God, we participate in him. To use Athanasius's formulation, he gives glory to those who glorify him. Discipleship winnows, and everything we hold onto as indispensable to our dignity as persons—our intellectual powers, our free choices, our possessions, our altogether natural desires—is chaff, to be burned away so that God's power in Christ might be all in all.

For the Christian vision of heroic discipleship, the Virgin Mary, or any other disciple of Christ, can never give up enough of herself to hear and keep the word of God. Whether one is a freethinker concerned about critical reason or an avant-garde artist eager to affirm personal experience, or just one of the ordinary folks overwhelmed by the daily demands of life, this Christian heroism seems a narrow and diminishing way of life.

How can self-denial be the way to life? How can self-emptying be anything other than a repudiation of our humanity, and become an ascent, as Camus so effectively describes, to a "lofty plain"? Are we not thus turned into automata? Are we not made into faceless soldiers in an ecclesiastical army? Thinned to an allegory of spiritual purity that takes on Christ-like form, like Saint Francis in Dante's *Paradiso,* do we not forget our fleshly reality, our need for the small and comforting anchors of everyday life? The vast modern consensus treats such questions as rhetorical rather than real. Of course depthless obedience diminishes, of course complete self-denial is inhumane, of course such a life is simply unrealistic. Anyone who takes such a call seriously is heaping frustration upon frustration. Surely we should be in charge of our own destinies. Surely we should take responsibility for our lives. Surely we should live on the broad plains of "experience" rather than the high summits of a sanctity that we cannot even claim as our own.

The standard explanation of the modern reluctance toward the risky ambitions of Christian discipleship is Augustinian, and it emphasizes human pride. For Augustine, our souls are characterized by a profound dynamism. We cannot help but seek after that which is greatest, best, most excellent. We are programmed to seek the highest good, and to bend the knee in worship. However, this love of what is best comes to be mixed with our love of ourselves. We rebel against the idea that what is greatest might be beyond our ken. We hate the thought that our worship must be so radically other-directed that we must deny ourselves in order to love the highest good. In order to resolve this difficulty, we adopt a remarkable solution. We convince ourselves that *we* are the highest good. Our powers of reason, our creativity, our cultural achievements, our intuitions and experiences are the indispensable basis and proper objects of admiration. Thus, we come to satisfy our desire for what is best by worshiping ourselves. For Augustine, this self-deifying impulse necessarily resists the authority of Jesus' call. We cannot worship both God and ourselves, and forced to choose, we will deny Jesus and follow the commandments we give ourselves. We will glorify our humanity rather than Christ in his divinity.

This Augustinian analysis is adopted by many critics—and defenders—of Christianity. Critics may find such pride a sign of the maturity of our age. The great discoveries of the human intellect that constitute modern science, the transformative victories of freedom that define modern democratic society, the urgent creativity of the human spirit: all these achievements militate against the Virgin Mary's passive acceptance.

Our time is one of critical and moral adulthood, we are told, and we can no longer believe in the authority of the scriptures. We can no longer act as though we are children dependent on the benevolent commandments of a heavenly Father. We rightly demand room and scope for ourselves against the oppressive demands of authoritarian religion. Achilles stands against Abraham: the perfect human specimen enlarged by a purely personal passion resists the desert nomad defined by promises made by God. The critic urges us to choose the hero who is great because of who *he* is and what *he* has done. The freethinker urges the achievements of reason; the avant-guard artist, the personal passions of creativity; ordinary folks default to everyday demands and expectations. However, in each case, whether the ambitious critical independence of the freethinker or the more modest aspirations of sanity and a pleasant weekend that animate ordinary folks, the glory worth having must come from achievements of a purely human sort. A glory born of divine achievement is neither real nor glorious; it is an alien illusion that diminishes the intrinsic dignity of our humanity.

The critics of Christianity have no monopoly on this Augustinian explanation of the modern resistance to self-denying obedience. Many defenders of the classical patterns of discipleship assume that the present age preens with arrogant self-confidence and shape their polemics accordingly. Man, we are told, wishes to make himself a god and cannot tolerate his role as a creature. We want to dive into the treacherous waters of genetic engineering. We imagine that we can solve the problems of war and poverty with heroic interventions and radical re-education. We fantasize about our ability to design computers of surpassing intelligence. At every turn, then, Christian discipleship clashes, we are told, with the limitless scope of human ability and ambition, and we must choose between Achilles and Abraham. Only the latter type of heroism, that of obedient discipleship, will deliver us from illusions of grandeur and self-command and bring us to the lasting glory of faith.

For centuries of Christian reflection, this collision of Achilles and Abraham has preoccupied the imagination of great thinkers. Augustine's great story of his soul, the *Confessions*, turns on this axis of pride and obedience. As an ambitious young man, he wanted fame, and even after reading Cicero and submitting himself to the quest for wisdom, he wished to attain the mountain peaks of insight on his own. God must fit his understanding. He must be the pinnacle of a syllogism that Augustine could discover and defend. But Augustine failed to be a hero of that sort. His Achillean ambitions fell before the power of the gospel, and his life was shaped into the obedient form of Abraham's heroism. He left his mistress and his brilliant career as a teacher of rhetoric. He left Italy, the center of Roman culture and the place where men of surpassing ability made their marks and secured glory, and in obedience, he went to the North African city of Hippo and became a servant of the church. Augustine followed the way of Abraham rather than Achilles.

To a great extent, from Athanasius's *Life of St. Anthony* through Spenser's *Faerie Queene* to Milton's remarkable poetic output, Christian literature has sought to show the necessity of the turn away from the expressive potency of Achilles and toward the evacuative obedience of Abraham. Anthony must undertake the spiritual disciplines of desert solitude; Redcrosse Knight must enter the House of Holiness in order to drain away the imprisoning illusions of pride, and its inevitable echo, despair. Milton's heroic savior, Jesus, must resist the temptation to undertake a heroism independent of God in order to stand and await the role that God has ordained. At every turn, Christian heroism is not Achillean, and it does not turn on a distinctive potency or achievement that is unique to the individual. Athanasius is careful to underline Anthony's dependence on grace, and Spenser's allegory, however vigorous in dramatic action, consistently emphasizes the Christ-like structure of true heroism. Against pride and its fantasies of singular and unique achievement, Christianity proposes a heroism of recapitulation; the disciple manifests Christ, who works in and through the life of the faithful. It is not us, but Christ in us, who secures the glory.

As teachers of this literature, and as observers of contemporary culture, we are struck by the increasing irrelevance of Augustine's story, and the waning of the traditional Christian concern to defeat pride and its aspirations toward an independent and purely human heroism. To be sure, our age, like past ages, has its Promethean moments. There are confident rationalists such as Bertrand Russell who scoff at the weak-minded believer, committed sensualists such as D. H. Lawrence who truly believe in the redemptive power of sexual desire, and ardent racial propagandists such as Joseph Goebbels who preach the triumph of collective will. But notice that these three great exemplars are dead, and their heroic ambitions have become largely empty cliches. They do not represent towering Promethean moments of inflated self-pride, but signal increasingly conventional aspects of our fragmented postmodern society. Pride may go before the fall, but after the fall it can take on silly and domesticated forms.

It is our conviction that the most common contemporary objection to Abraham comes from the implicit antiheroism of ordinary folks, and not the fantasies of heroic achievement that animate the now conventional freethinker and tenured avant-garde artist. By and large, we observe that a rejection of heroic discipleship stems from calculated judgment rather than offended pride. At issue is not a defense of purely human excellence and achievement against the submissive demands of an obedient faith. Rather, the constant demands of normalcy militate against any form of ambition, Christian or otherwise. For this reason, our students find the Homeric world as strange as the biblical; Achilles is as alien and repulsive as Abraham. Achilles is awesome, no doubt, but to our students, he seems rather self-involved, inscrutable in his violence, and unpleasant to his friends. Aeneas may found a great city, but he seems to have no life. His repudiation of Dido is cold-hearted and his role as founder of Rome too mechanical, too impersonal. The elusive Socrates can appeal, for his ambiguous form is so easily shaped into what we want to see. He is a great freethinker, a defender of conscience, a debunker of communal conventions—but even Socrates fails to fire the imagination. He seems altogether determined to die, unwilling to make the sorts of compromises that we all know are necessary. No, these classical heroes, with a greatness closely bound up with their unique identities, destinies, and accomplishments, do not fire the imaginations of our students. Their stories are assigned in countless surveys of Western Civilization, but like so much of what students read, after the papers are written and exams taken, they yellow with the lecture notes that are filed away never to be read again.

The Christian apologist can imagine such disinterest in classical heroism a gain for faith. No longer will the inflated ego aspire to a human excellence that contests with grace for glory. Now, such an apologist might imagine, the medicine of authority and submission will go down more smoothly. The freethinker is defeated by a skeptical temper that is unwilling to pass judgment on either faith or unbelief. The constraints of ordinary life discipline the avant-garde artist. We are not eager, however, to celebrate the demise of these two venerable modernist heroes of reason and self-expression. For they fall because of a widespread crisis of heroism and not the conviction that faith fulfills reason or that discipline prepares one for divine glory. No, however antagonistic the modern adversaries, however comical their delusions of grandeur might seem in our been-there, done-that age, at least the freethinker and avant-garde artist are driven by ambition. For both, Christianity is resisted, not because it is too heroic, but because it is a false and delusory heroism that must be set aside in order to achieve a genuine, humanistic heroism.

To overcome this humanistic ambition by championing the eclipse of heroic endeavor yields a false victory for the Christian apologist. The seminal figures we have considered—Paul, Athanasius, Spenser, and Milton, and even the antiheroism of Bonhoeffer—do not take this approach. They seek to take ambition captive to the purposes of discipleship rather than drain it away as futile. The path of heroic discipleship involves an evacuation of self, to be sure, but such self-denial prepares the way for God to fill us with a supernatural vocation that is every bit as glorious, even more so, than the classical aspirations of Homer, Plato, and Vergil. Athanasius's *Life of Anthony* is so striking because he intends the desert ascetic to light the fires of ambition in the reader. The greater glory of divine life is the proper end of Anthony's obedient discipleship. The same holds true for Spenser and Milton: the life of faith has epic scope, and it involves achievements that participate in the "Above Heroic" greatness of God. For Paul and Bonhoeffer, the distinctive personal content of discipleship is muted, even renounced, but not in order to disappear but so that the follower of Jesus might become more perfectly transparent to the Master. In short, for Christianity, discipleship is not simply evacuative; it is a heroism that recapitulates the surpassing and divine heroism of Jesus. Thus, if our age is allergic to heroic ambition and inured to the attractions of excellence, then it cannot respond to the intensely transformative ideals of Christian discipleship. If Achilles lacks appeal, then the ambitions of those who accept Abraham as the father of a heroic faithfulness cannot capture the imagination.

We do not think that our students and their collective alienation from the heroic are idiosyncratic. They bear witness to the world in which they live. The perceived necessities of professional certification, the demands of economic success, the constraints of social acceptance: these many mean disciplines and requirements of submission are readily accepted. The suburbs are full of pigeon-holed professionals, palliating their dissatisfaction with a paycheck, or worse, full of laid-off workers, middle-aged managers who have endured the knife of downsizing, and who find out that fifty year olds are not easily re-employed. Pundits tell us that we need to prepare ourselves for multiple job changes, even career changes in the new economy. The same suburbs are just as full of divorcees and single parents whose primary goal is to hold together the basic elements of family life. Raised in this atmosphere of survival, students are altogether too aware of the minefields of marriage and parenting. They reflect the cruelty of the world that nurtured them. Their peer groups provide no shelter, as adolescents develop elaborate petty hierarchies and think nothing of cruel exclusion, even as they regurgitate the platitudes of tolerance and diversity fed them by educators. There is, in short, little room or scope for Promethean ambition. Christianity is not alien because it is evacuative. Christianity is alien because it pursues excellence without limit and seeks glory everlasting. Christianity remains a distant prospect, as distant as the triumphs of Achilles and the founding labor of Aeneas, because it is heroic. It is not Anthony's hair shirt that troubles, but the confidence and expectation with which he wears it.

How, then, could heroism become so alien and remote? We suggest three related influences that reinforce the broader sense that normalcy and comfortable survival are goals enough for ordinary folks. The first influence is an egalitarian piety that is closely related to Camus's affirmation of the intrinsic value of human solidarity. Heroic ambition, we worry, can be corruptive of the kinder, compassionate virtue of those committed to the equal dignity of all. This makes us suspicious of heroism, both classical and Christian. The second influence is a cynicism about the public markers of excellence and the ideals of great achievement. A critical sensibility that unmasks patterns of power and self-interest underneath the veneer of social hierarchies habituates us to distrust the heroes put before us for admiration and imitation. Finally, and most pervasively, a supine indolence tends to make us uninterested in and bored with heroism. Even as dreams are shattered by closed factories and broken promises, we float on an ocean of pleasant distraction. The anodynes of consumption both soften the blows of fate and weaken the fervor of ambition. Let us look at each in turn, for these influences, far more than the now conventional exhortations of the freethinker and tenured radicalism of the avant-guard patron of self-expression, make Christian heroism seem alien and unattractive.

Egalitarian Piety

Achilles triumphed on the plains of Troy, but Homer never suggests that this triumph was anything less than the outpouring of a unique and almost superhuman man. Achilles was stronger, swifter, more handsome, and ultimately, more driven by the singular power of his spirited nature than any other hero at Troy. Achilles, then, did not make himself a hero; he manifested the conquering power of his greatness. He was a "natural leader," a "born warrior." The avant-garde artist is a modern Achilles. He recuses himself from the standard economy of bourgeois respectability and lives in a Bohemian combination of poverty and freedom. The garret becomes a foundry of authenticity, and then, with a purely personal voice, the avant-garde artist reenters the fray of culture with conquering innovation and a sharp clarity of vision. Though triumphant, the avant-garde artist is, of course, unrecognized. He surpasses the conventional frames of reference, and cannot be incorporated into standard schools of thought or trends of artistic production. Only the privileged few, fellow heroes of authenticity, can grasp his true achievement. Nonetheless, the creative fruits of his vision, poems, novels, canvases, and sculptures that are monuments to his genius endure, and subsequent generations come to see, recognize, and glorify his heroism.

The avant-garde artist has succeeded beyond his expectations. Nineteenth-century Paris gives way to late–twentieth-century postindustrial culture, but the platitudes remain constant. The insights of genius are above judgment; the authenticity of experience transcends conventional standards; the future will vindicate revolutionary innovation. These clarion calls to artistic heroism become certainties, and in the hands of educational theorists, "genius" reverts to its original meaning. Everyone has a genius, of sorts, and all of us can make a claim to unique experience. "Silenced voices" are championed; everyone is urged to have courage for self-expression. In the therapeutic milieu that dominates our approaches to personal life, we reassure ourselves that our choices, as long as they reflect our "real needs," are justified. We believe that our children will come to see the necessity, even the essential rightness, of our divorces. Everyone has the right to escape unhappiness, and once the young see how narrow is the path toward happiness, they will forgive us our mistakes. In this way, we are all avant-garde artists of our own souls, implicit heroes of self-expression, true to ourselves very nearly by default. The conventional morality from which the avant-garde artist struggled for freedom now evaporates into an ether of "personal opinion" and multiplying "lifestyle choices" as we accord all others the dignity of personal genius and the right to self-expression that we claim for ourselves.

If all of us are heroes of individuality, then none of us can claim or even recognize excellence. The housewife's life is as legitimate, as worthy and heroic, as any other, "if that is what she wants." The high-powered medical researcher who seeks to make great discoveries and who covets a Nobel Prize is equally heroic, "if that is what she wants." Our lives are vindicated by our choices, and in the grip of egalitarian piety, we clear away invidious distinctions and objective standards that might impede self-expression. Every student at Anywhere High School is a valedictorian. Everyone has the right to be a hero. Like a banana republic that prints money with abandon, we mint rewards and praise and honors that are worthless. Existence itself becomes heroic. If you breathe, you triumph, or at least you can make a claim to the empty symbols of victory in battles never fought, races never run, tests never endured. Every competitor gets his trophy. The only failure is inauthenticity, but even here the confidence of a higher standard crumbles. Authenticity stems from the self-justifying truth of personal experience and the authority of pure individuality, and for just this reason, it is not at all clear how *anyone* can be inauthentic. We all have "experiences"; we are all "individuals." Some have a genius for self-command, others a genius for submission. Who are we to judge one the greater?

This reduction of heroism to the simple state of being a person cannot be sustained. Our egalitarian piety is limited by the claims that genuine excellence makes on our souls, and we do recognize some as more admirable than others. Great athletes evoke praise and adulation. Captains of industry enjoy celebratory profiles in financial magazines. Courageous individuals who resist tyranny or who commit themselves to social change are held up as exemplary heroes of conscience. However, our egalitarian piety will tolerate neither a Homeric nor a Pauline explanation of these forms of heroic achievement. There are no noble souls by birth, nor are there souls transfigured by grace. There is only achievement won by hard work, available to all who would make the effort. The platitude of high school graduations is constant: "If you work hard enough, you can do anything. You too can be a hero." This is not a Promethean claim of pride, but an assumption necessary to sustain our egalitarian piety. Heroism must be an act of the will, the sum of small disciplines and insignificant sacrifices, and not a consequence of good fortune, good birth, and strong genes, not the result of a grace inscrutable and given by God to some, but not others. Achievement and excellence, our thin world of self-help tells us, are within our reach, if only we will buy the latest book and follow the five easy steps to personal success.

For sensibilities constrained by egalitarian piety, then, heroic recognition is not an honor we bestow on liminal men and women whose gifts outstrip the ordinary and whose wills draw on a power we can barely imagine, and which no amount of self-discipline, no amount of hard work, could ever create. Achilles does choose; he does act and, in so doing, "make" his destiny. But when he draws his sword, from the sinews of his rippling muscles to the horrifying determination in his eyes, his adversaries see a force of nature, not a man who has piled up effort—graduate degrees, stock portfolios, certificates of achievement—like a careful bricklayer in order to "make" himself a great warrior. The same holds true for Anthony. His triumphs may read like a resume of saintly achievement, but as Athanasius makes clear, Anthony never made himself holy. Christ triumphed in him; all his victories were divine in origin, and they secured an everlasting glory.

There is an ascetical element in this egalitarian piety, a self-renunciation that insists that everybody is a hero or can become one with sufficient effort. This conviction requires evacuating the mind of insight into human nature, and it produces a careful discipline of verbal behavior. For example, when speaking of moral matters, our students compulsively qualify their judgments: "in my opinion," "from my point of view," "for me." They never want to impose their standards on others, for to do so would imply a higher, impersonal standard by which to judge the character of all. In this solipsism, the exigencies of egalitarian discipline are strenuous: never, never impose your opinions about human greatness on others. Eventually standards do impose themselves; the finish line is the great adversary of egalitarian illusions. However, we reassure ourselves that all heroes have earned their excellence by the ordinary means of hard work, accessible to all. If everyone is not a hero, actually, then all are heroes, modally. We *could be* heroic if we work hard enough at our goals. In both cases, the demands of egalitarian piety force a renunciation of surpassing excellence. The horizon of heroism must be domesticated and the range of achievement constrained so that all might think themselves worthy, actually or potentially, of the palm of victory.

Cynical Suspicion

Here, the freethinker, who so cherishes the cold dictates of objective observation and the stringent requirements of logic, cannot help but rebel. Surely, nothing we know about human beings provides evidence that human excellence is universally available. No amount of hard work will allow most of us to dunk the basketball. Endless hours of study will not unlock the mysteries of topology for those untouched by the spark of mathematical aptitude. To insist otherwise is to fall victim to illusions born of an irrational piety. The sharp critical demands of the freethinker may puncture our egalitarian piety, but the upshot is not a renewed enthusiasm for heroism, either classical or Christian. Quite the contrary, the relentless unmasking that characterizes critical examinations of human culture also undermines the heroic. After but a few courses in social science and cultural studies, students adopt a cynical stance toward pious claims and high ideals. The purely evacuative demands of critical judgment disenchant the heroic and devalue the glory of excellence.

As Max Weber recognized, disciplined scientific inquiry is a spiritual vocation, and involves renouncing the pleasing outward features of human culture in order to penetrate underneath comforting fictions to examine the inner workings of society. The upshot is what Weber calls a "disenchantment of the world." The glorious veneer must be peeled away, and the common materials of our humanity—our violent impulses, our covetousness, our fear of death, our desire for security—exposed in their diverse forms and manifestations. To endure without illusions requires rigorous commitment to rational inquiry, as well as the determined conviction that insight, however remote from the high ideals and pious hopes of one's childhood, is sufficient reward for the hard labors of science. This self-restraint and acceptance of the thin rewards of critical inquiry is, for Weber, a moral achievement. We desperately want to believe that we are destined for a greater glory, for something like the Rome that Aeneas founds, or the divine glory that Paul so confidently claims as the possession of all who are reborn in baptism. But such ambition and hope cannot endure critical scrutiny. Vergil's Rome was governed with brutal imperial principles, and Paul's faith cannot withstand the tests of rational justification. Thus, the Weberian scientist must be a veritable Milton of critical reason: he must see and handle and analyze, and yet abstain. The only possible heroism is to resist the temptations of heroism.

The same sensibility has interpretive consequences when carried over to the more fulsome heroes of Homer and Athanasius. Gifted students have little trouble analyzing the *Iliad.* They see that Homer's depiction of Achilles reinforces the patriarchal system of violence and oppression. The hero stands above communal restraint and reshapes social mores to serve his interest in power and domination. Thus, the *Iliad* functions to legitimate the dominion of the powerful over the powerless. The same analysis can be performed on Athanasius's account of Anthony's life. By depicting a Christian saint who submits himself to orthodoxy and divine authority, Athanasius is reinforcing his ecclesiastical power, and justifying his persecution of heterodox groups. At every turn, then, the hero is a mask for vested interests and cruel practices. Heroic literature, concludes this critical sensibility, attempts to gain our loyalty and legitimate the pleasant illusions that disguise the unattractive features of human nature and social interaction. As the bright armor of the warrior and the radiant glow of the martyr are transfigured by critical insight into the grey machinery of culture, a cynical suspicion of the heroic comes to predominate.

Supine Indolence

Prudence triumphs over the risks of excellence, and this, we believe, more than anything else, undermines our capacity to see and admire the heroic, in ourselves or others. Parents urge their children to work hard in school, to fill their resumes with just the right sorts of activities, to get good job experience. But this advice has not a tinge of real ambition. We need to lay up a treasure of skills and credentials in order to protect ourselves against a dangerous world. The *labor et virtus* of our time—and surely we live in an age of intense self-discipline, long hours at work, and seemingly boundless activity—does not strive toward the founding of a new city. We compact our souls; we pour ourselves into jobs and projects—but with a defensive purpose. Our achievements are little more than an electric fence we erect around our egos, our families, and our retirements. We do not extend ourselves in the risks of ambition governed only by the lure of excellence and blind to the dangers of failure. The so-called risk takers—the entrepreneurs, the wealthy middle-aged professionals who try to climb Mount Everest, the artists who pose against the background of transgression—are nothing more than gamblers looking for a big payoff. They want to add to their personal account—their bank accounts and their ego accounts. They simply calculate in larger sums than most of us.

Prudence mounts constant assaults on our imprudent and often uncontrollable desire for excellence. For example, we worry about the fate of gifted children. Such a child should not "feel" different from his or her peers. The concern is not to inculcate Christian humility, for that entails driving the gifted beyond the horizons of their surpassing abilities toward the vision of an achievement higher still. Rather, we worry about talented children because of our collective preoccupation with plain vanilla happiness. Precocious children must be properly socialized; they need to enjoy the playground. As they grow older, they need to feel comfortable in the pinched world of adolescent isolation. They need to fall under the sway of anxieties about fitting into their peer group, about whether or not they have the right clothes, the right car, and the right date for the prom. God forbid that a talented child miss out on normalcy; otherwise, she or he will never "fit in." If talented children are recognized, then they will feel the endless lash of expectation and ambition. Faced with Achilles' choice of returning to his family and enjoying the home and hearth, or the cold and isolating steel of battle, they might, like him, be unable to embrace mediocrity and its soft pleasures. Buffeted with anxieties about our own happiness and numbed by the comforts of postindustrial plenty, we think such a fate terrible. Better to encourage a "normal childhood."

The triumph of a fearful and sated prudence is the greatest threat to Christian discipleship. The freethinker can be met in the open contest of argument and evidence, and cynical suspicion is sufficiently confident of its critical truths that the Christian apologist has an opportunity to undertake his or her own Socratic battles with the city of reason. The avantgarde artist and the domesticated cult of self-expression that animates our egalitarian piety also have weaknesses. The potent experiences of the saints and the sheer radiance of discipleship that Athanasius thought so self-evident have the power to convict and convert. However, both anxious and well-fed, the supine indolence of the present age can be indefeasible. The Virgin Mary seems a strange and disturbing figure because she signals dangerous territory where we fear our psyches cannot survive. The very idea of virginity is terrifying. It is so . . . *abnormal.* Could I really endure such renunciation? Could I survive being so different from ordinary folks? And toward what end? What are, thinks our calculating prudence, the compensations? But within the patterns of heroic discipleship, chastity is no more than the urgent physical center of any number of rings of risky renunciation: property, family, and communal loyalty. At every turn, the intense ambition of Christian discipleship challenges our sense of what is reasonable, humane, even possible. Abraham is not a threat to our reason or our freedom of self-expression. Most of us have little loyalty to argument and evidence; inconvenient facts and inferences are repressed. We have little confidence in our personal genius, and we are more concerned about "finding our voice" than speaking our minds. Nor is Abraham a threat because he is obedient. We are largely followers rather than leaders, and prudence dictates conformity and submission most of the time. Rather, Abraham is terrible because his obedience is so singular, so extreme, so heroic.

In his massive account of the history of the world, the *City of God*, Augustine undermines the classical world's claim to heroism. The achievements of Rome were not justice and peace, Augustine argues, but only the cessation of vicious conflict, an absence of violence made possible by threat and domination. The virtues of such a civilization, he continues, were nothing more than glorious vices, able to command admiration in their time. But these virtues were hollow, and according to Augustine, they lacked the everlasting glory of God, for the achievements of classical heroism were defined by a city of men whose vision was limited and whose ambitions were crimped by the implacable realities of suffering and death. Neither Homer, nor his ancient readers, nor Achilles himself, could do more than glimpse a heroism beyond the ebb and flow of human conquest and the uncertain outcomes of our collective struggle for the satisfactions of vengeance, the restoration of earthly honor, and the glory of dominion. Yet, in his polemic against classical ideals of political and personal achievement, Augustine is no more antagonistic to the underlying human ambition for glory than Athanasius. Augustine's goal is to capture our desire for excellence and to direct it toward an end supremely worthy of our ambition, an end that certainly surpasses the human frame of reference, not tragically, but redemptively. As a result, for Augustine, not all virtue is an illusion. Faith, hope, and love are true virtues, and they bring us to participate in the glory of God in Christ, a glory that is everlasting.

It is our conviction that Augustine's decision to write a Christian epic of world history signals a basic truth about the literary and poetic atmosphere in which Christian faith flourishes. The glamor of discipleship and the real glory of Christian virtues are most visible in the context of fulsome heroic discourse. However dangerous the temptation of pride, Christianity has no interest in reinforcing the egalitarian piety and cynical suspicion that make heroism seem so scandalously elitist or hopelessly naive. And Christianity certainly should not contribute, with therapeutic preaching and the cheap grace of an easy, accepting God, to the supine indolence of the present age. Christians should actively embrace Abraham, not shrink from the extremity of his obedience. Milton's vision is crucial. He knew the temptations of pride and feared the blandishments of earthly glory as much as any Christian writer, and yet, his approach was not to undermine human ambition, but to bring it to the forum in which such ambition might be realized in an "Above Heroic" achievement. Milton does not shrink from heroism; he took its heroic discourse captive in his poetry in order to entice his readers toward the extremity of Abraham's obedience.

Christian education and engagement with heroic literature ought to follow Milton's lead. Athanasius wants us to marvel at Anthony and his achievements, and in order to fall victim to Anthanasius's intentions, we must train and stretch our imaginations beyond the pinched confines of egalitarian piety and cynical suspicion, and we must certainly free our souls from the many chains of supine indolence. Spenser wishes to incite us toward an active faith that quests toward high goals, and in order to follow his poetic arguments, not just analytically but personally, we need to develop a living vocabulary of the heroic. At each point, these Christian writers have not renounced heroism. They have not rejected excellence. They have reclaimed heroism and excellence on behalf of the highest good. We should do the same.

Notes

Chapter 1   The Challenge of Christian Heroism
1. Friedrich Nietzsche (1989).

Chapter 2   The Presence of the Hero: Achilles
1. This task is itself a "heroic" undertaking; Hainsworth (1991:8) says that the epic poet "must be, like the heroes of whom he sings, 'great-souled' and not flinch at the problems posed by grim fate, stern duty, and the inscrutable purposes of the gods."
2. The line numbers that appear are those of the Greek. All translations are our own. Some modern translations of the *Iliad* adhere to the Greek line numbers; others do not. The line numbers of Richmond Lattimore's 1951 translation follow the Greek and therefore will be identical to ours. We also recommend Robert Fagles's 1991 translation. Its marginal line numbers, however, apply only to its own translation; the equivalent Greek lines appear in brackets at the top of Fagles's pages.
3. Cf.Nagy 1979, especially chapter 2.
4. *Iliad* 9.343 and Griffin ad loc. (1995:115). Briseis herself will later weep over the body of Patroclus and say that he promised to marry her to Achilles (19.297–99), but a similar lost hope is never expressed by Achilles. He does receive her back from Agamemnon, and in the last scene in which he appears, he is sleeping beside her, as a final, pictorial resolution of the quarrel of book 1 (24.675–76). Cf. also Taplin (1992:212–18) on the significance of Briseis.
5. So inauspicious are these narrative conditions that Finkelberg even suggests that the "incongruity" between Achilles' need to enact his *aretê* and his singular concern for *tîmê* might invite the question whether the *Iliad* is "the work of a single poet" or the product of "multiple authorship" (1998:27–28). The incongruity she interprets as the overflow of one age's ethics into another we read as the narrative consequence of Achilles' overflowing excellence.
6. Griffin 1995:134, note to lines 524–26.
7. Griffin 1995:21 Achilles' speech is "the point at which we see how extraordinary a hero Achilles is, and at which we judge his decision not to come to terms with Agamemnon."

8. The terms "competitive" and "cooperative" are those of Adkins, from his influential study *Merit and Responsibility* (1960), chapter 3. They are now in general use (cf., e.g., Cairns [1993] and Zanker [1994]) though not without dissent. Finkelberg, for example, suggests that *tîmê* is a "distributive" rather than a "competitive" value (1998:16).

9. Nestor (9.104–13), Odysseus (19.181–83), and even Agamemnon himself (2.375–80, 9.115–20, 19.137–39); also Poseidon (13.111–14).

10. The most influential articulation of this interpretation is Parry 1956. The most careful study of the language of Achilles and its originality is found in Martin 1989. Cf. also Taplin (1992:66–73), Zanker (1994:73–92), Gill (1996:124–54).

11. A glorious death is also a conveyor of *kleos,* as the choice of Achilles implies; but in this as in all else, Achilles is the exception rather than the rule.

12. Redfield (1975:105) calls Achilles' great speech in book 9 "Sarpedon's speech inside-out or in negative print." Achilles, however, has a special knowledge of his own mortality; to what degree and when this knowledge becomes part of his motivation is unclear. For an interpretation that puts great weight on Achilles' knowledge of his brevity, cf. Zanker 1994:77–84.

13. Taplin (1992:50) expresses it most clearly: "*Tîmê* entails questions that are in the broadest sense 'ethical.' What does some particular one deserve *tîmê* for, and how much? Who should grant it? What form should it take? Much of the *Iliad* is, in my view, spent on disputing just such questions as these, issues of just desserts, approval, disapproval, credit, and blame." Cf. Gill 1996:70.

14. Gill 1996:134 n. 129

15. Claus 1975:24 "Achilles must be paid, but he cannot be bought." Modern readers might compare recent past discussions of Michael Jordan's "worth" to the NBA, which have little relation to his salary or his recognized excellence.

16. How Agamemnon has this right of redistribution is not made completely clear in the text. Nestor says that Agamemnon is preeminent because "he rules the most men," and the catalogue of ships confirms that Agamemnon's contingent is the largest. Recently, Taplin (1990:67–70) has suggested that his position is due to his relationship to Menelaus, the wronged party, and that as his brother, Agamemnon is in charge of this expedition. Whatever the reason, Agamemnon does not come off favorably in the text. The inequity of Agamemnon's share is also a charge of Thersites (2.225–33), who is silenced without being contradicted.

17. This third is not novel. The ethical systems supplied to frame the actions of Achilles often set up some sort of dichotomy to contain him or define him as inside or outside, e.g., Redfield 1975:103: "Achilles . . . looks back at culture from the outside." Achilles consistently reveals the inadequacy of dichotomies or of systems to contain him, as he goes "beyond" or is "spe-

cial" in his relationship to them. See notes 18 and 20 below. The ethical systems described, whether they are based on competitiveness or reciprocity or affection, are not inaccurately identified, just inadequate; hence Achilles as "special." It is his "specialness" that we are trying to explain.

18. Zanker ranks "affection and a sense of fairness" as "the ultimate motivation" for cooperation within heroic society, and he adds, "Competitive honor is presented as the more compelling proximate motive" (1994:22). Zanker's argument is cogent, but as he also notes, Achilles has "a special view of the value of honor" (77–78) which strongly suggests that he has a different sense of what is ultimate and what is proximate.

19. He does not speak again of leaving, but he claims that he will not return to the fight until Hector's attack reaches his own ships (9.649–55).

20. This is a point too often overlooked. Achilles feels an isolation from others, whether he still participates in the system or not. Mark Edwards points out that Achilles does not understand why no others reject Agamemnon's authority, and he belittles them for it (1986:233–34). Achilles says that his own men fault him for his intransigence (16.198–206). Although Gill argues for a "participant-objectivist" reading of Achilles, in his analysis of Achilles' exchange with Ajax he says: "To this extent, it seems that Achilles pushes to (or even beyond) the limits of acceptibility, and intelligibility, the implications of the ethics of the generalized reciprocity, and of the gratuitous gesture, as he interprets these" (1996:152). It is the implications of the "beyond" that we are concerned with.

21. We refer especially to the works of Adkins (1960), Redfield (1975:113–19), and Cairns (1993:48–146); Cairns provides a useful bibliography.

22. Cairns is careful to explain that no single English term covers the expanse of *aidos* in Greek, which includes aspects of "shame, embarrassment, and respect" (1993:14, passim). *Nemesis* comes closer to being captured by our sense of "righteous indignation."

23. Hera's response, however, suggests that Apollo may not speak for *all* the gods in saying this (24.55–63). Cf. Cairns 1993:131–32 and n. 257.

24. Cf. Cairns 1993:97: "in some individuals *aidos* can be powerful to the point of being undesirably so. It should be no surprise that it is not powerful in every individual."

25. Redfield 1975:118: For Achilles, "*nemesis* is purely personal. . . . Achilles has made of his own will a moral law."

26. There is some question about the appropriateness of this Meleager tale, which itself stretches the boundaries of unity, to the dilemma of Achilles. Meleager's withdrawal is due to his mother's curse, which goes unactivated in Homer, and which he earned for killing her brother, his uncle. The relation of that event, and of the Calydonian boar hunt, to the siege of Calydon by the Couretes, and of the whole to the parallel with Achilles and Troy, is confusing. It seems likely that the story of Meleager has been manipulated

to fit the scheme of the *Iliad,* and in so doing, ends up an uneasy hybrid. Cf. Griffin 1995:134–36.

27. Hector usually addresses Paris with reproach in the epic (3.38–57, 6.325–31, 13.765–73). Likewise, Trojans view him as the cause of the war, and some wish his death (3.451–54, 7.344–97).

28. Supplications between gods are always successful; some supplications between men are not. For example, four Trojans who face death on the battlefield ask for mercy and are killed (Adrestos: 6.37–65; Dolon: 10.454–57; sons of Antimachus: 11.122–47; Lycaon: 21.71–119). Supplications between men and gods also meet varying success. Cf. Pedrick 1982:132–40. Most notably, Achilles prays to Zeus after sending Patroclus into battle, asking that Zeus give Patroclus success in battle and then that he come safely from battle. Zeus grants the first and denies the second (16.232–52).

29. In fact, the poet makes the connection: Patroclus's words at 16.273–74 are identical to Achilles' at 1.411–12. Taplin seems right on: "Patroclus is a pale reflection of Achilles' own fate" (1992:181).

30. Edwards (1986:264–73) is particularly good on these foreshadowings from books 16–18.

31. Patroclus recounts it himself as a ghost to the sleeping Achilles (23.84–90).

32. Taplin 1992:252

33. Cf. Segal 1971:51–52

34. Taplin (1992:181–82) notes that the yoking of a mortal trace-horse, which dies, to the immortal horses for Patroclus (16.154) prefigures the relationship of Patroclus to Achilles. These same horses mourn Patroclus and speak to prophesy Achilles' death (17.432–40 and 19.404–17).

35. A concise, intelligent overview of the role of the funeral games is found in Macleod 1982:29–32.

36. The time frames in book 1 parallel those in book 24: Achilles grieves for eleven days after Agamemnon dishonors him (1.421–27, 488–95) and defiles Hector's body for eleven days after the funeral games (24.31). Cf. Macleod 1982:32–34 for this and other structural parallels.

37. Taplin discusses this *kudos,* 1992:263.

38. For a comparison of passages, see Macleod 1982:20–21.

39. 24.580–95. Andromache envisions Hector naked and vows to burn the clothes that he will never wear upon the pyre (22.510–14). Cf. Segal 1971:45–47 and Taplin 1992:274.

40. For the significance of this word and this concept, see Zanker 1994:127–54.

Chapter 3   Irony of Presence and Absence: Socrates

1. The formal genre of tragedy was born in Athens, mid- to late sixth century B.C.E., a hybrid of lyric, choral, and dialogue meters and forms. The influences on Greek tragedy were extremely diverse and not limited to Homer, but the figure of Achilles, desolate and implacable, provides perhaps the single strongest reference for the tragic condition.

2. Diogenes Laertius 3.5. It is unlikely, however, that Plato did not meet Socrates until he was a young man. Socrates was well-known enough in Athens to be mocked in comedies as early as 423 B.C.E., when Plato was a child, and Plato's maternal uncle, Charmides, was devoted to Socrates. Socrates frequented public places—the agora, the gymnasia—where the young Plato certainly must have gone.

3. Tragedians recognized the dramatic value of the forensic setting. The *Eumenides* of Aeschylus is extant; in plays that we know only by title or fragments tragedians presented the trials of Palamedes and the judgment of Achilles' armor. Socrates expresses an interest in talking to Palamedes and Ajax, victims of "unjust judgments," in the afterlife (*Apology* 41b).

4. The accuracy of Plato's account of the trial of Socrates is a notorious and long standing scholarly problem. (The best review of evidence and summary of scholarly opinion for both the "accuracy theory" and the "fiction theory" can be found in Brickhouse and Smith 1989:2–10.) Socrates, like Jesus, was a historical figure; and like Jesus, Socrates' words are recorded for us by others. Moreover, like the stories of Jesus, Plato's accounts of Socrates are highly intentional: he wants us to see the real Socrates, his distinctive character as the wisest of men. This does not mean that Plato sought factual or stenographic accuracy. Quite the contrary, as we will see in Plato's very conception of true excellence, a scribal recapitulation of Socrates' words or a pedestrian catalogue of his daily actions would cause the reader to founder on outward and inessential features, thus failing to see Socrates as he *really is*. So, like the art of accusation or defense in the courtroom, Plato must write in such a way as to manifest the excellence proper to his hero; he must bring to bear, in an effective way, what will sway us and bring us to recognize and appreciate Socrates. As such, we will read the *Apology* as a faithful account, faithful to the fact that Socrates triumphs in his speech, and in this way manifests his heroic excellence.

5. On the conflict between Socrates and Athenian traditions, see West 1979:78–80. Socrates' relation to Iliadic heroism is paradoxical. Eisner (1982:13) says, "In the Platonic dialogues we have moved, as their author intended we should be, a world away from the timocracy and shame culture of the *Iliad*," but the Iliadic world and its values are invoked and redefined.

6. All translations are our own. We refer to Plato by the conventional Stephanus pages of the Greek text, which are subdivided into five parts indicated by the small letters *a* through *e*. Most modern translations include some reference to these ancient divisions.

7. Aristophanes' *Clouds*, which Socrates cites specifically (19c), is the best extant example of such a characterization. In all likelihood, there is some truth to it. In the *Phaedo* (96a–100b), Socrates gives evidence of his early interests in science and natural philosophy before he began ethical philosophy.

8. The specific influence of Aristophanes' *Clouds* is difficult to judge. The play that we have is a partially revised version of the one produced in 423, which finished last in the comic competition. In the Platonic works, Socrates cites

it here and Alcibiades is made to quote from it in the *Symposium* (221b); other Platonic passages may also be read as covert responses to Aristophanes (cf. Vander Waerdt 1994a:52 n. 17). Socrates was a frequent target of comedians: in 423, the same year of Aristophanes' *Clouds*, Ameipsias also produced a comedy about Socrates titled *Konnos*, of which only fragments remain. Aristophanes and Eupolis, another comic poet whose works exist only in fragmentary form, found the idiosyncratic and well-known Socrates an easy butt of jokes, as others must have. Cf. Aristophanes *Birds* 1282, 1553–64, produced in 414, and *Frogs* 1491, produced in 405.

9. West explains the narrow constraints of Socrates' self-presentation before the court in a manner analogous to our own: "Only if truth and beauty, philosophic and political speech, could be united would a successful and truthful defense of Socrates be possible. This would mean that the 'foreign dialect' of philosophy would have to learn how to speak the language of the political community, in order to show that philosophy and philosophers can be at home in the city. To do this, philosophy would have to discover a way of telling the truth that is politically responsible and respectable—one that could evoke from common men the conviction that the truth is noble, and that it can defend justice from injustice" (West 1979:80).

10. The evidence of the *Phaedo* (96a–100b) argues that these things *once* occupied him. Aristophanes' *Clouds* presents Socrates as substituting a cult of the clouds for the cult of the mysteries of Athens. It is possible that Socrates experienced an early "conversion" of sorts, away from natural to moral philosophy, but the nature of that conversion must remain speculative.

11. Strauss 1983:40.

12. In the heroic world (as in the industrial world), old age may bring with it the virtue of wisdom, but more often senescence borders on irrelevance. In the *Iliad,* Nestor is painfully aware of his own diminution: his opportunities for glory are things of the past; the prize that he wins in the funeral games for Patroclus is an expression of charity, because he cannot compete (*Iliad* 11.668–70; 23.615–23).

13. Whether Socrates had a substantial reputation before the oracle's pronouncement is unclear, nor is the date of Chaerephon's visit to Delphi known. Scholars who read the *Clouds* as accurate, for example, assume that Socrates was known to Delphi for the sophistic practices caricatured in the play; others assume that his reputation was already based on his wisdom. Reeve surveys these arguments and points out, in contrast, that the oracle often replied with answers contrary to expectation—when asked for the happiest man, the oracle names someone unknown or already dead; when asked for the wisest man, it names a poor peasant. Reeve concludes that Socrates need not have had a substantial reputation before the oracle; he need only have been self-knowing in the way that led to his particular interpretation of the oracle (1989:28–37).

14. Socrates says that he was "commanded" by the god "through oracles and dreams and with every way that one divine portion or other has ever commanded a man to do anything" (33c4–8). Socrates, of course, lacks the essential unwillingness of Heracles, and he undertakes his mission as a "service to the god" (23c1)—but Brickhouse and Smith miss the heroic parallel when they insist "Socrates' sense of obligation to the god derives from his already-held belief about the requirements of piety, not from the direct command issued through the Delphic oracle" (1989:95).

15. As Socrates says, "Indeed it is necessary to reveal my wandering to you, as if I were fulfilling labors, in order that the oracle not be reproached" (22a). The Greek employs a redundancy, "as if I were laboring labors" (*ponous tinas ponountos*), which is the standard phrase to describe Heracles' labors. Heracles uses this of himself, for example, at the end of Sophocles' tragedy *Philoctetes* when he appears as the *deus ex machina* (1419). The Greek word *ponos*, like the Latin *labor*, may mean both "labor" and "misery."

16. Ancient authors were well aware of Heracles' dramatic ambiguity, employing him as an epic, tragic, comic, and philosophical hero (see Galinsky 1972). For the philosopher Prodicus, and others who followed him, Heracles "suggested himself as Everyman," a hero whose character has an inclusive scope (Galinsky 1972:102).

17. Socrates does cite something that would bring him shame: "doing and saying everything to escape the sentence" and "to flee death" (38d2–39a1).

18. Socrates himself defines (or redefines) irony, as even the ancients noted: the Roman grammarian Quintilian notes that irony (*ironia*) may characterize an "entire life" (*vita universa*), and his sole example is Socrates (*Institutio Oratoria* 9.2.46). Of course, this makes any definition of the nature of his irony surprisingly difficult. Scholars, who note this difficulty, have offered several different definitions. Most famously, Vlastos states that there is no hint of intentional deception in Socratic irony, as the Greek word *eironeia* implies, but that his irony is "complex," that Socrates "both does and does not mean what he says" (1991:21–44), hence the modern use of the word. Other scholars contend that Vlastos stops short and ignores the "dramatic" dimension of the Socratic irony in the Platonic dialogues, where there is an audience who understands and one who does not (Gottlieb 1992; Gordon 1996), which resurrects the possibility that the one group on the outside is deceived; there is also the audience of the dialogues themselves, into which we fall. Both aspects of Socratic irony, the complex and the dramatic, come together in our discussions of his essential irony, heroic and ordinary, recognized and condemned.

19. As Burnet points out in his commentary, this is "another way of putting the requirement of care of the soul (29e1)." The Greek has no denominative word for what we translate as "interests": "the things of himself" is more literal. The implication is that everyone's primary care should be for the self,

the soul, first and foremost; and afterward, for health, wealth, honor, or any other "interests" or circumstances and properties of the soul. The same is then said for the city itself.

20. The verb used here to propose a penalty is *timasthai,* at the root of which is *tîmê.* Since *tîmê* is that which is due to a person, it implies both punishment and reward.

21. Xenophon pointedly observes that "Socrates ever lived in the public eye" (*Memorabilia* 1.1.10).

22. Alcibiades captures this facet of his irony, *Symposium* 221c–d.

23. See Long 1988:152: "Though Socrates' philosophical principles clamoured for replication and interpretation, there could be no dissemination of the whole man, on the basis of all the sources, either as a paradigm on whom to model one's life or as a more abstract set of theories. Socrates was too complex, too individualistically contoured, to be appropriated in full by any single philosophical school."

24. In another heroic analogy, Alcibiades says that "Ajax is more vulnerable to iron than Socrates to money" (*Symposium* 219e1–2).

25. Clay (1972) draws parallels between the mules ("half-asses") and heroes ("half-gods") in Socrates' conversations and Socrates' own irony.

26. Plato may have in mind here another heroic allusion. The Greek archer Philoctetes received Heracles' bow after Heracles' death. As Philoctetes was sailing to Troy before the start of the war, he was bitten by a serpent. The wound was not fatal but excruciating and repugnant, and the Greeks abandoned Philoctetes on the island of Lemnos. For the duration of the war he remained on Lemnos until a prophecy revealed that Troy could not be taken without Philoctetes and Heracles' bow. Sophocles wrote an extant tragedy, one of his greatest, on the subject. Alcibiades suggests that Socrates' influence is more determinative of character than Philoctetes' fateful snake bite.

27. Patterson (1982:87–90) argues for the "tragedy" and "comedy" of Alcibiades in terms set forth by Plato in the *Symposium* and other dialogues.

Chapter 4   The Fate of Achilles: Aeneas

1. See Hornsby 1987:13, "Homer hinted at the need for some other *modus vivendi* than the heroic code and Vergil took up the challenge." Hornsby, however, would probably disagree with our statement, since he holds that Vergil is expanding on Homer's vision, not denying it.

2. Scholars do not often frame their interpretations in terms of change and continuity per se, and it is sometimes difficult to know which they think is the case. Otis (1995:305–12) argues clearly for change, but points to the "conversion" of the sixth book.

3. This equivocation generally puts the interpretive burden on those who read change in Aeneas, because the usual narrative markers that indicate a char-

acter's change are not present in Aeneas: he speaks little, he has no epiphany, nor is it clear exactly what he learns nor when he learns it. Other characters do experience realizations and express their emotions and insights, while Aeneas moves steadfastly, if sometimes blindly, toward the realization of his destiny. For a rhetorical and political explanation of Aeneas's "taciturnity," see Feeney 1983.

4. A single example may suffice. In his passage "home," Aeneas is detained for a swift year of love by Dido, as Odysseus is by Circe; but Dido is very human, devoted to the memory of her first husband, and surrounded by suitors, as Penelope is in the *Odyssey*. By mingling parallels to Circe and Penelope in Dido, Vergil complicates the question of the rightness of Dido and of staying in Carthage with her.

5. Vergil does not engage Odysseus's heroism, almost dismissing it. As Lyne notes, "we find that characters themselves have views about the roles being played" in the Iliadic allusions (1987:108), but the same does not happen in the "Odyssean" books. No characters compare themselves with Odysseus. Stanford puzzles out this "oblique form of depreciation" (1963:133). Odysseus is mentioned, of course. In the vivid second book, Odysseus (whom the *Aeneid* calls by his Latinized name Ulixes, hence Ulysses) is the architect of Troy's fall through the deceptions of the Trojan horse and the false tale of Sinon. He is a metonymy for treachery: Laocoön cites him specifically in his warning (*sic notus Ulixes?* 2.44). Aeneas laments that the Trojans were "captured by deceptions and forced tears, we whom neither Diomedes nor Achilles, nor ten years nor a thousand ships overcame" (2.196–98). Odysseus may offer an alternative form of success, but not a legitimate form of heroic enactment for the *Aeneid*. If Aeneas is merely donning a (false) role in the enactment of his destiny, then the epic fails.

6. We follow other scholars in this division. Cf. Pöschl: "The sorrowful memory of Troy . . . is a recurring leitmotif in the first third of the *Aeneid*. . . . The middle third contains, as it were, the hero's emancipation from the burdens of the past" (1962:36, 37, and 181 n. 6).

7. The line numbers that appear are those of the Latin. All translations, unless otherwise noted, are our own. Few modern translations of the *Aeneid* adhere to the line numbers of the Latin text. The most available translation is that of Robert Fitzgerald. Its marginal line numbers, however, apply only to its own translation; the line numbers of the equivalent Latin lines appear at the top or bottom of the page.

8. Scholars haved debated whether *pietas* has the affective sense in the *Aeneid,* especially for Aeneas, as we maintain. Arguments against such a possibility (e.g., Lee 1979:17–23) often point to the "contradiction" between duty and affection rather than to conflicts of different affections. Saller (1994:105–14), by contrast, presents cultural evidence for the devotional and affective dimensions of *pietas.*

9. Otis describes Vergil's style as "subjective" in comparison with Homer's "objective" style (1995:41–96). Segal (1981) studies this passage with an emphasis on the dialectic between "authorial" and "participatory" voices.

10. These lines are notoriously compressed and difficult to translate. The Latin of 461–62 runs: *sunt hic etiam sua praemia laudi, / sunt lacrimae rerum et mentem mortalia tangunt.* There is a temptation to translate grandly, as if this were a tag for the entire epic and its effect, but Vergil discourages that by calling the mural an "empty picture" (*pictura inani,* 1.464). Better is the translation that focuses Aeneas's relief on his assumption that the Carthaginians feel pity for the *Trojan* suffering. Compare Fitzgerald's translation: "Even so far away great valor has due honor; they weep here for how the world goes, and our life that passes touches their hearts."

11. Apollo 3.94–98; hearth-gods (*penates*) 3.154–71; Celaeno 3.247–57; Helenus 3.374–462. *Ausonia,* more exactly southern Italy, is one of Vergil's poetic equivalents for Italy.

12. For example, see 4.65–66 (on Dido); 9.446–49 (on Nisus and Euryalus); 10.501–9 (on Turnus and Pallas); 10.791–93 (on Lausus).

13. Dido recognizes that she has a *similis fortuna,* "tossed through many toils" (1.628–30).

14. In the *Confessions* 1.13 (chaps. 20–22), Augustine famously reproaches himself for such tears; he shed them while he viewed his own spiritual death with dry eyes, he says.

15. Austin 1955:89, note to line 260: The Dido-smitten Aeneas is "a glimpse, seldom seen, of Virgil's hero as a happy man." Incidentally, "Virgil" is an alternative spelling of the poet's name, common in Britain but also used by some Americans.

16. Cf. 1.35, 1.514, 3.178, 3.638, 5.34, 5.283, 7.36, 7.288, 8.311, 8.544, 8.617, 10.787, 10.874, 12.700. Aeneas is not described with this adjective in book 4. Lyne (1989:181–85) rightly notes that *laetus* "may connote *disaster-prone* happiness, happiness which disaster awaits" (emphasis his). In none of his examples, however, does he adduce the *laetitia* of Aeneas, whose happiness is significantly less ominous.

17. Many, especially young readers, protest that he never *really* loves her. It is true, as Wiltshire notes, that "Aeneas never uses *amor* in his conversations with Dido" (1989:108). But Vergil is unequivocal: "Duty bound, Aeneas . . . shaken at heart with great love, nevertheless follows the orders of the gods" (*pius Aeneas . . . magnoque animum labefactus amore, iussa tamen divum exsequitur,* 4.393–96. When they met in the Underworld, Aeneas "wept and addressed her with tender love" (*demisit lacrimas dulcique adfatus amore est,* 6.455). At question is the equivalence of his love. In Hades, Sychaeus "equals her love" (*aequatque Sychaeus amorem,* 6.474), something that Aeneas apparently never does.

18. For many readers, alienation from Aeneas is matched with an association with Dido: *she* is the real hero of authenticity. Though Vergil does not intend this reading, many are drawn to it. Cf. Van Nortwick 1992:120, 123: Aeneas is "a man who has lost all track of who he is . . . the struggle of Aeneas for a richer life is over before it starts."

19. There are several examples of other characters who put on someone else's armor, always with disastrous results; the most notable, of course, is Turnus, who puts on the armor of Pallas, which incenses Aeneas (12.940–44). Hornsby (1966) discusses this motif.

20. The failures that attend these falsifications again underscore the implicit rejection of Odyssean heroism for Aeneas.

21. Cf. Moorton 1990:159: "As Aeneas and Dido were once united in that bed by the metaphorical fire of sexuality, so she and his effigy will be united in the literal fire of cremation. Her death will be like her love."

22. As Dido knows. Cf. 4.321–23: "Because of you, my reputation for modesty is gone, and my former fame, the one thing by which I wrote my name among the stars!"

23. This is captured most clearly in line 449: *mens immota manet, lacrimae volvuntur inanes* (His mind remains unmoved, his tears roll down in vain). Cf. Pöschl 1962:46

24. This is an intensification of what many other scholars have noted. Austin (1964:xvi) speaks of discipline and Lyne (1987:107) of subordination, for example. They emphasize these as the by-products of *pietas,* and in so doing, they suggest that Aeneas must return to or simply become more of what he is, *pius.* There is certainly a continuity in his essential quality of *pietas.* We argue that his destiny necessitates a change in that continuous *pietas;* it is the nature of that change that we attempt to explain.

25. Cf. Otis on Aeneas's descent to the Underworld (1995:281) : "He must undergo the death out of which alone rebirth could come. Virgil's problem in the sixth book was to express the theme of death and resurrection . . . in terms appropriate to his hero's mood and situation."

26. The meeting with Dido is Vergilian artistry at its best and most complex. In this scene, Vergil closes the story of Dido, reiterates Aeneas's emotional ties in a moment of transition, and provides an etiological explanation for Roman and Carthaginian enmity, which resulted in the three Punic Wars (all won by Rome). It is sobering to note that this picture is really the only one in the *Aeneid* of a happy, nurturing love—and it exists in Hades, in the "Fields of Mourning" (*Campi Lugentes*).

27. This "paradise" is not mentioned during Odysseus's visit to the Underworld in *Odyssey* 11, but in book 4.561–69, Menelaus receives a prophecy from Proteus that he will be transported to Elysium since he is Helen's husband, therefore son-in-law to Zeus.

28. Pöschl sees in this scene "the most comprehensive interpretation of the

poem. Here the connection of the legend with the two spheres of which the poetical partakes—Universal order and the Roman order of the world—is most patently visible . . . Aeneas realizes the connection of mortal life with world order and that of his own destiny with the history of Rome" (1962:27).

29. Penelope mentions the gates as she tells her dream to the disguised Odysseus (*Odyssey* 19.563–67).

30. The basic conclusion of Otis (1995:304) and Austin (1977:276).

31. Otis 1995:341.

32. We translate *virtus* here as "heroism." The English word "hero" is a derivation from Greek via Latin, and it appears in its Latin form in the *Aeneid* (see, e.g., 6.649, 8.530, 12.502, 12.723). But the Latin word that captures that sense is *vir*, which also means both "man" and "husband." *Virtus* is the quality that constitutes manhood; it also serves conventionally as the epitome of manhood, hence heroism, in the Roman mind.

33. Action is paramount over destined goal and consequent difficulties; for this reason Aeneas offers Hector to Ascanius as another paradigm (12.440). Aeneas makes no mention of *pietas* in his self-description, the one area in which he exceeds Hector (11.291–92).

34. Regarding the relation between *pietas* and battle, some scholars seem to think that when Aeneas is under the influence of one, he is not under the influence of the other. Putnam (1995:134–51) identifies "polarities" of passion and *pietas* throughout the work; he sees the activation of Aeneas's *pietas* in Lausus's death as happening *too late*. It is our argument that any polarity between passion and *pietas* is not an essential one, but a result of Aeneas's natural retrospection and human ignorance: as these are shed, the polarity vanishes and is overcome in the final scene. To see it otherwise is to privilege the *ideals* of destiny and humanity over their enactment.

35. Turnus's death is the critical watershed of the work. Generally put, if Turnus dies justly, then the work is imperial, bright, "Augustan"; if he dies unjustly or tragically, then the work is pessimistic, dark, subversive, private. Interpretations tend to be polarized on this point. For excellent articles that take opposing views, see Stahl 1990 and Thomas 1998.

36. This is the interpretation of Servius, Vergil's fourth-century commentator.

37. During their final battle, Jupiter raises a scale "with a level balance, places in it the diverse fates of the two men, one whom the toil would doom and whose death would follow the sinking scale" (*quem damnet labor et quo vergat pondere letum*, 12.725–27). Thomas (1998:296–97) traces how Aeneas "becomes Jupiter" through the analogies of storm and thunder; Putnam, through Turnus's supplications of him (1995:4). Achilles is also "god-like," but in his wrath, his *menis*. This word is used only of divine wrath in the *Iliad*, with the exception of its application to Achilles. The *Iliad*, however, emphasizes the distance between Zeus and Achilles, and Achilles' awareness of that distance; the *Aeneid* ends with the greatest likeness of god and man.

38. Thomas (1998:275–83) explores this assimilation cogently. His assessment of the parallel lines linking Aeneas's fear in the storm with Turnus's death is excellent: "Turnus becomes what Aeneas had been when we first saw him, isolated and facing death" (1998:275).

39. Since the epic gives voice to Turnus—literally through direct speech and subjectively to his perspective—this reading has textual support. Jupiter is described as "savage" (*saevus,* 12.849) as he dispatches a Fury and terrifies Turnus, and Juturna recognizes Jupiter's deadly and "haughty commands" (*iussa superba,* 12.877); her lament lingers over the final scene. Turnus realizes his error at the end, when he acknowledges Jupiter as "my enemy" (*Iuppiter hostis,* 12.895). This reading is essentially a tragic one; it sees Turnus as individually ennobled by his resistance to his loss of identity and authenticity, threatened by Aeneas and the Trojan domination of Italy.

40. Lyne (1987:81–83) believes that Jupiter speaks rhetorically, "glossing the truth, packaging a fact that will be unpalatable to Juno. She is going to get a great deal of what she wants, but not all she wants." That is to say, "Trojan-ness" will not be entirely obliterated in the new mixture. Lyne again: "The Trojans will make vital contributions to the new race besides their stock: religion and civilization."

41. Cf. Stahl 1990:209: "it is indispensable to see that Turnus is called an Achilles only to the extent that he revives and repeats a past threat to the Trojans, but that he is a priori doomed to fall at the hands of an even greater hero, a new super-Achilles, so to speak, who is Aeneas."

42. Stahl (1990:205) overstates the case; he sees the reader "being impregnated with antipathy against cruel Turnus."

43. Cf. Pöschl 1962:95: this "moment of retardation . . . focuses and enhances his tragedy."

44. Wiltshire 1989:16: ". . . the tremendous public achievement of Octavian on the one side, the costs exacted by that achievement on the other." Her book, however, is far more than a tallying up: she traces eloquently and assesses positively the "precarious balance" and "the ways by which, with the greatest of difficulty, Vergil keeps public and private together" (1989:4, 20).

45. Johnson eloquently expresses this dualism, the "unique equilibrium of light and darkness, without which his poem becomes superior propaganda or remarkable melodrama" (1976:20).

46. Cf. Hainsworth (1991:146): "The finest examples of epic poetry explore some theme, as the *Iliad* explores the idea of heroism and the *Aeneid* that of empire"; and Johnson (1976:133), who sees the *Aeneid* as more "about the nature of history."

47. Thomas 1998:275: "The Augustan critics depend on their ability to dismiss as 'modern' or 'Christian' any tendency to see excess in the actions of Aeneas." Thomas is correct, but he is targeting the darker political readings of the *Aeneid.* Those who see the work as a celebration of Augustus's

accomplishments tend to deprecate the pessimistic readings that focus on the "tragedy" of Turnus and on the "failure" of Aeneas's pity.

48. There is no doubt that readers were meant to see Augustus as a contemporary successor of Aeneas. A political reading of the *Aeneid,* however, cannot equivocate: either Vergil supported or did not support Augustus, either the human costs were worth the end of civil war, or they were not. Implicit disapproval is disapproval all the same. Much modern scholarship, with its focus on the humane and political dimension of the *Aeneid,* reinforces the sense that one must adhere to one or the other polarity; Johnson (1976:2–16) traces the history and content of these two "schools." We believe that the *Aeneid* is politically celebrative, not subversive. But politics are only a backdrop to the work. The *Aeneid* is as much about politics as the *Iliad* is about war. Both are works about the excellence of one man, and both works strive to set forth that respective excellence as clearly as possible, with all its attendant glories and failures that attract and repel.

49. The *Aeneid* was read as a Christian allegory for centuries: Aeneas is the "lover of virtue" and Dido is the "lust of the flesh," for example. Medieval commentators and illustrations in medieval manuscripts of the *Aeneid* are fascinating for their reach in bringing everything into a Christian frame. Dante's *Divine Comedy* is an intricate reworking of Vergilian material. Christian approaches to the *Aeneid* are not just medieval: in this century Eliot read Aeneas as "proto-Christian" (1957), and Haecker read Vergil as an *anima naturaliter Christiana* (1934).

Chapter 5   *Messianic Triumph: Jesus*

1. Homer served as the educational text for the Greek world, and Paul seems to have acquaintance with certain Greek philosophic and tragic texts.

2. One significant difference is historical perspective. Rome exists, and Vergil weds his hero to a proven fact of greatness with revelations of Aeneas's future that catalogue Rome's glorious past. Matthew weds Jesus to a historical prophecy, but one still unrealized.

3. Cf: von Rad 1965 for an account of the ways in which messianic expectation is intensified across Old Testament history and prophecy.

4. See Calvin 1948:502. In Rom. 14:11, where Paul appeals to a messianic prophecy, "As I live, says the Lord, every knee shall bow to me," Calvin comments, "This is a remarkable passage for the purpose of confirming our faith in the eternal divinity of Christ: for it is God who speaks here [in the prophecy Paul quotes from Isaiah] and the God who has once for all declared that he will not give his glory to another (Is. 42:8). Now if what [God] claims here to himself is alone accomplished in Christ, then doubtless he in Christ manifests himself."

5. For an explanation of the spiritual consequence, for the reader, of a seemingly deliberate literary strategy of obscurity, see Origen 3.1.17. Of those

sickened by sin, Origen writes, "If I may speak paradoxically, God heals them by not healing them, lest a premature recovery of health should render them incurable." Referring to veiled speech, of which the author of Mark makes great use, Origen observes, "The Lord wanted to prevent the unready from being too speedily converted and only cosmetically healed." The Gospel's opening clarity, followed by a continuously difficult and opaque narrative, is motivated by just this concern. The author of Mark delays recognition so that we might avoid a facile repentance and faith. Even more, the author depicts false recognition as a mirror for his reader, so that we may see how superficially, partially, and falsely we recognize the Son of God.

6. See, for example, Augustine's explanation of the true, but false, testimony of the demons in Mark 1:24. "Those words show clearly that the demons have much knowledge," writes Augustine, "but entirely lack love." The demons saw with their eyes, but their hearts were closed to Jesus. So, instead of conforming to him in love, they fled him in fear (*City of God* 9.21). Augustine also sees the loveless testimony of the demons as a warning to our own blind ways of seeing. "The devils confessed Christ, but lacking charity it availed nothing. They said, 'What have we to do with you?' They confessed a sort of faith, but without love. Hence they were devils. Do not boast of that faith that puts you on the same level with devils" (*Tractates, on the Gospel of John* 6.21).

7. The two-fold treatment is given extended expression the way in which the author of Mark arranges all the healing stories. Austin Farrer argues that in Mark the cures may be categorized according to the type of ailment: possession, illness (unto death), defilement and incapacity of hand, foot, ears or eyes (see *St. Matthew and St. Mark,* pp. 24–37, especially p. 34, note 1). If we accept this view of the division of the cures, then we see a pattern. The first healing in each category is done in private with exhortations to secrecy. The second healing in each category is done openly and without the imperative of secrecy. In this way, the first healing of the blind man encapsulates the extended pattern of all the healings. Christ's powers of renewal have two stages: first, a power the results of which we cannot see clearly, and second, a power which is entirely manifest and evident. Thus, not only in the particular healing of the blind man at Bethsaida but also across all the healings we can see a pattern of partiality leading to fulfillment, of ambiguity leading to clarity. In this way the author of Mark uses the healings to reinforce the momentum of the text toward the moment of greatest narrative clarity, Jesus' death.

8. Exactly who these "Herodians" might be is rather mysterious, especially since Herod and "Herodians" drop out of the narrative altogether after this point. The only subsequent mention occurs in 8:15, when, in the general ambience of anxiety about food, Jesus warns his disciples to be on their guard against the leaven of the Pharisees and of Herod. Unlike Luke's account, in Mark, Herod and his associates have no role in Jesus' fate.

9. Farrer (1954:14) suggests this foreshadowing in his study of the literary patterns in Mark. Farrer also reads John's death as a recapitulation of Elijah's trials at the hands of Ahab and Jezebel, a reading suggested not only by the triangle of prophet, manipulated ruler, and manipulating queen, but also by the fact that Herod's advisors have Elijah very much on their minds, though, like Herod, they have the relationship between Jesus and John reversed. This, in turn, provides the crucial background for Jesus' response to the disciples' question on the descent from the mount of his transfiguration: "Why do the scribes say that first Elijah must come?" (9:11). The recapitulation of Elijah's fate in John's execution allows the reader to understand Jesus' enigmatic reply to the disciples' question: "I tell you that Elijah has come, and they did to him whatever they pleased, as it is written about him" (9:13). Jesus is referring to 1 Kings 19:10,14. The prophet of the restoration of righteousness has come, and he has met his fate in rejection and death, as it is written. Now the way is clear for the Messiah to come, and as Jesus has already taught (8:31), he also shall suffer rejection and death.

10. Farrer (1951:40) suggests the prefiguration of the hours of the passion. He also detects another clue. Within the apocalyptic discourse is the echo of tribulation prophesied in Daniel, where we read of the "half-week" of desolation (9:27) which precedes the establishment of God's everlasting kingdom. With this in mind, we turn to the passion, and, lo, the half-week pattern holds. Thursday's preparations for the Passover feast send Jesus to his destruction on Friday. The struggle with the devouring power of death on Saturday (see Daniel 7:23) is resolved on Sunday morning as death's dominion is taken away (Daniel 7:26). In the hands of readers intimate with the apocalyptic visions of Daniel, Jesus' discourse evokes the half-week expectation that points forward to the passion.

11. See MacIntosh 1912:288–92 for a cogent discussion of the category of hero in relation to Jesus.

Chapter 6   Transparency and Imitation: Paul and Early Christianity

1. In his letter to the Galatians, Paul claims that he did not learn the gospel from others but "received it through a revelation of Jesus Christ." He describes the events told in Acts 9 very briefly, but adds the temporal detail that three years elapsed between his conversion and his introduction to the other disciples in Jerusalem, during which time he sojourned in "Arabia" (Gal. 1:11–18).

2. Such interpretations are fairly common from commentary and pulpit, and the letters do suggest a moral looseness, both active and passive, within the Corinthian church. Paul reproaches the church for this in 1 Corinthians 5–6.

3. In Acts 18, Luke writes that Paul arrived in Corinth shortly after the emperor Claudius expelled the Jews from Rome in 49 C.E. (cf. Suetonius, *Claudius*

25), that he met and worked with Aquila and Priscilla, a Jewish couple converted to Christianity, and that he remained in Corinth for eighteen months. When he departed, he took with him Aquila and Priscilla, who remained at Ephesus, while he traveled back to Antioch, where he stayed some time before beginning his next missionary journey. During that next journey, Paul's third, an Alexandrian Jew named Apollos, who had converted to Christianity, arrived in Ephesus, where he too met Aquila and Priscilla and received instruction from them. When he desired to go on his own mission, he was sent to Corinth; how long he stayed there, we do not know. After his departure, the church apparently desired his return, and Paul encouraged it, but Apollos demurred, preferring to await the "right time" (1 Cor. 16:12).

4. The factions may have "developed along house church lines if the patrons of the house churches favored different apostles" (Witherington 1995:87), or factions devoted to different rhetorical schools and teachers influenced the ways that the Corinthians approached Paul and Apollos (Winter 1997:185). The Corinthians may have divided themselves along the lines of their individual conversions, that is, they recognized themselves as the converts of one evangelist or another. Jewish converts of Peter may have been present in Corinth, and witnesses of Jesus after his resurrection, whether in Corinth or not, were for the most part still alive and available for confirmation (1 Cor. 15:6). But loyalty owed to the individual evangelists cannot account completely for the factions, since Paul's faction would necessarily be quite large, and Peter's, by contrast, would be quite small.

5. Witherington finds a faction of Christ "hard to conceive of" and suggests "It is very unlikely that there was a Christ party in Corinth" (1995:84 nn. 9, 87).

6. There is a parallel between the relationship of Paul and Christ and that of the individual congregations to the "church of God" as a whole. In Corinth, before there were church buildings or any denominational faith, Paul speaks both of "churches" (*ekklêsiai,* 1 Cor. 14:33;16:19; 2 Cor. 8:1) and of the "church of God" (2 Cor. 11:22; cf. Gal. 1:13). That there is both a partiality and a wholeness in every congregation is underscored by Paul's analogy in 1 Corinthians 12 of the body—with its many members it is still an organic whole. Similarly, Paul seems to feel that there is an integrity that he possesses both with Christ and in himself. For Paul's view of the *ekklêsia,* see Witherington 1995:90–93.

7. Cf. the well-known passage from Ephesians 6:12–13, in which Paul expands on the image by drawing out each piece of God's full armor, perhaps studying, as some have thought, the panoply worn by the Roman soldiers who guarded him: "For our struggle is not against enemies of blood and flesh, but against the rulers, against the authorities, against the cosmic powers of this present darkness, against the spiritual forces of evil in the heavenly

places. Therefore take up the full armor of God, that you may be able to withstand on that evil day, and having done everything, to stand firm."

8. Cf. 2 Cor. 5:21: "For our sake, he made him to be sin who knew no sin, so that in him we might become the righteousness of God."

9. Ignatius attributes any wish for his safety to the devil: "The prince of this world wants to kidnap me and pervert my godly purpose. None of you, then, who will be there, must abet him" (7.1). If Ignatius does not suffer because of the intervention of the Romans, he says "it will be because you hated me" (8.3). Ignatius has decided (how, he does not say) that God's will for him is to die a violent death in Rome, and he never considers otherwise: for example, that God may wish to save him miraculously or through the efforts of the Romans; that God may wish to spare him by having him die naturally; that God's will is a mysterious thing.

10. Bowersock discusses the language of Ignatius and the absence of certain terms: "If μάρτυς had meant martyr at that time, Ignatius would undoubtedly have availed himself of the word" (1995:77). But Ignatius is not unaware of, and does not avoid, the corollaries of martyrdom, including the phenomenon of visibility: "For if you quietly leave me alone, people will see in me God's Word" (2.1); "I shall be a convincing Christian only when the world sees me no more" (3.2).

11. There is little evidence that there was a conception in the mind of the disciple who faces martyrdom to then shape his or her actions to a form of heroism. We focus only on the tendency to attribute heroism by the audience, the non-Christian and Christian communities alike, who see in the act of suffering the sufferer more than the cause.

12. The manuscript of his martyrdom contains a brief postscript that gives a history of the text from one found among the papers of Irenaeus, himself a disciple of Polycarp, to the present copyist Pionius; this pedigree asserts the authenticity and the contemporaneity of the account.

13. A note of the metaphorical creeps into the description of the actual immolation of Polycarp. The flame refused to consume him, but walled him in as if it were an oven or a furnace, and Polycarp a loaf of bread or crucible of ore. The author claims that Polycarp gave off a scent "as of incense or of other expensive fragrances" (15.1), likening him to Christ, who gave himself for us "as a fragrant offering" (Eph. 5:2). To modern readers, the similarities to details of Jesus' life strain credibility, but the anonymous author is reporting what he saw and believed. His standard of veracity is the scripture, most importantly the Gospels, and the conformity of details confirms his recognition of Polycarp's greatness.

14. All quotes are taken from *Athanasius: The Life of Anthony and the Letter to Marcellinus*, Gregg, (1980). The text of the *Life of Anthony* is cited by reference to paragraph number.

15. Augustine, *Confessions* 8.6.

16. Cf. the preface to R. Gregg's translation of *The Life of St. Antony*, where W.

Clebsch speaks of "the ladderlike quality of the saintly life, in which each higher step risked a harder fall" (1980:xv).

Chapter 7   The Poets of Christian Heroism: Spenser and Milton

1. For a subtle reading of Dante's account of Francis, see Auerbach 1984:79–98.
2. The Reformation came about in two principal movements, the Continental Reformation, led by Luther, Calvin, Zwingli, and Knox, and the English Reformation, first grounded in Henry VIII's break from the Catholic church and followed later by more theologically driven reformers. The English Reformation was a gradual, splintered process, beginning in earnest with Elizabeth's coronation in 1558, according to some historians, and culminating in the Glorious Revolution of 1668. We do not suggest that there is a uniform "Protestant" theology, neither in its inception nor now, but we believe that we can safely locate its essence in its emphasis on grace.
3. All quotations of Spenser come from the 1978 edition by Thomas P. Roche, Jr., and C. Patrick O'Donnell, Jr.
4. Evans (1970:36) states that "iron runs through the imagery of the poem as a symbol of all the forces of the earth which have dragged man lower than he need be."
5. For a discussion of scholarly controversies surrounding this seemingly clear stanza, see Gless 1994:146–50.
6. See Watkins 1995:107: "like the souls of the Romans and like Aeneas himself, Redcrosse must fulfill his historical obligations." Spenser knew Vergil extremely well, as well as commentaries on Vergil. For scholarship on their relationship, see Watkins 1995:180, n. 11, and Watkins 1995:passim.
7. See Evans 1970:126: Cymochles "represents the innate quality of human passion to flag when it has spent itself and then to flare up anew on the next occasion." The names are all Greek (*pyro-* meaning "fire" and *kyma* meaning "wave").
8. Verdant suggests "green-giving" (Italian: *verde*) and "spring-giving" (Latin: *ver*) and he replaces Mortdant, whom Guyon finds dead in the first canto of the book.
9. *Areopagitica*, 728–29. All quotations from Milton are taken from *John Milton: Complete Poems and Major Prose*, 1957.
10. Fish's influential study discusses this "singleness" in Milton's mind: in Adam and Eve's sin were *all* sins; in the command to obey God was the entire Law; and "Faith, discipline, obedience—they are one, along with heroism and love; and none of them can be invoked to sanction a movement away from God" (1967:158–59).
11. Cf. Fish's chapter 4, "Standing Only: Christian Heroism" (1967:158–207).
12. Low (1984:338): "Satan urges the Son to lift all the hardships from life."
13. For this reason, Low and others see the genre of *Paradise Regained* as "heroic georgic." Cf. Low (1984:351): "Like the *Georgics, Paradise*

Regained does not describe a pastoral retreat from responsibility but instead dwells on small, recurrent actions, often trivial or inglorious in themselves, that nevertheless converge toward a turning-point in the world's history that will be truly apocalyptic."

Chapter 8   Twentieth-Century Antiheroism: Camus and Bonhoeffer

1. Smith examines the nature of Bonhoeffer's heroism and "martyrdom" (1997:316–36).

2. Our reading of *The Plague* follows the basic interpretive suggestions of McCarthy.

3. Camus 1991:276. All quotations are from this edition; hereafter, page numbers will be given in parentheses.

4. For particularly effective evocations of the ordinariness of Oran, written before *The Plague,* see "The Minotaur, or Stopping in Oran," published in the collection *L'Été* in 1954 (available in English in *Lyrical and Critical Essays,* ed. Philip Thody, trans. Ellen Conroy Kennedy, [New York: Vintage Books, 1968] 109–33). Camus's humor mixes with a perceptive grasp of the heroic impulse in intellectual pretension when he writes, "No one, on the boulevards of Oran, discusses the problem of Being, or worries about the way to perfection." This is no great loss. In the place of world-historical posturing, Camus observes, "There is only the fluttering of wings, the flaunting of outspread tails, flirtations between victorious graces, all the rapture of a careless song that fades with the coming of night" (1991:115). For Camus, this frivolity is the enduring power of humanity. As he says later in the essay in an aphorism typical of Camus, "Isn't mediocrity itself eternity?" (1991:125).

5. Roland Barthes argues that *The Plague* fails because of this elision of resistance from the political and social into the biological and medical (see his essay, "Sur *La Peste* d'Albert Camus," *Club,* Bulletin du Club du Meilleur Livre, février 1955, reprinted in Jacqueline Levi-Valensi, *Albert Camus La Peste,* [Paris: Gallimard, 1991], 183–89). Camus's response is also reprinted in Levi-Valensi's volume, 190–92.

6. Camus's other novels reiterate the theme of dangerous and dehumanizing spiritual ascent. His depiction of the Luciferian narrator of *The Fall* assumes a darker, more damning will-to-spiritual-superiority. Jean-Baptiste Clemence 1960:260–61 sought a career as a supremely righteous attorney. He wished to live as a man of surpassing virtue, to attain the "supreme summit," and to remain "living aloft." From these heights, Clemence enjoyed looking down on humanity, and the pose of superiority is the germinal seed of his descent into misanthropy.

7. Elsewhere, Camus suggests that abstraction and isolation are necessary for both knowledge and moral endurance. "To understand this world," he writes, "one must sometimes turn away from it; to serve men better, one must briefly hold them at a distance" (*Lyrical and Critical Essays,* 109).

8. In his open correspondence with Roland Barthes, Camus suggests the central role of Rambert. See "Letter to Roland Barthes on *The Plague*," in *Lyrical and Critical Essays*, 338–41.

9. Bonhoeffer 1995:59. All quotations are from this edition, hereafter, page numbers are given in parentheses.

Glossary

agôn (Greek): A struggle or contest of strength or words.

aidôs (Greek): Generally, shame; in Homer, the emotion provoked by the thought of being seen by others while failing to act appropriately to one's social and moral roles.

aretê (Greek): Excellence in a peculiar or general capacity; virtue.

kleos (Greek): Glory; poetic renown.

labor (Latin): Suffering; toil, a hard or difficult effort.

nemesis (Greek): A sort of righteous indignation; the emotion provoked in those who witness a failure of action appropriate to the agent's social and moral roles.

nomos (Greek): Custom; law.

pietas (Latin): Devotion to duty, including duty to family, country, and gods.

tîmê (Greek): Honor; recognition; that which is due to a person.

virtus (Latin): Manhood (*vir* being "man"); courage; heroism.

References

Adkins, A. W. H. 1960. *Merit and Responsibility.* Oxford: Clarendon Press.

Auerbach, Erich. 1984. "St. Francis of Assisi in Dante's 'Comedia.'" In *Scenes from the Drama of European Literature.* Minneapolis: University of Minnesota Press.

Austin, R. G. 1955. *P. Vergili Maronis Aeneidos Liber Quartus.* Oxford: Clarendon Press.

———. 1964. *P. Vergili Maronis Aeneidos Liber Secundus.* Oxford: Clarendon Press.

———. 1977. *P. Vergili Maronis Aeneidos Liber Sextus.* Oxford: Clarendon Press.

Bonhoeffer, Dietrich. 1995. *The Cost of Discipleship,* trans. R. H. Fuller. New York: Simon & Schuster.

Bowersock, G. W. 1995. *Martyrdom and Rome.* Cambridge: Cambridge University Press.

Brakke, David. 1995. *Athanasius and the Politics of Asceticism.* Oxford: Clarendon Press. Paperback: *Athanasius and Asceticism.* Baltimore: Johns Hopkins University Press, 1998.

Brickhouse, Thomas C., and Smith, Nicholas D. 1989. *Socrates on Trial.* Princeton, N.J.: Princeton University Press.

Brown, Peter. 1983. "The Saint as Exemplar in Late Antiquity." *Representations* 1:1–26.

Cairns, Douglas L. 1993. *Aidos. The Psychology and Ethics of Honour and Shame in Ancient Greek Literature.* Oxford: Clarendon Press.

Calvin, John. 1948. *Commentaries on the Epistle of Paul the Apostle to the Romans,* trans. John Owen. Grand Rapids: Wm. B. Eerdmans Publishing.

Camus, Albert. 1991. *The Plague,* trans. Stuart Gilbert. New York: Vintage Books.

Claus, D. B. 1975. "*Aidos* in the Language of Achilles." *Transactions of the American Philological Association* 105:13–28.

Clay, Diskin. 1972. "Socrates' Mulishness and Heroism." *Phronesis* 17:53–60.

Clemence, Jean-Baptiste, 1960. *The Collected Fiction of Albert Camus.* London: H. Hamilton.

Edwards, Mark. 1986. *Homer, Poet of the* Iliad. Baltimore: Johns Hopkins University Press.

Eisner, Robert. 1982. "Socrates as Hero." *Philosophy and Literature* 6:106–18.

Eliot, T. S. 1957. "Virgil and the Christian World." In *On Poetry and Poets,* 135–48. New York: Farrar, Straus, & Cudahy.

Evans, Maurice. 1970. *Spenser's Anatomy of Heroism: A Commentary on the Fairie Queen,* Cambridge: Cambridge University Press.

Farrer, Austin. 1951. *A Study in St. Mark.* London: Dacre Press.

Farrer, Austin. 1954. *St. Matthew and St. Mark.* London: Dacre Press.

Feeney, Denis. 1983. "The Taciturnity of Aeneas." *Classical Quarterly* 33:204–19.

———. 1991. *The Gods in Epic.* Oxford: Clarendon Press.

Finkelberg, Margalit. 1995. "Odysseus and the Genus 'Hero.'" *Greece & Rome* 42:1–14.

———. 1998. *"Timê* and *Aretê* in Homer." *Classical Quarterly* 48:14–28.

Fish, Stanley. 1967. *Surprised by Sin: The Reader in Paradise Lost.* Berkeley, Calif.: University of California Press.

Forsyth, N. 1985. "Having Done All to Stand: Biblical and Classical Allusions in *Paradise Regained.*" *Milton Studies* 21:199–214.

Francis, James A. 1995. *Subversive Virtue: Asceticism and Authority in the Second-Century Pagan World.* University Park, Penn.: Penn State University Press.

———. 1981. "Pagan and Christian Philosophy in Athanasius' *Vita Antoni.*" *American Benedictine Review* 32:100–13.

Galinsky, Karl. 1972. *The Herakles Theme.* Totowa, N.J.: Rowman and Littlefield Publishers.

———. 1988. "The Anger of Aeneas." *American Journal of Philology* 109:321–48.

Gill, Christopher. 1996. *Personality in Greek Epic, Tragedy and Philosophy.* Oxford: Clarendon Press.

Gless, Darryl J. 1994. *Interpretation and Theology in Spenser.* Cambridge: Cambridge University Press.

Gordon, Jill. 1996. "Against Vlastos on Complex Irony." *Classical Quarterly* 46:131–37.

Gottlieb, Paula. 1992. "The Complexity of Socratic Irony: A Note on Professor Vlastos' Account." *Classical Quarterly* 42:278–79.

Gransden, K. W. 1984. "The *Aeneid* and *Paradise Lost.*" In Martindale 1984:95–116.

Gregg, Robert C., trans. 1980. *Athanasius: The Life of Anthony and the Letter to Marcellinus.* New York: Paulist Press.

Griffin, Jasper. 1995. *Homer, Iliad Book IX.* Oxford: Clarendon Press.

Haecker, Theodor. 1934. *Virgil, Father of the West.* Trans. A. W. Wheen. New York: Sheed & Ward.

Hainsworth, J. B. 1991. *The Idea of Epic.* Berkeley, Calif.: University of California Press.

Hornsby, Roger. 1966. "The Armor of the Slain." *Philological Quarterly* 45:347–59.

———. 1987. "The Refracted Past." *Vergilius* 33:6–13.

Johnson, W. R. 1976. *Darkness Visible.* Berkeley, Calif.: University of California Press.

Lee, M. Owen. 1979. *Fathers and Sons in Virgil's* Aeneid: Tum Genitor Natum. Albany, N.Y.: SUNY Press.

Long, A. A. 1988. "Socrates in Hellenistic Philosophy." *Classical Quarterly* 38:150–71.

Low, Anthony. 1984. *The Georgic Revolution.* Princeton, N.J.: Princeton University Press.

Lyne, R. O. A. M. 1987. *Further Voices in Vergil's* Aeneid. Oxford: Clarendon Press.

———. 1989. *Words and the Poet: Characteristic Techniques of Style in Vergil's* Aeneid. Oxford: Clarendon Press.

MacIntosh, H. R. 1912. *The Doctrine of the Person of Jesus Christ.* New York: Scribner's Sons.

Macleod, Colin. 1982. *Iliad. Book XXIV.* Cambridge: Cambridge University Press.

Martin, Richard. 1989. *The Language of Heroes. Speech and Performance in the* Iliad. Ithaca, N.Y.: Cornell University Press.

Martindale, Charles, ed. 1984. *Virgil and His Influence: Bimillenial Studies.* Devon: Bristol Classical Press.

McCarthy, Patrick. 1982. *Camus.* New York: Random House.

Milton, John. 1957. *John Milton: Complete Poems and Major Prose,* ed. Merritt Y. Hughes. Indianapolis: Odyssey Press.

Moorton, R. F. 1990. "Love as Death: The Pivoting Metaphor in Vergil's Story of Dido." *Classical World* 83:153–66.

Nagy, Gregory. 1979. *The Best of the Achaeans.* Baltimore: Johns Hopkins University Press.

Nietzsche, Friedrich. 1989. *On the Genealogy of Morals,* trans. Walter Kaufmann and R. J. Holingdale. New York: Vintage Books.

Origen. 1966. *On First Principles,* trans. G. W. Butterworth.

Otis, Brooks. 1995. *Virgil: A Study in Civilized Poetry.* Norman, Ok.: University of Oklahoma Press. Reprint of original edition published by Clarendon Press, Oxford, 1964.

Parry, Adam. 1956. "The Language of Achilles." *Transactions of the American Philological Association* 87:1–7. Magnolia, Mass.: Peter Smith Pub., Inc.

Patterson, Richard. 1982. "The Platonic Art of Comedy and Tragedy." *Philosophy and Literature* 6:76–93.

Pedrick, Victoria. 1982. "Supplication in the *Iliad* and the *Odyssey.*" *Transactions of the American Philological Association* 112:125–40.

Pelling, Christopher, ed. 1990. *Characterization and Individuality in Greek Literature.* Oxford: Clarendon Press.

Pöschl, Viktor. 1962. *The Art of Vergil: Image and Symbol in the* Aeneid. Trans. by G. Seligson. Ann Arbor: University of Michigan Press. Originally published as *Die Dichtkunst Vergils,* Wiesbaden, Rohrer, 1950.

Putnam, Michael C. J. 1981. "*Pius* Aeneas and the Metamorphosis of Lausus." *Arethusa* 14:139–56.

———. 1995. *Virgil's Aeneid: Interpretation and Influence.* Chapel Hill: University of North Carolina Press.

Rabel, Robert J. 1997. "Sophocles' *Philoctetes* and the Interpretation of *Iliad* 9." *Arethusa* 30:297–307.

Redfield, J. M. 1975. *Nature and Culture in the* Iliad. Chicago: University of Chicago Press.

Reeve, C. D. C. 1989. *Socrates in the* Apology: *An essay on Plato's* Apology of Socrates. Indianapolis: Hackett Publishing Company.

Roche, Thomas P., Jr., and C. Patrick O'Donnell, Jr., eds. 1978. *The Faerie Queene,* by Edmund Spenser. New York: Penguin Books.

Saller, Richard. 1994. *Patriarchy, Property and Death in the Roman Family.* Cambridge: Cambridge University Press.

Segal, Charles. 1971. *The Theme of the Mutilation of the Corpse in the* Iliad. *Mnemosyne* Supplement 17. Leiden: E. J. Brill.

———. 1981. "Art and the Hero: Participation, Detachment, and Narrative Point of View in *Aeneid* 1." *Arethusa* 14:67–83.

Smith, Lacey Baldwin. 1997. *Fools, Martyrs, Traitors: The Story of Martyrdom in the Western World.* New York: Alfred A. Knopf.

Stahl, Hans-Peter. 1981. "Aeneas—An 'Unheroic' Hero?" *Arethusa* 14:157–77.

———. 1990. "The Death of Turnus: Augustan Vergil and the Political Rival."

In *Between Republic and Empire: Interpretations of Augustus and His Principate,* ed. K. Rauflaub and M. Toher. Berkeley: University of California Press.

———. 1998. *Vergil's* Aeneid: *Augustan Epic and Political Context.* London: Duckworth.

Stanford, W. B. 1963. *The Ulysses Theme.* Oxford: Basil Blackwell Publisher.

Strauss, Leo. 1983. *Studies in Platonic Political Philosophy.* Chicago: University of Chicago Press.

Taplin, Oliver. 1990. "Agamemnon's Role in the *Iliad.*" In Pelling 1990:60–82.

———. 1992. *Homeric Soundings: The Shaping of the* Iliad. Oxford: Clarendon Press.

Thomas, Richard F. 1998. "The Isolation of Turnus: *Aeneid* Book 12." In Stahl 1998:271–302.

Van Nortwick, Thomas. 1992. *Somewhere I Have Never Travelled: The Hero's Journey.* Oxford: Clarendon Press.

Vander Waerdt, Paul. 1994a. "Socrates in the *Clouds.*" In Vander Waerdt 1994b:48–86.

———. 1994b. *The Socratic Movement.* Ithaca, N.Y.: Cornell University Press.

Vlastos, Gregory. 1991. *Socrates: Ironist and Moral Philosopher.* Cambridge: Cambridge University Press.

von Rad, Gerhard. 1965. *Old Testament Theology,* vol. 2. Trans. P. N. G. Stalker. New York: Harper & Row.

Watkins, John. 1995. *The Specter of Dido: Spenser and Virgilian Epic.* New Haven: Yale University Press.

West, Thomas G. 1979. *Plato's Apology of Socrates: An Interpretation, with a New Translation.* Ithaca, N.Y.: Cornell University Press.

Wiltshire, Susan Ford. 1989. *Public and Private in Vergil's* Aeneid. Amherst: University of Massachusetts Press.

Winter, Bruce W. 1997. *Philo and Paul among the Sophists.* Cambridge: Cambridge University Press.

Witherington, Ben. 1995. *Conflict and Community in Corinth: A Socio-Rhetorical Commentary on 1 and 2 Corinthians.* Grand Rapids: Wm. B. Eerdmans Publishing Co.

Zanker, Graham. 1994. *The Heart of Achilles: Characterization and Personal Ethics in the* Iliad. Ann Arbor: University of Michigan Press.

Index